*You're
the
Boss*

You're the Boss

Joe Robinson

ST. MARTIN'S PRESS • NEW YORK

Design by Jeremiah B. Lighter

Library of Congress Cataloging in Publication Data

Robinson, Joe.
  You're the boss.

  1. New business enterprises.   2. Success in business.
I. Title.
HD62.5.R59 1987   658.4'2   87-16149
ISBN 0-312-01027-3

First Edition
10 9 8 7 6 5 4 3 2 1

For my parents, who encouraged
me to follow my dreams;
and for Vicki,
whose love and support
sustains them.

Contents

Acknowledgments

GETTING through to some of the most incessant workaholics in America was an entrepreneurial adventure in itself. Interviews were set, canceled; set, canceled; set, canceled. After all, these were people who were running some of the fastest-growing companies in the country, if not the world. They had plenty of things to do besides talk to writers.

Thanks to a lot of efficient secretaries, assistants, and PR professionals, though, precious time on the calendars was cleared. I'd like to take this time to thank from the bottom of my heart all those who helped get their bosses to sit down long enough to talk to me, particularly Nancy Ross at The Sharper Image, Joanne Snyder at Banana Republic, Lana Lundgren at OP, Sandy Missett at Jazzercise, and Dee Cravens at Televideo.

Obviously, my greatest debt of gratitude is to the entrepreneurs themselves. Their willingness to be grilled on times and struggles some would have just as soon forgotten is what made this whole book possible. They were gracious, informative, illuminating, and inspiring. I'll be forever grateful to all of them for giving me the entrepreneurial education of a lifetime.

Because of space limitations, there wasn't enough room to include the stories of all the entrepreneurs I interviewed in this book. For those whose stories were left out, or abbreviated, I can only say that every effort was made to feature as many profiles as possible. Your spirit and your cause, if not your actual circumstances, are represented throughout. Thanks very much.

There were many people who provided key encouragement and support along the way. I'd like to thank Chuck Thegze and Gene Sculatti for the advice and encouragement that helped get me going. Thanks to the Merlin's gang—David Lees, Stan Berkowitz, Mason Buck—for their commiseration and counsel; to Jim Bickhart for reviewing extraneous, unwieldy drafts; and to Phil Waters for graphic support.

I'd also like to thank several others who made important contributions—Marty Herman, Jim Lustgarten, Bradley Frederick, and Anna-Maria Wiig. Thanks for trans-Pacific solidarity to Jeff Sievert and others along the way—Mort Maron, Ray Davies, Keith Reid, Gary Brooker, Donald Fagen, Bob Marley.

In addition to unfailing moral support, David O'Connell, Jill Harris, and Canyon Design provided key financial backing. Thanks, awfully.

Many entrepreneurship experts were kind enough to share their thoughts on the subject. Ivan Light of UCLA provided important leads that enabled me to pinpoint the rise of entrepreneurship. Richard Buskirk at USC was invaluable in helping me uncover and develop the corporate dropout phenomenon. I'd like to thank all the expert sources—from economists to psychologists—who were interviewed during the course of this saga.

On the editing side, Shelley Lowenkopf was a major factor, straightening out things when they got discombobulated. Thanks to Brian DeFiore for his editing skills and enthusiasm for the project, and also to Christopher Skala at St. Martin's and to copy editor Judith de Rubini.

The person most responsible for this book being in your hands is Barbara Lowenstein, agent extraordinaire. Her advice, determination, and patience turned a kernel of an idea into a full-fledged, definitive volume. It couldn't have happened without her. Thanks for sticking with it through thick and thin. You're the greatest!

Last, but not least, I'd like to thank my parents, John and Helen Robinson, for their support on all levels at all times, and for their lifelong tolerance of my passions and projects.

One person went through more than I did in the writing of this book. My wife, Vicki, had to not only live with this project for two and a half years; she had to live with me. Her understanding, encouragement, wisdom, and love proved equal to the task. This one's for you. You made it happen.

Introduction

*T*HIS IS NOT your typical business book. Nor is there anything typical about the way I wound up writing it. I came to these pages and the subject of entrepreneurship not by way of business school or a lifelong craving to run my own multinational conglomerate. It was a meandering path through the workaday world, and the galling frustrations of being a wage slave that deposited me on the doorstep of enterprise.

My call to the self-made world came in a manner that many of my generation—the notorious baby-boom brigade—have experienced over the last decade. Weaned on the individualism and idealism of the sixties, yet locked into a corporate vise; burning to achieve, yet stifled by bureaucratic hierarchies, I found myself considering something I'd never thought about before, a business career.

Like many of my generation, I hadn't tabbed business as a major priority in my formative years. I was more concerned with the new Kinks album than with what I would do for a living. I took liberal arts courses and got a degree in journalism, and did my best to stall off "real business" type employment. I traveled the globe for a while. When the call of funds could no longer be ignored, I settled on a halfway measure; I went to work for a corporation, but one that didn't seem like one—a major record company.

It was as good as working for other people could get. My job was to advertise the music I loved. I went to free concerts, got to meet some of my heroes, like Ry Cooder and Procol Harum, and never lacked for free albums.

As I approached my thirties, though, it became obvious that whatever the perks, and however well disguised the informal corporate setup, I was still a cog in a big, fat, political, bureaucratic machine. There was no chance for advancement.

My bosses were buffoons. I was trapped. Until a way out appeared. Entrepreneurship.

Although I didn't know it at the time, tens of thousands of my compatriots across the country were discovering the same escape hatch. Peaked out in corporate jobs, or being laid off in droves by downsize/merger mania, a generation of stifled mavericks was rediscovering individualist ways. The search for a more meaningful, fulfilling, profitable life was leading wage earners to trade in the esteem and security of the corporate grind for the risks and promise of self-made careers.

My old sense of independence and nonconformism came rushing back as I blasted out of corporate orbit with adrenaline racing. I started a business marketing a novelty/gift item, the celebrity window waver, a lifesize cutout of a famous person that attached to a car window. My celebrity passengers (Rodney Dangerfield, Joan Rivers, Ronald Reagan, Marilyn Monroe) had a spring-action hand that waved to passersby with the motion of the car. The product was sold from Bloomingdale's to Dodger Stadium (Fernando Valenzuela model) and from Tokyo to Switzerland. I wound up on "Entertainment Tonight," and even Johnny Carson got into the act, demonstrating one of my items on his show. My products could be seen waving down the highways and byways of all fifty states.

It was an incredible three-year odyssey, filled with disasters and triumphs, and it whetted my appetite for the entrepreneurial life, where there was no one to report to, and no limit to achievement other than one's own imagination. My business was marginally successful, though I didn't make the big score. I decided there was more I needed to know before my next venture, so I began to dig deeper into the process of entrepreneurship.

Having just gone through the wild and woolly experience of starting a venture, my curiosity focused on those earliest, critical moments of a business. My experience on the front lines had taught me that those first days can be mind-boggling, if not overwhelming, for the beginning entrepreneur. It's a time of total bombardment, of incessant questions for which there are precious few real-world sources to turn to for advice and counsel.

Getting your hands on the details, the day-in, day-out practicalities of getting a business going, and living with its risks, are hard to come by in a hype and headline culture. Things like where *exactly* you can find a marketable idea; how *precisely* you can find funds and investors; how *specifically* you can talk, negotiate, and deal with banks, suppliers, and factories; just what kind of pitfalls await you; and what the straight scoop is on taboo issues like rejection, sacrifice, setbacks, failure, and luck are glossed over in favor of generalities, theories, and buzzwords. We're left with evangelical success seminars, frothy "go for it" volumes, turgid textbooks, and one-minute TV interviews.

I wanted to get beyond the usual clichés that all it takes is the right idea, hard work, etc.; beyond the power of positive thinking, scholarly theories . . . I wanted to get to the real stuff: what really happens out there. What was it—precisely—that got immensely successful entrepreneurs, starting at the same base as you or I, out of the blocks from ground zero? What was the whole sequence of events that got them from Point A—a dead-end job—to Point B—a thriving venture?

A record of the actual experiences, the strategies and moves that steered these entrepreneurs through their early make-it-or-break-it days, would create a startup primer rooted in the realities of the fray, not based on surmises, theories, or platitudes. It would show the rollercoaster ride of entrepreneurship the way it really is, filled with highs and lows. It would describe not only what preeminent entrepreneurs did to get to the top of the heap, but also how they felt along the way, touching on their fears and uncertainties as well as their triumphs.

This is the story, then, that I set out to explore—the unvarnished road to entrepreneurial success, the whole story from start to finish. No camera pan from startup to instant millions. No Lifestyles of the Rich and Famous. I was less concerned with how many yachts my subjects had in their backyards than their first awkward, tentative steps on the way to self-employment.

I wanted the stories of my entrepreneurs to be as relevant as possible both to the lives of readers and to current market conditions. So I developed the following criteria for selection in *You're the Boss*:

The entrepreneur (1) had to have started with little or no money or have raised it himself, (2) could not have inherited the business or have gotten any handouts from rich relatives to get going, (3) had to have started the venture primarily within the last 10 years—15 years at the outside, (4) must have had a product or service with a national scope, and (5) needed to be actively pursuing growth.

There are two kinds of entrepreneurs—the mom-and-pop type (whose major goal is produce a wage) and the ones whose major goal is to produce growth. According to David Birch, one of the leading experts on small-business development, as many as 80 percent of the nation's entrepreneurs fall into the "income substitution" category. My focus in this book is on the other 20 percent, those whose drive for innovation and expansion are fueling today's entrepreneurial economy.

These growth-oriented types had to meet a minimum annual sales requirement of at least $1 million. As it turned out, all but a handful of the people I selected were well over the $10 million mark, ranging up to $503 million in the case of Compaq Computer. Because satisfying, self-made careers come in all sizes and shapes, I chose to cover as wide of a variety of success stories as possible, from companies on the rise to those in orbit, with products as diverse as the entrepreneurs who began them.

I also wanted to find out why the boom in entrepreneurship was happening now. After watching so many of my peers bail out of stalled corporate careers my hunch was that the independent ways of the sixties generation had something to do with it.

This generation, I discovered through my research, was

different than those before it. It wasn't resigning itself to a salaried life, as its parents' generation had. The seeds of discontent had been sown in the late sixties and early seventies, as big corporations and institutions fell out of favor with an independent-minded generation.

Perhaps not so coincidentally, the story of our modern era of entrepreneurship began shortly thereafter. The nation's self-employment rolls, on a downward skid for a hundred straight years, suddenly went up in 1972, and has edged upward ever since.

A generation with a propensity for doing its own thing was gravitating increasingly to entrepreneurship, to fulfilling, self-realized careers more in keeping with their unconventional ways. It was a generation of "Great Expectations," as author Landon Jones described in his book of the same name. This group wouldn't settle. They wanted more. And what they wanted was something that had been obscured by corporate fealty for too long: the American Dream.

This generation, with its emphasis on ideals and independence, had bought the Dream big in youth. But their rugged individualism didn't assert itself immediately in an economic context, as in traditional American lore. They didn't go from high school to their own hot dog stand. They were led to believe that opportunity and achieving was in the corporate sphere, so they gave that a try first. It's when that course proved futile that they began to make the break for self-made pastures. Liberal arts majors, math-phobics, and people who never thought they'd be running a business were suddenly doing just that.

The corporate dropout route to entrepreneurship, sparked largely by certain generational values and attitudes, is a new phenomenon, and one which I decided to explore through relating the stories of the entrepreneurs, as well as summarizing our independent times, in a separate chapter called "Revolt of the Wage Slaves."

One of my major goals in this book is to demystify the

business process, which is much more accessible than you might think. There may be a number of arcane things you have to learn to run a business, but they all can be figured out. You don't have to be a whiz with numbers, stay up to read the treatises of economists, or even care what the Dow Jones averages are. Furthermore, you don't have to be an expert at power lunching or be able to bowl over people with your magnetic personality.

We tend to glorify those who have achieved great success and power, forgetting one simple fact: everyone has to start somewhere. No matter how exalted their lot today, the people you are about to meet started from the same place the rest of us must begin—square one.

Starting isn't glamorous, so it doesn't attract much attention. In a TV age of perfect smiles, perfect wits, perfect bodies, perfect clothes, and nonstop experts, it can seem like you're the only greenhorn in town. You're not. Behind every "overnight sensation" there's an entrepreneur who struggled to find his or her course, went through countless trials to get a product or service on the market, and fought epic battles to get it accepted.

This is the side of success you'll discover in *You're the Boss,* the roots, the process of success, not the gilded result. Starting a business can be a baffling, disorienting, and humbling experience, but it can also be a thrilling, exciting adventure, as our veteran beginners will demonstrate.

Individual profiles show how each entrepreneur got going from the earliest stages. You'll see how the individual extricated himself from a bad job and fumbled around with a notion until it became a viable commercial product or service. You'll learn about all the fits and starts of producing, marketing, and distributing a new product; the scrapes and setbacks that were overcome; and the key events and decisions that made the difference in a successful launch.

Each profile also illustrates a particular lesson in the how-to chronology, from finding a marketable niche to raising seed capital to withstanding the pressures of chronic risk. The chapters will take you from the first inklings of the entrepreneurial life—a belief you can do better for yourself ("Starting from Scratch")—through an exhaustive examination of the idea process ("The Big Idea"), to testing the waters ("Basic Training"), to raising money ("Capital Offense"), to avoiding start-up pitfalls ("The Real World"), to living with risk ("Down to Zero"), to bouncing back from failure ("The 'F' Word"), to acquiring and utilizing breaks ("What's Luck Got to Do with It?").

Chapter 11 then summarizes all the lessons you've learned, taking an extensive look at the California Cooler story, one that demonstrates just how far you can go when you're "Starting Smart."

You'll find—as I did in my interviews—that as successful and powerful as these entrepreneurs may be, they exhibit a distinct lack of superhuman qualities. They have drive, vision, risk-taking ability, yes, but no inate genius or ability to leap tall buildings in a single bound.

Their achievements are undoubtedly awe-inspiring. I was impressed strolling through Michael Crete's 135,000-square-foot spread for California Cooler, pumping out some twenty million cases of Cooler a year. I was boggled to hear my voice echo in Philip Hwang's parquet-floored, roller-rink-sized office, the war room for his Televideo computer empire. Yet I was struck by the fact that every high achiever I met could be interchanged with any other ordinary, hard-working soul who came up with the right notion and plan of action. Many of the entrepreneurs I talked to readily admitted as much. The Sharper Image's Richard Thalheimer noted that his "genius," for instance, was simply putting one foot in front of the other for an extended period of time.

As you discover the humble origins from which these empires grew, you'll be inclined to agree that the most ordinary beginnings can produce extraordinary results.

Books about success usually offer a neat list of precepts, which, if followed, will lead instantly to the big time. I've taken the opposite approach, because entrepreneurship is not a tidy affair. It's not easy. It's often a messy, no-holds-barred marathon in which the rules of the game can be maddeningly ambiguous and subject to change without notice. Flexibility, imagination, and resourcefulness better serve the cause than conscientious adherence to rules. There are no Ten Commandments of entrepreneurship that can ensure the Promised Land.

I've tried, instead, to present a more realistic, in-the-trenches view of the quest for career independence. It takes a while to get there. You need to know all the facts—the good, the bad, and the ugly—to steel yourself for the long march ahead. Pat answers and pet theories won't see you through the hair-raising dilemmas of the start-up years. What will, though, is practical advice from those who've been there.

You're the Boss gives you the specifics, the tips and tricks used by successful entrepreneurs to bull their way through similar critical moments. Whether it's how to persuade that first customer to buy your product, how to talk to printers, or how to collect money from your clients, every detail you need to start and run a successful venture is contained in the pages that follow—all taken from the actual experiences of today's top entrepreneurs.

Beyond details, there's something else I believe this book provides, something crucial for budding and in-the-thick-of-it entrepreneurs alike. Solidarity. Entrepreneurship is by definition a solitary exercise, a self-made, self-risked, self-propelled journey through the marketplace. It can be short on company sometimes. *You're the Boss* provides a link with others who share the spirit.

I found a host of kindred souls willing to risk job security and egos, to live on the fringes, and devote every ounce of energy to the realization of their dreams. Their stories certainly energized and inspired me. I hope they're able to do the same for you, to give you what you need to become successful in your own business.

If one advances confidently in the direction of his dreams, and endeavors to live the life he has imagined, he will meet with a success unexpected in common hours.

—Henry David Thoreau

Making the Break

A BAD JOB could be the best thing that's happened to you; it's the traditional starting point for almost every entrepreneur.

Job dissatisfaction has been shown to be a key element in the decision to go out on your own. St. Louis University professor Robert Brockhaus has found that entrepreneurs tend to come from the ranks of employees "significantly less satisfied" with their jobs than the general population. Unfulfilling work, poor job conditions, intolerable bosses and co-workers, combined with no possibility of advancement, "push" the achievement-oriented person to take things into his or her own hands and become an entrepreneur.

It takes a drastic impetus to, as Andrew Carnegie said, "plunge into and toss upon the waves of human affairs without a life preserver in the shape of a salary." So a job that's going nowhere could provide just the intense motivation needed to take a walk on the wild side of entrepreneurship. Don't suppress your restlessness. Allow it to build and force you into a more productive direction.

The story of the entrepreneurial endeavor is the story of the negative incentive, of unhappy circumstance forcing people to take action to turn things around. If you're in a job you don't want to be in, use it as a springboard to career independence.

Many of us would like to move into a self-made world where we can control our own destiny, but we can't break the hold that the corporate routine has on us.

Desire is one thing. Building the energy to make the break requires a cold, hard look at the way we lead our working lives. The security of the weekly paycheck must be compared to the price we pay to get it. We need to take an unflinching look at what most of us really get for our money in the corporate world.

No real security anymore. In an era of rampant layoffs, mergers, and global economic convulsions, few jobs today are truly secure. Uncertain times have underscored the bottom line for anyone who works for someone else—you're expendable.

No fulfillment of creative aspirations or personal potential. Every job sets an artificial ceiling on what its workers are permitted to achieve. That ceiling can be reached in two hours, two weeks, or two years. From that point on, achievement horizons narrow to a tiny sliver of tasks within the specialized job description assigned by our employer. Personal and professional growth ends before we've hardly gotten started.

No recognition. Our contributions are taken for granted, lost in layers of bureaucracy, belittled, or just plain ignored by the powers that be. The merit system, reward for effort, goes out the window, as our working fate hinges on the more unpredictable world of company politics, nepotism, inept supervisors, red tape, sexual politics, and runaway gossip.

Not enough money. Whatever the salary, we never make enough to really get ahead of the game. Working for someone else never gives us the money to really do the things we want, or the financial security we need to keep pace with the skyrocketing cost of living. A company wage is no match anymore for the price tag on a new home, the kids' college education, and particularly major medical care.

No freedom to move. An employee lives according to the employer's schedule. Daily activities have to be fitted around the job. It is the employer's convenience and employer's whims that determine the hours and days of work and the tasks that are tackled. Creative design of work schedules, flexibility in merging and alternating work and personal activities is impossible. We can't live our own lifestyle. We live the boss's.
   We toe the line and try to preserve a little bit of ourselves

inside, apart from the fray. We can see the problem, but it's hard to visualize the solution. We may be living in an economy ripe for new ideas and individual possibilities, but visions alone don't put bread on the table.

We stick with what does, and the best years of our lives are pumped dry, our peak energies and ideas gobbled up. As time passes our recourse to independent action fades into the distance. Overtime, suicidal deadlines, and endless business luncheon-function jive—all we have to show for them is an income equal to our means, or below it, and a precarious dependency that could end when we're least prepared.

And for all that effort, that expenditure of ourselves, only 27 percent of us are "completely satisfied" that we can move up the ladder, according to a Roper poll. And very few of us will actually achieve our expectations.

In an article in *Personnel Journal*, "Will Career Plateauing Become a Bigger Problem?" management reflects on the "problem" of achievement-oriented employees, noting that employees of the sixties and seventies have the audacity to "assume that hard work and education should be rewarded by increased power." The article's advice to the nation's employers is: "It is to nobody's advantage to hire mainly superstars with high mobility expectations. We must seek out individuals who can perform competently at work, but have other interests in which self-esteem is anchored." Calling all drones. Corporate America wants you.

TURNING THE TABLES ON THE NINE-TO-FIVE

When great expectations and career stagnation collide, chronic job dissatisfaction sets in. In this predicament, you can either abandon your aspirations—the traditional response—and make the best of a bad situation, or abandon a sinking occupational ship before your hopes and dreams go under.

The same job that can break your spirit with tedious drudgery can also be the critical first spur for you to make it on your own. The trick is to make your job work for you, instead of the other way around. Begin to see the world in an entrepreneurial light, see that behind every problem lies an opportunity.

This book will give you what you need to know to turn the tables on a dissatisfying job, to break out of the workaday rut and get your piece of the opportunity society. You will learn the practical techniques of becoming an entrepreneur by seeing how some of today's most successful entrepreneurs made the break from wage earner to career independence. From their real-life examples—not clichés or platitudes—you'll discover the nuts and bolts of getting a venture going from nothing. You will learn the techniques of:

Starting from scratch

Developing entrepreneurial creativity

Testing and researching your idea

Getting your start-up stake without going to the financial establishment

Making the financial establishment work for you

Surviving the marketplace

How to live with risk and survive setbacks

Making your luck

Using brains instead of money

The word from the front lines is that anyone can—and many are—achieving financial independence. Enterprise is for everyone. Here are just a few examples of the men and women you'll be meeting, people just like you, former employees who decided to follow their entrepreneurial dreams and who now run some of the most exciting, successful ventures in the U.S.

—Pauper day-care teacher Lane Nemeth got fed up

with her $5-an-hour wage, and the limited horizons of professional babysitting. Why don't I try something completely different? she asked herself. Something that could lead somewhere. So at twenty-eight, Lane started her own business, an educational toy company, Discovery Toys, which now brings in revenues of $40 million annually.

—**Harried commodities trader Stuart Bewley** felt trapped in his high-pressure, low-satisfaction occupation. His aspirations ran headlong into a stone wall of bureaucrats and bosses. He concluded that things didn't have to stay that way. At twenty-six, he opted out of the nine-to-five and, with his partner, **frustrated beer salesman Michael Crete,** who drove a truck for Coors, Bewley co-founded California Cooler. Starting with just $10,000 between them, within five years they were selling $150 million worth of wine coolers per year.

—**Stifled journalist Mel Ziegler, and his equally hampered illustrator-wife, Patricia,** were at the end of their ropes butting up against restrictive editors on the *San Francisco Chronicle*. Instead of spiritual resignation, they chose a letter of resignation. With $1,500 they started a company over which they would have full editorial control. Today their firm, Banana Republic, a travel and safari clothing empire, grosses $50 million a year.

—**Bored senior managers Rod Canion, Jim Harris, and Bill Murto** were in their mid-thirties and plateaued-out in the corporate confines of Texas Instruments. They huddled together and decided it was time for a new play to avoid the lifetime stall-out. They'd do something themselves. They formed Compaq Computer, whose first-year sales of $115 million made it the fastest-growing company in American business history. Within three years it reached an annual gross of $503 million.

—**Exasperated high school chemistry teacher/football coach Ron Rice** knew he was never going to achieve his potential in life through secondary education. So he taught himself how to make suntan oil. The twenty-eight-year-old teacher mixed up a potion in his garage that has become one of the world's leading suntan products, Hawaiian Tropic Tanning Oil. With $500 start-up capital he created a company, Tanning Research Labs, that today has revenues of $120 million each year.

—**Stymied advertising copywriter Faith Popcorn** had a well-paying job in the advertising business, but it didn't compensate her for the lack of creativity and achievement curbed by corporate policies. Grating at a boss "who had half my intelligence and instincts," she exercised the option of independence rather than grit her teeth in perpetuity. At twenty-eight, with a friend and $20,000, she started BrainReserve, a market research and consulting firm. Today it grosses $23 million a year and is ranked in the top sixty women-owned firms in the U.S. by *Savvy* magazine.

As these entrepreneurs would be the first to tell you, starting a business and achieving success takes a lot of hard work and commitment—but it *can* be done. And getting started is easier than you think. It all begins with a simple resolution: "Today I start taking control of my life."

THE PRIMARY ASSETS

If it doesn't take experience or money to be an entrepreneur, what does it take? It takes a certain group of personal attributes. These can be called the Primary Assets. They are the basis for all entrepreneurial endeavors. You can start without background or cash reserves, but not without this private backing.

Belief. All of us have doubts from time to time, even entrepreneurs, though they don't like to admit it. Belief is a superior confidence in your own worth that deflects those doubts and doubters by enormous reserves of conviction. You have to have rock-solid faith in yourself and your instincts. As Philadelphia psychologist Joan Harvey says, "It's a tendency to be internally validated and not have to look outside yourself for some kind of validation of your own ideas or your own feelings." You don't need someone else to tell you what to think. Strong self-belief awakens the first entrepreneurial urge, that you owe it to yourself to do better; it sustains you through the long hours and crises.

Certain types of behavior and attitudes indicate a good foundation of this Primary Asset.

1. You feel you can do the job better than others.

2. You've decided that the successful people of the world aren't supermen or women, and have no more on the ball than you do.

3. You don't go with the flow. You aren't a joiner.

4. You don't mind advocating a position no one else shares, or being the lone dissenter in a group decision.

5. Rejection and criticism are not a deterrence, but an incentive.

6. You have a stubborn streak, and lots of willpower.

7. You make high demands of yourself.

8. You are accustomed to doing activities on your own.

9. You have great self-pride. You put in your best effort no matter the task.

Aspiration.   Whatever the motivation for your venture, it has to be stronger than even your faith in yourself. The hunger must be relentless. Aspiration is not mere desire, or the coach's cliché of "wanting it more" than the next guy. It's not a "want" at all. It's a matter of soul-sating need. Nothing less than the most consuming need can generate the courage to break from the past and the energy to start over. These needs cause a craving that can't be slept off, bought off, or written off until satisfied.

The signs of that hunger are a need

1. To achieve, to master a challenge.

2. To create.

3. To achieve financial security.

4. To prove your worth to a particular person or the world at large.

5. To control your own destiny.

6. To get revenge for past wrongs of employers, family members, or society.

7. To have power and influence over others.

8. To grow and advance; to be fulfilled.

9. To beat the competition.

10. To live your own lifestyle.

Imagination.   This supplies the means to accomplish your nagging objective. It attaches a shape, a course, a destination to the amorphous quest for alternatives. The entrepreneurial imagination doesn't require the pure creative genius of a Salvador Dali or a Charlie Parker. It's more a case of being a keen interpreter than a creator. It's an ability to take observations and information and twist it around, add to it, and recombine it into a next logical step that will not appear logical to others for maybe quite some time.

Entrepreneurial imagination is marked by

1. Alert observation of life and human nature, understanding people's likes, dislikes, and how those change.

2. Avoiding routine to seek out the fresh and new.

3. A high level of curiosity, even about areas you may have had no prior interest in.

4. Asking questions, no matter how elementary they may be.

5. An active critical faculty, able to not only spot problems but offer solutions.

6. An instinct for anticipation, for someone's next move.

7. An ability to think beyond the present tense, and plan ahead.

8. Energetic daydreaming. A willingness to entertain improbable and seemingly impossible thoughts, to imagine how things can be different than they are.

Initiative. You can have an ample supply of the other three Primary Assets, but they're useless for entrepreneurial purposes without initiative. Action is what separates the entrepreneur from the rest of Homo sapiens. You have to be able to move on your dreams and plans. No one is going to make them happen unless you do. You don't have to be a compulsive dice thrower to manifest this asset, but you do need to know how to analyze the pros and cons and make quick decisions, accepting the possibility that some may be wrong ones. The more comfortable you are with decision-making, the easier it will be to deal with the risks of initiative.

Entrepreneurial initiative is demonstrated by:

1. A hatred of standing still, and an addiction to motion and forward progress.

2. A belief in change and your ability to effect it.

3. Assigning ultimate blame or credit for your actions to no one but yourself.

4. The realization that no one else is going to give you a hand. You have to do it yourself.

5. A refusal to second-guess the past, and get on with the next decision.

6. A dislike for playing it safe.

7. A large reserve of physical energy.

8. A capacity for spontaneity and an ability to improvise as the situation requires.

THE WAY OUT

Backed by the Primary Assets, a good idea, and an openness to new possibilities you can overcome the daunting double whammy of no experience and no money. Kevin Jenkins didn't know a thing about computers before he decided to switch careers from publishing to hi-tech. He wound up building a $35 million company, Hercules Computer, just by teaching himself how to do it. "Even if I don't know much about something, it doesn't stop me from getting into it," says Jenkins.

"Many times people tell me, 'Boy I'd like to get into something.' But they're afraid to try something new. I say, Who cares? It doesn't make any difference. To me it's a challenge to see how much you can learn."

Most people view a change of career with a combination of dread and outright terror. Fear of the unknown, fear of looking foolish, and most importantly, fear of admitting your present course isn't working, block the only way out of an unsatisfactory job—doing something different. It's tough to admit that your investment in time, schooling, and years in a given trade may not have amounted to much. Our society constantly admonishes us to not be a "quitter." So we soldier on year after year, plying a dead-end course.

To unlock your entrepreneurial potential, you have to see change not as a foe, but as your best friend. Advancement can only come through growth and the adoption of new approaches and career angles. Who cares what anyone else thinks? It's your life on the line, and you're the only one who can steer it to where you want it to go.

Ron Rice wasn't worried about what the neighbors thought when he started brewing up suntan oil in his garage in plastic garbage cans. The Daytona Beach, Florida, high school teacher and summer lifeguard didn't rule out a move to the suntan business because he wasn't "qualified" to do it, or didn't have a dime to sink into a new route. It didn't matter to him that he'd never been a chemist for Coppertone, or hadn't marketed a product before. He believed he could do it; he had a compelling need to do it; and he had the initiative to go into action. It was the only way things were going to turn around for him.

With only the courage to try something new, his resolve and $500 from his father, Rice created Hawaiian Tropic Tanning Oil. Today, with that product as his flagship, his company, Tanning Research Labs, takes in $120 million a year through the sale of tanning oil, the private label production of cosmetics, and a line of beachwear.

How was Rice able to graduate from high school to chairman of the board of the second largest tanning products company in the world without any apparent resources? As his story shows, it's not money or background that makes a successful entrepreneur; it's the inner qualifications—the determination to change your course in life, the imagination to find an exploitable idea, the belief that you have the ability to move in a new direction, and the courage to see your venture through.

USING THE OLD COCONUT
Ron Rice/Tanning Research Labs

The system controls you until you control the system. Ron Rice, of whom I have spoken before, was made painfully aware of that fact each time he looked at his paltry schoolteacher's paycheck, each time school administrators vetoed his ideas, each time he was called on the carpet for not conforming to rules and regulations, and certainly each year when he was sent packing to find a new job. In eight years of teaching, Rice worked at seven schools and got fired six times.

He was in one of those seemingly interminable cycles familiar to many in the working world. You're never going to get anywhere this way. Yet you don't have the resources to change the situation. Rice didn't make enough money to save any, and as a chemistry teacher/football coach, he wasn't "qualified" to do much else.

The entrepreneurial option seemed the only way out. He looked for an opportunity. A cheap one. But he couldn't find anything.

"Everybody told me, save your money, you're going to recognize the opportunity. It's going to come along, then you'll invest in it and that's what you'll end up doing. But that wasn't the case at all. Because nothing ever came along."

It had always been that way for Rice, always on the outside looking in, trying to figure out how to get off the ground. His family never had anything. As a result, he had learned the value of initiative at a young age. During summers growing up in the mountains outside Asheville, North Carolina, he sold walnuts, pecans, berries, and apples at a roadside stand. He also had his own cider mill. At Christmastime he would trim hedges and make Christmas wreaths to sell.

He worked his way through the University of Tennessee and was doing graduate work in geology when he concluded that "there were guys with doctorates and masters in geology who were making less than guys with bachelor's degrees in business." Quitting school, he went down to Florida, where he had been working as a lifeguard during summer vacations at Daytona. When the lifeguard season ended one fall, he had to get a job and wound up in a Florida high school, coaching the football team, and teaching chemistry and physics.

The years dragged on, teaching nine months, lifeguarding during the summer, getting fired from schools. But instead of being beaten down by it, the frustration was a constant incentive for him to find another way. His desire to play by his own rules, to get ahead in the world, and have the independence to live a "casual beach lifestyle," kept him on the lookout for opportunity. He kept probing for an idea.

And one day it came to him, looking, as it usually does, not as a pot of gold, but as a vague, random speculation. It was one of those instances where something you never take notice of because you're surrounded by it, is suddenly seen in a new light. As he looked up and down the beach from his lifeguard tower, at all those people glistening with suntan oil he saw something different. Perhaps there was room on the market for a new tanning substance, something more natural, like the kind he had seen used in Hawaii. If it was successful in the Islands, maybe it could be marketed in Florida, too.

It was something to play around with, anyway. An extra income on the side could help fill out that pauper's salary he got from the school board. He thought about it more and more over the following weeks. The concept, a coconut-oil–based tanning lotion, just might work. On a trip to Hawaii, he had noticed that local women rubbed coconut oil in their hair; other fruit, nut, and flower extracts were commonly used as beauty aids in the Hawaiian backwoods. The observation had stuck, as such curiosities often do in the mind of an entrepreneur. Years later, as Rice pondered suntan lotion one day, that Hawaiian recollection turned a mind's wandering into opportunity.

Did he have the credentials to pull something like this off? Not in the usual sense. But yet, as a chemistry teacher, he could probably figure out the right mix of chemicals. As a lifeguard, who could be more in tune with tans and burns and lotions than he was? He was beginning to see that his supposedly limited job skills weren't that limited after all, if applied to the right areas.

Money was the big problem. He didn't have any, and didn't know anyone who did. "Somehow, somewhere," recalls Rice, "my father came up with $500 and lent it to me to buy caps, labels, bottles, and oil. I bought a $3.25 garbage can and that's where I mixed it all up."

Starting with so little capital, Rice knew it wasn't going to happen overnight for him. But he thought if he took it slow enough, and kept costs to the bare minimum, he could gradually build the business from nothing. He held onto his teaching job while he mixed his potions at night and on weekends. The magic formula was elusive, but he didn't give up.

"It took years to create," he remembers. "Years of testing various formulas on beachgoers while I was a lifeguard. I'd put an 'X' on one arm, a 'Y' on another arm, a 'Z' on one leg, and then I'd see which one they liked best. Everybody didn't necessarily like the same items. It was a matter of which one did the most people like, and which did I think was the best product."

Rice's tanning laboratory was his garage, where he spent two years mixing every possible combination of ingredients. When he finally got the blend he wanted, he hired two eleven-year-old kids to help him fill bottles with a hose that ran out the bottom of his trash can/still, and he signed up a fourteen-year-old secretary to help with the orders and calls. Then Rice hit the beaches of Daytona with the first natural coconut tanning oil.

Although his resources were limited, Rice made sure his product didn't look like it came out of a garage. He knew that the little guy has a better chance if he looks like a big guy. He used only the most expensive packaging and ingredients and charged a higher price than his competitors. Although he knew nothing about business, Rice did have some valuable street/beach knowledge. He knew his audience and recognized that he had a gimmick that would appeal to them.

"I had the only natural suntan lotion before 'natural' was cool," he says. "All the other products on the market were just chemicals that were put together. When the natural craze hit there was no commercial suntan lotion available along that line. When everybody else was running around eating fruits and nuts, I was already out there with my product."

But he had to convince retailers to carry it. Stores never want to touch an unproven item, so selling those first few stores was Rice's toughest job. His lifeguard connection helped. He went first to the concessionaires of beach wagons, then to beach stores, and he got some lifeguards to use it. With no advertising, the first batch of Hawaiian Tropic somehow managed to sell out and reorders soon had Rice and his high school staffers filling up bottles into the wee hours.

With only the money he took in from sales to finance the venture, things grew slowly, bottle by bottle. As he could afford it, he would buy an automated filler or other equipment. But the operation stayed in the garage for a long time. He would teach in the morning, coach football in the afternoon, and bottle lotion at night. Weekends were his big selling period during the school year. During the summer his small crew worked around the clock.

There were no visions of fortunes in those early days. His philosophy was "Don't spend a penny unless it brings a return." And as someone accustomed to frugality, Rice knew how to pare expenses down to the bone. That meant no playtime in a place where partying is a full-time occupation. Socially, he had to answer the entrepreneurial call of hibernation.

"All my buddies were trying to get me to go out and party and get drunk," Rice remembers. "I wouldn't do it. I had no social life at that time. There was time for nothing but to eat, sleep, and work."

It wasn't until three years after he launched Hawaiian

Tropic that Rice made the decision to quit his teaching post and pursue suntan oil full-time. He admits to a "little panic when I didn't get a regular paycheck. But that all changed when I realized the business was going to make it."

Hawaiian Tropic was selling well, partly because of a key sales innovation dreamed up by Rice, who had never before sold anything to anyone. He gave his franchises away, instead of selling them. "If you sell somebody something, you're obligated to them," he points out. "If you give it to them, they're obligated to you. I gave them all a tremendous profit to inspire them."

His sales team—all amateurs, made up of his former lifeguard buddies and football players—was inspired enough to beat back a competing product from the huge Bristol-Meyers Corp., which was blitzing the country with Tanya. Proving that big corporations are vulnerable to a more innovative product in the hands of a hungrier sales force, Bristol-Meyers was forced to discontinue Tanya in 1974.

Rice showed that given the proper incentive and responsibility, many others like himself, who weren't given a chance, could rise to the occasion. In 1973 Rice gave the whole Australian market to a friend of his just out of Florida State University. Today Hawaiian Tropic is the second best selling tanning oil in the Land of Oz.

Rice says "the secret of our success is promotion. It's the way you present it to the public and to the business." His strategy here was to position Hawaiian Tropic as a quality, higher-priced tanning lotion, 25 to 75 cents more than the competition. Packaging, promotions, and advertising all helped create a prestigious image that allowed it to go from the beaches of Daytona to the shelves of the nation's better department stores, like Bloomingdale's, Macy's, and the former Gimbles.

The rise of Hawaiian Tropic was not without the usual share of scares and stumbles of a start-up. The oil crisis of the mid-seventies, for example, nearly cut off the supply of base oil, the central ingredient in his product. But Hawaiian Tropic didn't make any major blunders, and continued to grow until it had become the second leading seller of tanning products in the U.S. and an increasing force on the world market.

The company had diversified into private-label packaging, which Rice thinks will do three times the business of tanning oil. Major cosmetics firms like Revlon come to Rice's eighteen chemists with product problems or new ideas, and Tanning Research Labs makes the ingredients, bottles it, labels it, and ships it out.

Rice has made a fortune from a very small niche in the marketplace. Only 5 percent of Americans even use suntan oil, and only 2 percent are avid users. He has proven that a small concentrated target market can be a launching pad to riches. From those first two eleven-year-old kids and fourteen-year-old secretary, the company has grown to 2,000 employees worldwide. Rice oversees it all now from a $3 million beach mansion, pulsing with movers and shakers and beautiful people, and parties that have caused it to be known as Playboy Mansion East.

Working for himself has its advantages over his old school days. "For one," he notes, "I wasn't driving a $250,000 Lamborghini; I wasn't driving a 530, European cut-nose Porsche when I was a teacher. The most important thing, though, is the freedom to dictate my own schedule, to pretty much do what I want to do when I want to do it."

Rice feels he hasn't done anything other people can't do. You can do it, he says, but "you've got to be willing to take the time. Total commitment. Today there's more opportunity than ever before. People come up to me and say 'everything's been done.' But we all know that's not true because there's more opportunity than ever before. All they have to do is come up with the idea and just go do it. There were other suntan lotions on the market when I did mine. I just added a little twist to it. I found a better mousetrap and just pushed it out there until I beat my competitors."

THE AMATEUR'S EDGE

The overachieving efforts of millions of amateurs like Ron Rice is what gives life to the national ideal—that someone can start out with nothing and make it into something—and fuels our culture and business with a dynamism found nowhere else.

Going from last place to first place is an American tradition. None of us are ever completely out of the running. There's always a chance to redirect a poorly chosen course, or take control of one chosen for us.

In a crowded, technological age, though, some people let the opportunity option be dwarfed by forces which seem too strong and smart to take on. Decades of emphasis on the giant corporation, of making the MBA-graduated, multinational manager synonymous with "businessman," has built up a mystique about business, that it's a preserve for top-of-the-class types and requires years of training the average person could never match.

The age of specialization and a steady diet of "experts" in the media conspire to make all of us feel inadequate. The specialists make everything look harder than it is. We live in complicated times, say the experts, so everything must be complicated. So many authorities stressing complexity can make anyone hesitate to take the entrepreneurial leap.

But the experts are wrong. It's just the lack of extensive expertise that gives many entrepreneurs the edge in the marketplace. Mark Twain once said that the formula for success is "ignorance plus confidence." Experts are saddled with iron-clad views of what can or can't be done in a given field. The newcomer can look at opportunity in a new way, unrestricted by the baggage of routine and tradition, and come up with an approach the know-it-all could never imagine.

Michael Crete came up with an idea to put wine in beer bottles. It made sense to him that his California Cooler—if it were true to its name—should be an instantly quenching, single-serving drink. If it sat in the cold refrigerated display cases of liquor stores it could be featured, and moved, alongside other quick-selling beer items. The major liquor companies were aghast. "They said it couldn't be done," says Crete. "'How can you put wine in a beer bottle?'" Five years later California Cooler had $150 million in sales, and Gallo, Heublein, Seagram's, Anheuser-Busch, and over 100 other companies had followed his lead. Crete's amateur intuition had beaten billion-dollar companies to the punch.

Behind every millionaire entrepreneur is an idea that either didn't occur to, or was rejected by, so-called infallible experts. Chester Carlson, for example, tried to sell the idea of a photocopy machine for more than a decade, but the experts wouldn't buy it. Out of his invention Xerox was born. The biggest computer company in the world, IBM, concluded that there was no market for home computers—until the amateurs of Apple Computer convinced them otherwise.

For the body of established opinion there are things that just "can't be done." They're judged to be too risky or not technically feasible. Other ideas are dismissed because they're just not the "right way" to do things, too uncouth, too foolish, yes, even too simple for those in control.

The authorities in the weight-training business said no one could market a home gym. But an entrepreneur could. Jerry Wilson's idea of the home gym ran counter to every reigning principle in the field. Coaches wouldn't recommend lifting weights to their athletes, saying it would slow them down. Weight-machine manufacturers were convinced that the only market for their machines was the health clubs, certainly not home users. Engineers and fitness-machine manufacturers told Wilson that it was physically impossible to design a compact device that would do what he wanted it to. Says Soloflex founder Wilson: "Coaches and industry authorities are always the last ones to find out anything new. It always comes from the outside."

Outsiders and amateurs, assumed to be at a disadvantage in the formidable world of business, actually have the edge when it comes to creativity and innovation. They also have a big advantage in another key area: risk-taking. With little to lose, those who start with nothing are in a much better position to take the risks that are essential to propel a venture forward. As T. C. Swartz of Society Expeditions explains, "If you start out with nothing, anything you wind up with is better. If you end up with zero, at least you've learned something, but you're in no worse position. I don't see risk as risk because I started with nothing, so everything is a bonus."

CHANGE: OPEN DOOR FOR NEWCOMERS

The plain fact is that no matter how unapproachable the experts make business out to be, amateurs have as good a chance as anyone to carve out a piece of enterprise for themselves. The reason is change. The pros can never have things all locked up because things are constantly changing. Economist Joseph Schumpeter, father of entrepreneurial theory, described it this way: "Capitalism is essentially a process of economic change. Without change, capitalist society can't exist—without innovation, without entrepreneurs, without entrepreneurial achievement, there are no capitalist returns and there is no capitalist propulsion."

Instead of all positions being preselected, the players are always changing, and the giants are always being driven to the hills by energetic newcomers armed with better ideas. Consumer wants and needs are constantly shifting. Whoever spots the new direction first—and it could be any of us—has the opportunity to win the day.

Change is the great equalizer. It's what makes entrepreneurship the most democratizing force in society. It allows people with none of the prescribed attributes of the establishment to detour the system and come out on top. People without the right credentials, without the right entree; people who didn't come from the right part of town, graduate number one in their class, who weren't selected homecoming queen or named All-American; people who didn't know from the age of twelve that they were going to be a doctor or lawyer, and who struggled and flailed around looking for a direction—through change anyone can find an opportunity to get off the ground and begin achieving.

HIDDEN TALENTS

Starting is believing. You may not know exactly what you want to do, or you may not be sure that you have the money or experience to do something on your own, but the feeling is there. You believe you can do something better than someone else is doing it; you believe you deserve better; you believe there's a better life out there.

That's where it starts, the long road to career independence, with a nagging, insistent belief in yourself. Your employer may underestimate your worth, but you don't.

From there the next stop is to assess how your skills might translate into the business sphere. Surprisingly, even without any business experience, you already have some rudimentary entrepreneurial resources. That's because entrepreneurship is a generalist's job that borrows from many different walks of life. It depends more on the overall makeup of the individual than on any specific aptitude.

You can be a first-time businessman or woman, but still have valuable experience to bring to the job:

- Journalist Mel Ziegler knew how to research a subject from scratch, to find the information needed to get Banana Republic off the ground.

- As a dancer, Judi Sheppard Missett learned the self-discipline and interpersonal skills needed to build Jazzercise.

- Landscaper Avi Ruimi knew how to get his hands dirty, and his clothes wrinkled, a key ingredient for the hands-on entrepreneurial life-style that was required to successfully launch Auto-Shade.

*   *   *

There are many varied skills, then, that are transferrable to the business world. You just need to redirect what you have into a more profitable area. Making the jump to business doesn't require an MBA as much as it does a backlog of good work skills from any occupation.

People don't start companies because they're good in business. Ventures are begun—and sustained—on the strength of a saleable idea, and on the entrepreneur's belief that he or she has enough brains, drive, and resourcefulness to see it through. So, if you have confidence in your own personal inventory, it doesn't matter if you know anything about freight forwarders, die-cutters, or profit and loss statements. If you have reasonable intelligence and do your homework, you'll learn what's necessary as you go along.

When John Todd, a product manager for GAF Corp., started his hotel amenity company, Guest Supply, he didn't know anything about business. "I didn't even know what an invoice was," he says. "I didn't understand what terms were on invoices, credits and debits, or anything." But knowing that he had a good idea, and that he was a generally capable fellow, he assumed he would figure things out eventually. He did. His company is now listed on the New York Stock Exchange.

Joan Barnes can testify that you don't have to know everything to get started. She was making $5,000 as a children's program director for a Jewish community center in San Francisco when she decided to start a children's fitness company, Gymboree. Her knowledge of business was zilch at the time. "I didn't even know what a business plan was," she says. "Cash flows, accruals, it was all alien to me." She figured it out well enough to build a $7 million company of Gymboree franchises. Now she speaks at symposiums, seminars, and before assemblages at the Stanford Business School on the intricacies of entrepreneurship.

The business details are essential to the ultimate success of any venture, but they can be picked up along the way. You do need to start out with some knowledge, though, of the market you are entering. Most entrepreneurs start ventures in their current field, a related one, or in an area they're intensely interested in, either as a hobby or as a lifelong dream. In any case, they may be starting from scratch, but they are bringing extensive familiarity with their markets to the table.

Once again, it's a matter of transferring skills, of finding a way to adapt something you already know into a moneymaking endeavor. It's looking at your talents in a new light, determining how you can make them work for yourself for a change instead of for someone else.

Norm Pattiz sold television advertising. All it took for him to go from a sales wage earner to an entrepreneurial tycoon was to transfer what he knew about TV advertising to radio. He started advertiser-supported syndicated radio programming like they had in the TV world. The Westwood One empire was born.

As a sales rep for a surfing products company and a diehard surfer all the rest of his waking hours, Jim Jenks was a long way from MBA material. Yet once he applied his knowledge of, and passion for, surfing to a product—surf fashions—he was able to ride his nonbusiness experience to the top of the apparel industry with Ocean Pacific Sunwear.

It was the same thing with Lane Nemeth. The outside world could easily dismiss this English major and day-care teacher. But Nemeth didn't believe in standard qualifications. She believed in herself. She found a way to make her background work for her by taking the most unlikely business setting—classrooms full of preschool toddlers—and turning her observations into a major corporation, Discovery Toys, a $40 million marketer of educational toys. Her story illustrates that we all know more than we think, and that we can harness that knowledge and experience to exploit opportunities very close at hand.

CONVERTING CLASSROOM TO BOARDROOM
Lane Nemeth/Discovery Toys

When Lane Nemeth decided she was going to start a major toy corporation, she got the usual reaction of a typecast world. "I would classify it as amused skepticism," she states. "My mother asked whether I really wanted to quit the day-care center to pursue this dream? My father said, 'I'm sure it's a good idea . . . but . . .' He was sort of amused. The day-care people nodded their heads and said, 'Well, you'll be back teaching here in a year, but good luck.'"

On closer inspection, though, we see that many of the skills Nemeth had developed over a broad range of jobs had prepared her well for an entrepreneurial venture. Entrepreneurship is, in large part, a matter of psychological and mental fitness. Nemeth was tough enough, to be sure, having survived a stint with the New York City Department of Social Services doing job counseling and rehabilitation for drug addicts and murderers.

She had learned how to initiate and be autonomous, setting up new programs and marketing them for the YWCA. She had mastered communication and marketing skills as the community liaison for the Social Services Department of Eugene, Oregon. As director of a day-care center in San Francisco that she helped start from scratch, she managed a yearly budget of $200,000. Unlike those who tend to downplay the value of a broad range of personal skills in an age of specialization, Nemeth took hers to the next step.

Bored and frustrated with her $5-an-hour wage at the day-care center, she was ready for something new. Her inspiration came as the result of a bad day at the mall. She had spent all afternoon looking for a toy for a friend's one-year-old son but came up empty-handed. She wound up buying him some clothes. The quality toys she was looking for were not to be found. The kind of educational toys she used at the day-care center weren't available in stores. She decided they should be, and that she would be the one to get them out there.

That night she excitedly told her husband and father about her plan to open an educational toy store. She would sell the type of toys she had in her day-care center, and would conduct workshops for parents to teach them how their children should use the toys. Her father was pessimistic, but her husband thought it sounded interesting. His comment planted the seed that would eventually sprout into Discovery Toys: "It sounds like Tupperware." That was in February 1976. Lane Nemeth was twenty-nine-years old.

The store idea turned out to be too costly, so she decided to give the Tupperware/home-party approach a try. The toys she selected for her first demonstration came mostly from her daycare center, which had a lot of extra, unopened toys filling up the storehouse. She bought a few additional items that fit her concept for safe, intellectually stimulating, aesthetically pleasing toys in local stores, most of which were under-distributed European imports. She got eight of her friends to host demonstration parties, and wound up selling a few hundred dollars' worth of toys at each party. The test had proven she had something.

So with the faith that her product was needed by the market she knew so well, she plunged in with the barest of assets. "We were just short of living on food stamps," she notes. "My husband's business was going bankrupt. It was really tough." Instead of being immobilized by the lack of resources, though, Nemeth took advantage of it with the proper entrepreneurial attitude—with nothing to lose, there's only something to gain. "It didn't seem like it could get any worse. I knew I wouldn't starve to death. I always could get a job again."

She borrowed $20,000 from her grandmother and brother-in-law and she was off to put Discovery Toys on the map. Lane Nemeth, daring enterpriser, was in action. But Nemeth was actually not much of a daredevil; she was more like a homebody. On a trip from San Francisco to Los Angeles for her first toy industry trade show, she had to have a friend accompany her because she was afraid to fly by herself.

"When we got off the plane," says Nemeth, "my friend asked, 'Now what do we do?' I answered, 'How do I know?' I was thinking that she would tell me how to get to the hotel. She said instead, 'Lane, it's not my business, it's yours.' It was one of those crisis points where I almost said, 'I can't do this, forget it.' So I took a deep breath and thought, 'Yeah, I can do this. I've never done it before but I can do it.'"

Nemeth discovered that you don't have to be superhuman to be able to achieve. Homebodies and people who have doubts can be entrepreneurs, too.

The direct-marketing scheme she had in mind to sell her product had never been tried with toys before. The home-demonstration party had sold billions of dollars' worth of plastic bowls and cosmetics, yet it was also tailor-made for Nemeth's products. It appealed to several key instincts—new moms love to get together and talk about their kids; they crave tips on how to best stimulate and educate tots in the early years; and they want the best of everything for their children. The home party filled a social need as well as a bona fide market by offering toys that were learning tools as well as playthings. Nemeth used the potent entrepreneurial logic that if she were fed up with something, like useless dolls and war toys, there were other people out there who felt the same way.

Nemeth decided she would hire saleswomen to arrange toy parties, at which they would instruct the assembled mothers on the value of educational playthings. In the plan, each saleswoman or "educational consultant," would get a percentage of sales from the party, initially 17 percent (now 24 percent) and each hostess who staged the affair would be eligible for either free toys or big discounts.

The heart of the system is the sales force. Nemeth knew that she'd have to come up with some people who could sell like social activists with a cause. But how? She had "never sold anything in my whole life," and she had no big money to offer them. It was up to good old entrepreneurial conviction to do the job. "To this day I'm not sure why they did it, except that I was so excited," she says about her very first saleswomen. "They were all moms; they all had young kids. I had a mission . . . I didn't offer them money. . . . It was like . . . we're going to change the world and make kids better. I was just so enthusiastic, so excited, and understood my product so well that they immediately grasped that these toys were exactly what they'd been looking for for their kids."

This passion soon began to translate into sales. With just two outside saleswomen she managed to sell $250,000 worth of toys her first year in business.

With a further loan of $30,000 from relatives, she moved operations from her overcrowded garage to a small, unheated warehouse in Concord, at the southern end of San Francisco Bay. Ants and mice would carry off donuts and lunches, and in the winter Nemeth and her staff worked in masks and parkas.

There are much bigger problems, though, that can plague the start-up company in the early years. Nemeth soon was up to her neck in them. Although Discovery Toys had grown to a considerable $900,000 in sales its second year, it had spent more money than it had earned. Nemeth was out of cash. She owed $100,000 and didn't have a dime. It was January 1980, and her peak Christmas selling season was a year away.

She had to stall suppliers and find a way to raise some money. Her only option was a loan at an exorbitant 27.5 percent interest rate. The $100,000 didn't last long. By June she was broke again. "I couldn't meet payroll," she says, "or buy any new toys. I was desperate. I didn't know what I was going to do."

But because she still believed in her product, and wouldn't give up, she had positioned herself for an unexpected helping hand. Out of the blue it came—The Break. A venture capitalist whose wife had gone to a Discovery Toys demonstration party was on the phone. "He said, 'I'm a venture capitalist and I'd like to invest in your company.' I didn't know what venture capital was. I'd never heard the word before. I said, 'Great.'"

Saved by the bell, Nemeth received new financing and by

year's end had doubled her sales once again, to $2.5 million. Two years later she had skyrocketed to $10 million. Things were going well, too well. Discovery Toys had gotten so big its growth was becoming unmanageable.

There comes a point in the growth of a venture when a company needs more experienced business management, and Nemeth had reached it. She brought in new management to help get the firm to the next level. However, within ten months the company had gone from possible tumor to terminal cancer. Not only did the experts fail to stimulate the expected growth and shepherd the company from an entrepreneurial phase to a mid-size corporate stage, but they drained off the last few years' worth of profit. Payroll ballooned five times while sales only doubled.

For the first time Nemeth faced the prospect of failure. "I went home and told my husband that we were in bankruptcy and I was out of business. I took a tranquilizer and went to sleep. I woke up the next morning really numb and empty inside. I thought maybe I shouldn't even go to work. I was too tired."

She thought about selling the company. She had an offer from a conglomerate standing by. But she couldn't allow the product of so much blood and sweat to succumb without a fight. She fired the so-called professionals who had destroyed her firm and set about reorganizing and cutting back to save the company.

There was one last chance—Bank of America. However, the bank, which had been financing Discovery Toys for several years, decided not to support the company in its hour of need. Crocker Bank had been courting Nemeth for years, and finally she contacted them. Maybe, just maybe, they would overlook the troubled period and bail her out. They did. The money arrived a few days before Christmas 1983. If it hadn't, Discovery Toys would have been out of business by January 1, 1984.

Nemeth went on to rack up sales of $40 million in 1985, with $100 million projected by 1988. By 1986 Discovery Toys had introduced 25 toys of its own creation and was making inroads into the Japanese and British markets. It had a sales force of over 12,000 educational consultants.

The chairman of the board attributes her success to having a quality product, and an intense level of commitment to it. "I think the only time a business really succeeds is when it's coming out of a personal need, when you personally have a deep attachment to the idea and understand it completely. If I had started this company saying, I don't care what the product is and I don't care about the quality, but, boy, I'm going to make a million dollars, I wouldn't have gotten past the second year."

It was worth the struggle. Now Nemeth can "do what I want to do. The freedom to be creative is the number one thing, to know that people aren't going to say no to me."

MAKING A LITTLE DO A LOT

The other half of the start-from-scratch equation (no experience is the first half) that is used to stifle career independence is lack of money. This obstacle is a tough one, and can seem almost impossible to overcome. Yet even here, if you're persistent and resourceful enough, start-up capital can be acquired. You may have to tailor your venture to one that corresponds with the amount of capital you can raise, and it may take a drastic reduction in your lifestyle to bootstrap it on minimal funds, but it can be done. There are a host of little-known ways to get your company up and running on next to nothing (we'll examine them in detail in Chapter 5, "Capital Offense").

As I mentioned earlier, John Todd launched Guest Supply, which markets promotional soaps, shampoos, and amenities to hotels, on a $2,000 cash advance on his Diners Club card and a $10,000 personal loan from his bank. Seven years later it was making $35 million annually. Mel and Patricia Ziegler had only $1,500 to start Banana Republic. They used the money to buy their first product, a truckload of Spanish paratrooper shirts, which they sold at a San Francisco flea market. Sales at the flea market gave them just enough money to pay one month's rent on a storefront. They sold enough during their first month to pay the rent and add an item or two for the next month, and so on it went until they had a $50 million operation six years later.

The proliferation of service industries, which substitute brainpower and personal attention for costly inventories and production facilities, has made it easier to start up on less. It doesn't take Fort Knox reserves to open a consulting firm, or a maid service, or a fast-food home-delivery service. Also, the availability of credit for crafty entrepreneurs is wider than ever, with more competitive financial institutions aggressively pursuing customers with new credit deals.

There's no getting around it, though: starting from nothing won't be easy. It may require living on nothing for a considerable period of time. In the beginning, it could well be the end of things like social life, status, and spending for anything but the necessities of life.

Before the entrepreneur can buy the $3 million home and Italian sports car like Ron Rice, there is an extended pit stop at a much different place. The scene ranges from barns to basements to dining room tables. Mo Siegel's operations for Celestial Seasonings Tea were run out of a dusty, unheated barn in Boulder, Colorado. Audio Environments' Mike Malone's first office was a desk-sized space under a staircase at a recording studio.

T. C. Swartz knew he was in for spartan accommodations. With only $500 borrowed from his wife, the twenty-seven-year-old was looking at an extended period of bare walls and peanut butter sandwiches. But since that's all he had to get his adventure tour company started with, that's the way it would have to be. He didn't wait for a day when he would have a comfortable amount of money to launch his venture. That day would never come. If he reduced his standard of living and used his wits, he was convinced he would prevail. He had a great idea, he had himself, and, as his tale reveals, that would be enough to turn Society Expeditions into a $32 million company.

THE WORLD ON A SHOESTRING
T. C. Swartz/Society Expeditions

As a tour leader for a travel operator in Chicago, T. C. Swartz was pulling down a decent wage and traveling the globe, escorting groups of tourists through the South Pacific, South America, Mongolia, and parts in between. He seemed to have the ultimate job. But while Swartz may have been going places physically, his own personal progress had been grounded. He had no say in anything going on in the company. His ideas were routinely shot down or ignored.

"I was tired of thinking up all these great ideas and nothing ever happening," he says. "I would think of really great ideas that would save the company money in six and seven figures and not even get a thank you."

When the exasperation was capped by an arbitrary tongue-lashing by the boss, he made his decision. He'd do it himself, even though he had nothing to do it with. All he had to start with was the rage of self-belief, $500 borrowed from his wife, and an idea nobody else had thought of.

It wasn't something the world was exactly clamoring for, educational trips to Easter Island, a lonely outpost in the Pacific. But T.C. thought he had found his own small niche in the travel market. The seed had been planted by a Chilean friend who was an archaeologist on Easter Island. It was 1974 and the socialist government of Salvador Allende had decided there were better causes to fund in a crumbling Chilean economy than restoring the mysterious stone monuments on the island. Over a few beers with a friend at his apartment, it dawned on Swartz that he might be able to help raise money for Easter Island and himself at the same time. In an all-night session he and his friend outlined the course for the Society for the Preservation of Archaeological Monuments, later to be shortened to Society Expeditions.

As often happens with entrepreneurial projects, Swartz initially looked at it as an exploratory stab, as a way to do something he liked to do that might turn into something profitable, but not necessarily lucrative, down the road. He did some research on Easter Island and put together a mailer that friends printed up for him on net/whenever-you-can terms.

With his $500 he mailed out brochures to former customers he'd guided on other tours. Within a few weeks deposits on bookings started to come in. The first four $250 deposits provided the working capital for his company.

Swartz could get off the ground with so little capital, not just because of his frugality and friendships, but because he didn't have to manufacture products, maintain an inventory, or even employ a sales force. His story is a perfect example of the opportunities offered by a service business.

With no money for rent, Swartz and his new wife relocated to Seattle, where they moved in with his sister. His first office was a friend's dank and dirty coal cellar that he cleaned out and set up shop in for free. T. C. considers that humble lodging, plus the use of his friend's travel agency facilities for a nominal fee, as his first break. Without that support he probably never could have gotten going. "If I hadn't had a guardian angel like that, I don't know how I would have financed myself."

Some people are afraid to start companies on a shoestring because they're afraid no one would buy anything from so impoverished an operation. So they wait for the fictional day when they will have enough money to do it "right." Swartz had no such concerns, even as a one-person company working out of a coal cellar. He felt that as long as there is a need for the product, and you present it with conviction, there will be buyers.

"Once we got on the trips," says Swartz, "people would ask how many employees I had, and I would be honest with them. I'd say, 'You're looking at him.' Once I developed a relationship with the individuals it didn't matter to them whether my enterprise had one employee or a hundred. People don't buy from companies; they buy from people."

Enough people bought his concept to fill his first trip. He was off and tooling through the eerie, treeless plains of Easter Island, inexplicably dotted with 20-ton stone masks. His archeologist friend provided historical and cultural details. On the second day, Swartz, still a bundle of nerves, heard the word that's music to the entrepreneur's ear: reorders. Three people in the group asked what other destinations he went to.

The light bulb went on. His in-depth educational/adventure concept could be expanded indefinitely. But, as with all new ventures, tantalizing prospects were eclipsed by the stark realities. Although he took five groups to Easter Island in the first year, the cash flow was bleak. "I was so poor that I didn't go out to dinner for a year," Swartz recalls. "I took a sandwich to lunch, which my sister made for me. She basically housed me and fed me for about a year until I could afford to take a small salary from the company. I could pay for the gas to drive to and from work, bottom line. There was money for the postage and stationery and whatever I needed to operate the trips. But that was it."

His first year sales of $50,000, with a net of $5,000 and no salary, didn't thrill his wife, who thought he was "nutty." They divorced after six months. His relatives also tried to get him to give up his fixation on that weird island in the middle of the Pacific. They would say, "I understand your putting together these trips to Easter Island, but what are you doing for a living?"

After nine months he added the first employee to his payroll, a student who came to work after school for four hours a day and was paid $2.50 an hour. The typist's $50-a-week salary was all Swartz could afford. He also made his first big purchase for the coal cellar works—a $179 Smith-Corona typewriter.

Despite his severe lack of capital, Swartz was able to keep things moving because of lean overhead, and because of his cash-up-front policy on bookings. Since he had all the international connections from his prior job, all he needed was a telephone and stamps to mail his programs out to past customers. Sales doubled to $125,000 in year two, but he still had many entrepreneurial as well as travel adventures to undergo.

On one trip to Outer Mongolia Swartz and the 20 members of his group got stranded in Siberia. Soviet officials had no record of his flight confirmations from Irkutsk to Ulan Bator in Mongolia. The daily flights were full for the next two weeks. "It is pretty embarrassing," he agrees, "when you take 20 people out to an airport and you don't get on the plane, then all of a sudden you're not going anywhere."

The resourceful entrepreneur always finds a way. Swartz loaded his clients, mostly in their fifties, who had paid $5,000 each for the ten-day trip, into a crowded train for the two-day journey from Siberia to the Mongolian steppes. At night, Swartz went around to all his troops and gave them each a nightcap of cognac. They loved it. It was unplanned adventure, precisely what they had signed up for.

This was Swartz's market niche, a hint of adventure in truly out-of-the-way places. "You have to have flexibility. If you hear of a wedding that's taking place in New Guinea, which is very colorful, you reroute and go there. The flexibility is what gives people the excitement. You really feel like an explorer. You're doing something special that not everyone has done."

The breakthrough for Society Expeditions came with a risk, some good timing, and a trip to a continent nobody ever went to—Antarctica. Swartz chartered a German expedition ship for an Antarctic cruise and booked two trips with 145 people each. He charged $1,000 less than the only other competitor at the time, Lindblad Travel, and at $3,000 a head, Society Expeditions made a profit of $300,000. It was "more money than I had ever seen or dreamed about."

Swartz decided to put the whole $300,000 on the line by acquiring the German ship on a full-time, year-round basis for five years and pouring all resources into marketing. It was a gamble none of the experts thought would work. "Most people in the travel industry thought that was the end of us," he says, "that we would choke on it and that there was no way we could develop the market."

His technique was the only one open to an under-capitalized venture, "guerilla marketing warfare." He couldn't afford to advertise like the big companies, so he used press releases and publicity handouts to get stories written up on his company in various publications. The ads he did take out were small and unglamorous but effective. The campaign worked so well that after one year he wound up purchasing Lindblad's Antarctic ship to give him the only two expedition ships in captivity.

The gamble paid off and today Society Expeditions operates 50 cruises a year. It runs five private trains, including the refurbished Paris-to-Istanbul *Orient Express,* a Trans-Siberian express, and a Trans-China rail link. His cruise ships have been the first to be allowed into Saudi Arabia and Burma, and the first to sail the Northwest Passage west to east.

He projects his biggest adventure for some time in the 1990s, when he would like to take the first tourists into space. Swartz isn't at all worried that it might not pay off. As with all entrepreneurs, risk isn't really risk to him. His only concern is to find out what it is he has to do to make something work; he never worries about whether or not it will work. "The recognition of doing something that people say can't be done is what keeps me going. People say I can't send people to space. You just watch. Failure is not in my vocabulary."

What is, is success. The former student vagabond, who backpacked around the world on $35 a week in 1970, now has a net worth of more than $10 million. He owns 100 percent of Society Expeditions, which jumped from $17 million in sales to $32 million in 1986 and has almost 200 people on the payroll.

His advice is "to trust your intuition. Be committed to what you're doing. Pick something that you really enjoy doing. I can't imagine putting in this kind of time if I didn't enjoy my work. I believe that people can have their cake and eat it too. It's just a question of figuring out how to do it. I wanted to have my cake and eat it too, so I had to create my own job."

* * *

As the stories of T. C. Swartz, Lane Nemeth, and Ron Rice demonstrate, upstarts and amateurs can still have their day in the USA. Aided by the entrepreneur's best friend, change, first-time businessmen and businesswomen are overcoming limited resources and seizing opportunities as never before.

Changing tastes in travel opened the door for Swartz. Changing parental attitudes about children's toys gave the green light to Nemeth. Changing tastes of sun worshippers let Rice sneak in and carry off the natural tanning oil market. Wherever there's change, there's opportunity, and where there's opportunity, there's a chance for anyone from any background or financial status to spot it and act on it.

As John Gardner wrote in *Excellence*, "Much of human performance is conditioned by what the performer thinks is possible for him." Entrepreneurs think it's possible to do things their lot in life says they can't. If you're backed by the Primary Assets, and you think it's possible, despite your modest circumstances, despite what the experts say, despite the daunting presence of big business, and despite the hardships of beginning on a shoestring, you have already taken your first, and biggest, step toward career independence.

Now it's time to find a marketable idea, and explore the techniques of successfully executing it.

3

The Big Idea (Is a Small One)

PRACTICAL IMAGINATION

Creativity, like business, is shrouded by larger-than-life myths that keep the ambitions of many ordinary citizens under wraps. Visions of child prodigies and astonishing intellects are conjured up, images of a world populated by specially endowed creatures well out of the orbit of those of us who shop at Safeway and visit the dry cleaners once a week.

The fact is, just as it's possible for someone to be athletic without being an Olympic gold medalist, people can be creative without having to produce a Pulitzer Prize–winning novel or medical breakthrough.

The imagination required to come up with a new business concept comes more from keen observation than supercharged brainpower. It's a process not of the clouds, but solidly based on terra firma and the needs of its citizens. The entrepreneur only has to give a guy a better shave, not explore the meaning of beards; provide a sturdier musical instrument case, not compose a symphony; offer a thicker hamburger, not discover an artificial beef supplement.

PROBLEM SOLVING

In effect, the idea behind entrepreneurship is nothing loftier than basic problem-solving—you figure out a way to solve an everyday, common annoyance or insufficiency. As a troubleshooter, you spot the element that is going to make someone's life easier, cheaper, or more pleasurable. It doesn't take a genius to know that people have an insatiable appetite for convenience, savings, and fun in their lives. It just takes a little awareness, curiosity, and digging to find out what specific product or service can deliver the goods.

For a stimulus to entrepreneurial imagination you might try keeping an Aggravation Diary. Make a list of daily nuisances, and if they crop up often enough, you can be certain you're not the only one encountering them.

Two Israeli immigrants in their mid-twenties used this technique to haul in millions of dollars. When Avi Fattal and his friend, Avi Ruimi, arrived in Los Angeles they knew what they wanted to do—to come up with a simple, inexpensive idea that answered an everyday need. They started paying close attention to all the little hassles that plague us in a typical day. "We thought about what bothers you every day," says Ruimi. "In the shower, when you brush your teeth, when you get in your car."

It was that last seemingly uninspiring ritual that gave him a sizzling idea one 100-degree summer day in L.A. Getting into his convertible, which had been frying in the sun, he was nearly incinerated by the boiling upholstery and steering wheel. And thus was born the Auto-Shade, a cardboard sun-shield to cover the windshield of your car and provide artificial shade inside. His company Auto-Shade, Inc., sold $12 million worth of the shades in 1986.

Entrepreneurial inspiration has always been a response to the most obvious discomforts, inefficiencies, and unpleasantries of daily life. Whitcomb Judson hated to bend over to tie his shoelaces. So he set about inventing the slide fastener, which in time became known as the zipper.

When Daniel Gerber was recruited by his wife to feed his infant child one night, he was amazed how much torture it was to mash up peas by hand to a consistency the child could eat safely. Squashing peas with a spoon took forever, and the food squirted all over the kitchen. This was an ordeal he didn't want to go through again, and neither, he reasoned, did mothers across the land: Gerber Baby Food to the rescue.

THE MOMENT OF CONCEPTION

None of these ordinary annoyances would have been taken the slightest notice of if the entrepreneurs hadn't been alert to their possibilities. Their "flash of genius" was simple curiosity. They found inspiration in a routine chore because they looked for it. Had they subscribed to the usual flash theory, and waited for the moment of genius to strike from out of the blue and discover them instead of them discovering it, opportunity would have passed them by.

The myth of the lightning bolt probably has inhibited more people from discovering opportunities than any other single obstacle. Hopeful people wait for the big one to appear, and it never does. The real light source looks more like a distant lighthouse in a pea-soup fog, an orb fading in and out, seemingly changing directions with every shift in the wind. It doesn't find you; you have to steer your way toward it.

There is no Immaculate Conception of full-blown, marketable notions. Ideas, like stories, have beginnings, middles, and endings. There is advanced preparation, or readiness for something new, exposure to the stimulus, and then a tumbling around of the concept, a testing, research, and feedback phase that leads to a course of action. Even cases that look like classic lightning fare follow this pattern.

Norm Pattiz's big idea, for instance, came right out of the thin air that beamed the strains of "Ain't No Mountain High Enough" into his living room one day. Yet the radio broadcast that triggered his future fortune didn't feel anything like a thunderbolt of genius. It was a faint signal that needed a lot of fine tuning. How it grew into a $50 million communications company, Westwood One, and how it turned an out-of-work salesman into a radio mogul worth $27 million, is the story of the idea process.

ONLY DIANA ROSS HEARS SYMPHONIES
Norm Pattiz/Westwood One

Norm Pattiz was sitting at home with a friend wondering "whys" and the "wherefores." He had been "the ultimate company man" doing "a bang-up job for six years" as sales manager at KCOP-TV in Los Angeles when he was unceremoniously sacked. He'd been dumped in one of the entertainment business's favorite maneuvers, the nepotistic appointment. The general manager's nephew was given his job.

Pattiz was devastated that such a thing could have happened to a high achiever like himself. "I wanted to move up the corporate ladder," he recalls, "all the way to general manager of the station."

He felt betrayed, and wondered if maybe it wasn't time for him to do something where he wasn't so vulnerable, so expendable to corporate whims . . . something on his own perhaps. On the radio the sounds of Little Stevie Wonder's "Uptight" and Marvin Gaye's "Ain't That Peculiar" began to play on his mind. He was tuned to a station that was playing fifty-two straight hours of Motown hits. Somewhere between Smokey Robinson and Mary Wells a thought occurred.

"I turned to my friend," recalls Pattiz, "and I said, 'Gee, do they ever syndicate these programs and sell them to national advertisers?'" That was it, the beginning seed, no more than a moment of idle curiosity. It was the kind of musing we've all done countless times—stray wonderment that pops up briefly and then is never thought of again.

The Supremes' "I Hear A Symphony" might have been on in the background, but it sounded like anything but to Pattiz. More like a very distant melody. But Pattiz was curious enough, and eager enough, to want to hear the rest of the song. Now that he was unemployed, Pattiz was ready for anything. If he had still had his well-paid TV job, he probably wouldn't have had the time or the inclination to think about ideas concerning another, unknown medium. Without the mental boundaries of the work routine, though, and with all the time in the world, Pattiz was free to speculate further. He had to.

So he took the first key step in discovering an entrepreneurial idea. He followed it up, not knowing if it even was an opportunity. All he had was a vague notion about a business he knew nothing about. He moved on his impulse in the way that is critical for any potentially good idea. He acted immediately, before procrastination put an end to his curiosity. He was down at the radio station that aired the Motown program the very next day.

He found out from the general manager of the station that the syndicated programs so common in television were almost nonexistent in radio. It sounded like there might be something here. Exactly what, though, could only be found out by getting in there and nosing around. Pattiz wasted no time worrying about his lack of experience in radio. He quickly talked himself into a deal with the station to produce a 24-hour advertiser-supported program, "The Sound of Motown." The station would supply the studio facilities, Motown the artist interviews and music, and Pattiz would sell radio stations and advertisers.

When he started putting the program together, he didn't view it as the start of a major national company. "It just seemed like an interesting project to work on for a while," notes Pattiz. "It was fun and would take advantage of my strengths and my previous history in dealing with advertisers."

Unknowingly, Pattiz was pursuing opportunity from the two best starting points: (1) finding a field compatible to your skills, and (2) active exploration to uncover the dimensions of the idea. In the beginning most ideas don't sound like much, because there's not enough information to evaluate their potential. But an intuition backed by supporting evidence can begin to bring the small idea into bigger focus. In the nine months it took Pattiz to get the Motown show produced and distributed to radio stations, he "started to realize that there really wasn't anybody in the marketplace doing this on any kind of large or professional scale."

Most of the syndicated radio programs, like "American Top 40," were sold to stations for straight cash, for $50 to $100 apiece. They were put together by former disc jockeys and program directors, people with good radio credentials, but with no knowledge of advertising. As an advertising man, Pattiz knew that where there was a large audience of consumers, advertisers would shortly follow. It was his hunch that radio was being underutilized as an advertising medium, and that if he could package professional programs and sell them to radio stations across the country as syndicators were doing in television, he could get advertisers to support it.

Using old contacts, he lined up three national sponsors for his Motown special—Warner-Lambert, Schlitz Malt Liquor, and United Vintners. When the show turned out to be a hit, three of its biggest fans were the advertisers. Pleased with the audience delivered by Pattiz, they commissioned him to produce a number of regular programs for them—short features, interviews, and various rock and Hollywood news segments.

"When I created those other programs for the advertisers, that's when I realized this could be a real business," he explains. A year after the idea first appeared it had finally become a full-fledged entrepreneurial opportunity. Pattiz's idea obviously was the product of a very slow-moving bolt of lightning. With $10,000 in savings, Pattiz started his company, Westwood One.

Selling any new concept from scratch takes time. Sponsored pop music programming wasn't immediately embraced by radio stations or advertisers. Rock marketing still wasn't mainstream in 1974. Pattiz clung to his initial sponsors as his life raft in the early lean years. "The first two years were full of anxiety. When you're dependent on one or two national advertisers for your livelihood, things can happen ten steps down the line from you and your support might not be there anymore. Having a small base of support and being involved in areas that are brand new, dealing with banks and creditors, can be very frightening."

There were many moments where it required fancy footwork to keep his company alive. On one occasion he had produced a show and lined up all the radio stations to carry it, but the advertiser dollars to finance it couldn't be found. Pattiz needed an advertiser or he had to scrap the whole project, which was something his list of creditors told him he couldn't do. To get a reluctant sponsor on board, he took a cheap midnight flight to New York to try to get his target company's ad agency to agree to a deal. However, when he arrived at the agency, he was told that the buyer he had flown to New York to meet with was "unavailable."

"I saw my life passing in front of me," Pattiz remembers. "I thought, 'Shit, this whole thing's going to fall apart.' But then I thought, 'Have I done everything I can do, or should I just get on a plane and go home?'"

In classic entrepreneurial fashion, Pattiz didn't quit. He showed up first thing the next morning at the agency and camped out until the person he was supposed to meet walked through the door. He got his meeting and his deal.

Westwood One's precarious existence gradually grew more stable, but by no means was it meteoric, until Pattiz got a major break in his company's fifth year. The communications industry was deregulated in 1979. Airtime formerly allotted to news and public affairs was freed up overnight. Radio stations across the country were suddenly looking for new energetic programming, and Westwood One was there with countdowns, interviews, and live concerts.

Over the next five years the company exploded from eight syndicated shows to twenty-eight. Exclusive live concerts and innovative contemporary programming made Westwood One the increasing choice of deregulated radio over older, less dynamic formats, like those of its chief competitors, ABC and CBS. Soon its programs were on more stations, some 3,800, than those of its top rivals combined.

With growing ad revenues from new shows and staples like "The Dr. Demento Show" and "Off the Record with Mary Turner," Pattiz turned to expansion, adding mobile recording equipment and an earth satellite station to his lineup.

By 1984, Westwood One had become such a prized communications concern that it became one of the year's most successful initial public offerings. When the dust cleared, investors had paid twenty-six times earnings and three million shares had been sold. Pattiz had pocketed $7 million in the exchange. A further offering in 1985 boosted his worth another $20 million. In 1986, Westwood One became the second largest radio network in the country by acquiring the fifty-year-old Mutual Broadcasting Network, adding news, sports, and such top-rated shows as "Larry King Live." Altogether the combination was worth $50 million in sales, with a valuation on the public market of a staggering $100 million.

The ex-mailroom clerk, publicist, and unemployed salesman now runs a company with 150 employees and offices in L.A., New York, and London. He lives in Beverly Hills and drives a Miro. Like many of today's new entrepreneurs, he doesn't fit the archetypal mold of wheeler-dealer schemers plotting fortunes from an early age. The uncertainties of the modern age and new opportunities pushed him in the entrepreneurial direction.

"I never thought about being an entrepreneur, or being in business for myself," he says. "But once I got a taste of it, it was clear to me that it was going to be tough for me to work for anybody again. When you've got a company that's valued at $100 million it's not easy to go back to working nine-to-five for a salary again."

Pattiz's advice for entrepreneurs starting out is to trust their own instincts and believe in themselves. "In the beginning stages you have to convince yourself that you're a special person to be able to keep doing all the things you've never done before. Just remember that people who can take nothing and turn it into something are unique individuals. It's very important to give yourself the confidence to go forward."

When it comes to finding a great entrepreneurial idea, Pattiz thinks it's a matter of being open to thoughts from all directions. To get the imagination moving, he recommends "backing off from your usual routine, and setting aside some time to think in a relaxed environment."

REMOVING CAPABILITY BARRIERS

The reason Norm Pattiz was able to go forward with his program was that he gave himself credit for having a decent idea.

Unlike many, he didn't feel he needed special qualifications to be able to think and observe. He didn't dismiss his idea as being too small, unoriginal, or lacking in brilliance. He didn't sabotage his notion by giving in to the usual fears and insecurities that stunt creative growth.

To discover good ideas, you have to first eliminate common creative phobias. Here are three of the major culprits:

I.Q.-Phobia.   You don't need special genes to make jeans, or a PhD to develop a new chocolate-chip cookie. Once you realize the people at the top are no different than you are, you've made a significant step to getting there yourself. A major springboard for most entrepreneurs is the realization that the boss is no more special than they are. As Armor All's Alan Rypinski found out about the rich and powerful: "They put one sock on at a time just like I do. A lot of the people I met who were really powerful people weren't as ready as I was. I said to myself, 'If this is competition, you're set to go.'"

Unique-aphobia.   The fear of having to do something totally original prevents many people from taking their own creativity seriously. The reality, though, is that there's nothing in thought, word, or deed that's really 100 percent new. As the writer Henry Miller observed, "Who is original? Everything that we are doing, everything that we think, already exists, and we are only the intermediaries, that's all, who make use of what is in the air." The semiconductor came from the transistor, the transistor from the vacuum tube, and so on. Don't fall for the "original" sin and bypass ideas for some ultimate invention.

Solo-Phobia.   Most people who get an idea will immediately ask themselves, "If this is so good, why hasn't someone else done it already?" This is a natural avenue of inquiry for anyone researching a new concept. It's part of your homework. But some people take the fact that nobody's doing it as a sign that there must not be anything to the concept. This fear of being the only one out there misses the whole point of entrepreneurship. If somebody's already doing it, it's probably too late. Your job as an entrepreneur is to go where the crowd's not going. Yet. Waiting for the safety of numbers to ratify your idea is the surest way to kill a golden opportunity.

THINKING LIKE AN ENTREPRENEUR

Being able to spot opportunity and discover ideas begins with the belief that there is nothing mysterious or inherently brainy about the process. It's really just an awakening to our own possibilities and a willingness to act on them.

What is required is a radical shift in the dutiful thought process fostered in school and in our working careers. We have to move from the passive role of student/employee, always a receptor, doing what we're told, to an active, initiating stance.

Learning to get on the offensive and think like an entrepreneur requires a new way of looking at things. You can create this new frame of mind by using a three-pronged system. It consists of an initial Capability Phase, of convincing yourself that you have as much business as anyone else to start a business; an Inquiry Phase, in which you probe and explore for your kernel of opportunity; and finally, an Assembly Phase, where you take your rudimentary idea and try to shape it into a marketable product or service.

Here's a practical guide to the first step in activating your entrepreneurial imagination.

The Capability Phase
BELIEVING

1. Get to know or read up on people who've started successful businesses (and pay close attention to your boss, too). Include any neighbors or acquaintances. Notice they're not part of an elite class.

2. Try to recall if you've ever used the phrases "Why didn't I think of that?" or "I wish I'd thought of that." That means

an idea was so simple you felt you could have thought of it. See? You already understand that the most successful ideas are the obvious ones, open to everyone—even you—to discover.

3. Keep a mental tally on how many times the experts have been proven wrong.

4. How many things have you done in your life that you initially thought were impossible? But you still got the job done, right? Recall past difficult missions you completed from scratch.

5. Start taking on small, diverse challenges, not necessarily in business. Get used to setting goals and achieving them. Running, for instance, can be an ideal proof of your ability to conquer seemingly impossible odds. Ordinary, nonathletes begin to realize how much they can achieve when they start out barely able to run a mile and after months of practice wind up running four, six, or even ten miles routinely.

6. Consider the number of recent immigrants who have arrived with nothing, not even the basics of language, and who have built prospering businesses. They include a former boat person who runs a $3 million computer assembly firm in Santa Ana, California, and an Afghan with a chain of fried-chicken restaurants in New York. If they can do it, why not you?

7. Remember that you live in a country whose whole premise is that the ordinary can achieve the extraordinary.

Once you've decided you're capable of pursuing an entrepreneurial course, it's time to mobilize all your inquisitive powers. Enterprising minds want to know about anything and everything. The trick to finding the right idea is to be exposed to as many different ones as possible. Don't rule out anything until you've explored it thoroughly.

In the Inquiry Phase you begin taking on a new analytical

approach to things. You stop taking the world at face value and begin to question how things could be different. The search for a marketable idea is a search for change. Whether it's a new product or service, an improvement on an existing one, or a new way of looking at an old product, the entrepreneurial notion seeks to change the practice of business as usual.

That means junking old habits and exploring new areas. There's nothing like getting out of the old rat race to stimulate creative thinking and open the mind to new possibilities. We're all locked into our daily patterns, discussing the same things with the same people. But it's the people you don't know at the party, not your friends, who may lead you into a new area of investigation. It's the person sitting next to you on the plane or at a restaurant, who is liable to bring up new data that could trigger alternatives.

Many ventures are sparked by a casual comment from a stranger or a friend we haven't seen in years. What usually happens in these encounters is that we ask many more questions than we do normally. This results in a flood of new information from outside our usual orbit. One question won't provide an immediate revelation, but it can lead to another, which in turn can lead to several others, which in the end may suggest a possibility.

A few practical suggestions:

The Inquiry Phase
DISCOVERING

1. Be inquisitive. Find out how things work in all kinds of businesses by asking questions.

2. Be willing to learn. Don't worry about asking dumb questions. There's no shame in a quest for new knowledge.

3. Be alert. You won't find glaring and not-so-glaring holes in the marketplace unless you're ready to follow up even the smallest or most unlikely leads.

4. Be speculative. Allow yourself to wonder, make-believe, and muse.

5. Get acquainted with change. Break the routine. Take extension classes, sign up for recreational sports. Go to trade shows and learn about new industries. Expose your mind to new faces and places. Broaden your contacts.

6. Travel. New ideas are often picked up once you leave your everyday environment. You might discover some new type of business being done in another country or in a different region of this country. Bumping into people from different walks of life might stimulate thoughts in a new direction.

7. Brush up on new developments at such idea centers as libraries and trade shows.

8. Listen closely to the problems and complaints of people you come in contact with. Are there any patterns? Can a chronic problem be solved with a new product or service?

9. Be aware of social trends. Are people eating out more? Staying at home and watching their VCRs more? Having fewer children? What products might address changing behavior patterns?

10. Brainstorm with others. Let the ideas flow without critiquing them. Dare to be silly and let even the wildest suggestions out of their cages. Go for as much volume as possible and worry about quality later.

11. Relax with others. The informal brainstorming of a good conversation at dinner or drinks can trigger many new ideas.

As you begin to piece together your findings in a promising area, you have moved from the Inquiry Phase of the idea hunt to the Assembly Phase. This process takes the raw information gathered in your investigation and transforms it into a commercial property.

Here are some guidelines:

The Assembly Phase
BUILDING

1. Examine the opportunity and see if it can be made cheaper, more deluxe, smaller, more comprehensive, more fashionable, more timeless, longer-lasting, disposable, softer, more durable, more portable, more efficient, simpler, friendlier, sweeter, shinier, healthier, more attractive . . .

2. Borrow, adapt, transfer, add to, streamline, recombine the opportunity into a new consumer value.

3. Use trial and error. Keep putting different pieces together until, like a jigsaw puzzle, the picture emerges.

4. Try to construct a workable idea from as many different opportunities as possible. If one doesn't attain a marketable form, go on to the next one.

5. Compare your opportunity to similar ideas already on the market, if any. Study how others put their notions together.

Assembling your idea is the most creative part of the process, though for the most part it requires a technique any child has mastered: the art of make-believe. Wonder. Wonder what would happen if a product or service in a potentially profitable area was altered slightly, combined with something else, or maybe even copied from something that is in operation in another region or country. Allow your mind free reign to wonder "what if," and suddenly anything is possible, and something, perhaps, probable.

Bill Tillson, a former folk singer and English major who knew nothing about high technology or microwave television transmission, wondered so persistently that he wound up the head of the world's largest live satellite TV company, Netcom. Today he oversees a company that takes in $18 million, transmitting live news and such sports events as the Super Bowl and the Olympics. He is a partner with the British and French governments in the first live satellite channel for Europe. His story illustrates how you can unearth ideas in fields you've never heard of, if you're inquisitive enough.

THE WONDERER
Bill Tillson/Netcom, Inc.

It all started with Tillson's runaway curiosity. He had been a very independent child, leaving his New Bedford, Massachusetts, home at the age of fifteen to work in the civil rights movement in the South, then roaming through Europe for a couple years after high school on $3 a day. Like half the youth of the world in the Woodstock year of 1969, his ambition was to be a rock star. But the $10 a night take he earned for playing his guitar at Parisian cafés fell short of the earning power he felt a rock star deserved, so he returned to the U.S. and took a degree in English.

Then he was off again, to San Francisco, where he got a job at an art gallery "just to pay the rent." But the resourcefulness he'd developed on $3 a day wasn't lost on his boss, and he was soon promoted to general manager of Eastman Galleries, where he directed the acquisition and development of four new branches. With no business background, he was suddenly running a $3 million company, and picking up important business skills.

It was on one of his many trips to Eastman's Washington galleries that a fluke incident occurred, one of those that mean nothing at the time but sometimes lead to breathtaking opportunity. He bumped into someone from his college days who was working at a television production company. The firm needed some business advice. Maybe Tillson would like to do a little consulting on the side.

Tillson had always been fascinated with TV and show business. One of his childhood fantasies was to have his own TV network. By helping out his friend he might be able to learn a few things about the industry. The production company was involved in some of the early satellite feeds coming into the Washington area, mostly going to the embassies in town. As Tillson straightened out the books of the company, he became more and more interested in satellites.

Questioning everyone in sight on the ins and outs of satellites, he began to wonder if he might be able to do something in this emerging area. Finally, at a dinner one night with the principals of the production firm, he wondered his way to an idea.

"It was at the end of a long evening of liquid refreshment," he recalls. "We were all kicking around ideas and I kept saying, 'You mean if, you mean if, you mean if.' And they kept saying, 'Yes, yes, yes.' The whole genesis of Netcom was really in that room on that particular night in 1979. It became clear that through the use of satellites, in essence, one could have a television network without having to buy a TV station."

If Tillson's theory was correct, he had discovered a way to transmit live television signals at a fraction of the going rate. Until then live television was transmitted by the huge fixed satellite antennas and microwave equipment of the telephone company. But with increased demand for live coverage from the television networks, and the growing use of satellite-transmitted teleconferences by corporations, there weren't enough antennas to go around, and what was available—from AT&T—was overpriced.

Tillson stepped into the breach with a typically outrageous entrepreneurial vision. Why not assemble a network of free-lance dish antenna operators who could link up the nation with their own mobile antennas instead of AT&T's costly and inflexible fixed equipment? Needless to say, Ma Bell did not tremble at the thought of a couple of dozen guys hauling antennas around in boat trailers and pickups to satellite receiving sites around the nation.

Every part of the network, every independent dish owner

had to be in the right place at the right time, come rain, sleet, or snow, for the live hookup to work. The skeptics naturally said there was too much human error involved. If it could be done the experts with the huge budgets, like ABC or CBS, would have done it. How could this art gallery manager who hadn't spent a day in the TV business pull it off?

Even more amazing is the fact that he had no money behind his grandiose plan. But he was blessed by the fact that it was 1980 and he was one of the first through the door of the newly deregulated broadcasting industry. Deregulation meant he could start up quickly and cheaply without years of costly delays. It took him a year to find a partner to put up $15,000 in start-up capital (he bought the partner out six months later for $50,000) and to track down his first customer.

His first client was the publisher of a financial newsletter based in Hong Kong he had met when he was with the art gallery. World Money Analysts signed up for a $100,000 show. The complex affair would be handled by two people working out of Tillson's house in San Francisco. Netcom's job was to broadcast the company's annual convention in Hong Kong back to the newsletter's subscribers at hotels in seventeen different U.S. cities.

"That first show," Tillson says, "was one of the most complicated international television shows to ever take place. Thank God we didn't realize it at the time. Part of starting a company is working without fear because you don't know any better."

As is the pattern with shoestring companies, Netcom lived on customer rations at the beginning. That first account gave Tillson the income to get a second customer, the second customer paid enough to get a third, and so on. With no product to sell in a service business like Netcom's, each of those early customers is especially important, because in a sense that client is the product. Each job is the product of the moment. Your customer is your inventory, and if you have a narrow customer base, the entire ranch can be on the line with each job.

Closed-circuit boxing matches made up the bulk of Netcom's early customers. Tillson's one-day network of portable antennas and transmission facilities was able to lop 90 percent off the rates charged by AT&T to televise closed-circuit prizefights.

Collecting payment from fight promoters can be as wild as Don King's hair. Luckily for Tillson, the satellite transmission business was so new, the competition so thin, and the costs so high that he was able to collect half of each bill up front. Even Don King complied. "The ability to take in that pre-money kept us afloat in the early days," he says. "We literally financed the company with the deposits from the next show."

A serious cash crunch, nevertheless, threatened to close down Netcom a year after it started. Suppliers had to be paid and customers were overdue on their balances. Tillson needed $50,000 in five days. He had the receivables to cover it, but the bank was refusing to lend him the money because he hadn't been in business for the three-year minimum to be eligible for a loan.

In a stroke of luck that was Netcom's lifesaver, the loan officer who had been refusing to lend money to the struggling firm was transferred to another branch. His replacement thought Tillson had been treated shabbily and went out on a limb to deliver a thirty-day $50,000 loan. "Without it," Tillson admits, "I was out of business."

With that reprieve Netcom's credit line was established and he was able to borrow all the money he needed to finance his rapid march to the top of the transmission industry. Demonstrating the vision and the negotiation skills of his idol, CBS founder William Paley, Tillson landed one top event after another and began diversifying into a dizzying array of areas. His company built two $75,000 mobile transmitter trucks, got into live rock concert/FM simulcasts, satellite distribution of syndicated programming, and was early on board in the video revolution, renting video filming and projection equipment and offering video production and post-production facilities.

All the major sporting events started going his way: the

Cooney-Holmes fight, the largest closed-circuit boxing match in history; the Super Bowl beginning in 1984; and the international telecasts of the '84 Olympics. The networks began to rely on Netcom for much of their major live remote telecasts. When Dan Rather reported from the Geneva Summit, Netcom transmitted the pictures. Cable News Network, the Financial News Network, and many other cable outlets also were scooped up as clients.

The obvious question is, Why didn't the networks, with all of their broadcasting resources, take on this lucrative natural extension of their business? Why did it take a private entrepreneur to do the job? The answer is that like all big companies the networks had enough to occupy them, and couldn't do it as cheaply as Tillson. He doesn't use union help. And he's more efficient. "The reason the networks use us," he explains, "is that the events we do are extremely important to them. That network has got to work. They know we're the best at what we do. Our survival depends on it."

By 1986 Netcom had become one of the dominant forces in the transmission business. There were 40 staffers, 2,000 subcontractors, 300 transportable satellite dishes, and teleport facilities in New York and Los Angeles.

How did it happen? Tillson feels it was his entrepreneurial edge. With no cumbersome boards or bureaucracy to answer to, he could take the risks and stay ahead of the pack. Much may have to do with his own relentless drive to seek out new areas, new knowledge, new frontiers. Like a lot of aspiring members of his generation, Tillson was raised to believe that the sky was the limit. "My parents instilled in me the belief that I could do anything," he states. "Most people look at life and figure out what they can't do. They spend most of the time trying to respond to situations that they feel control them. My problem is not finding opportunities, but to narrow down the opportunities I see and try to pick the best ones."

The key to entrepreneurial success, says Tillson, is that "you have to be willing to work very, very hard for a long period of time. You have to be honest with yourself. When it's not going well, you need to chop it off. When it's going well, push harder."

Tillson's drive and curiosity have taken him a long way. How far was made vividly clear to him on a trip to Paris to negotiate with the French government on the creation of a live European channel. He found himself lodged in a penthouse suite at the venerable eighteenth-century Crillon Hotel, home to dukes and diplomats. "I hadn't been to Paris since 1968, when basically I was a hippie with a guitar. To go back and be feted by the French government . . . I like it better on this side than the other side, living in suites instead of the streets."

PLANNING FOR CHANCE

There are two distinct styles of discovering opportunities, one very methodical and planned out, the other a random sampling of prospects that are tossed up in the course of life. As entrepreneurship and its viability as a career alternative has risen over the last decade, so has the number of people who are trying the more concerted route.

One of the foremost advocates of the systematic technique is America's leading management expert, Peter Drucker. In his book *Innovation and Entrepreneurship,* he argues that entrepreneurs have to come out of the dark ages and "learn to practice systematic innovation." His view is that you have to map out a calculated path to opportunity, that you can't rely on the coincidences of life to meander into an opening. Systematic innovation, he says, "consists in the purposeful and organized search for changes, and in the systematic analysis of the opportunities such changes might offer for economic or social innovation."

Drucker might have been talking about the way Rod Canion, Jim Harris, and Bill Murto conducted their quest for the opportunity that became Compaq Computer. It's probably not surprising, with Canion and Harris being engineers, that the approach the three took to finding a business of their own was as systematic as you can get.

It began with the three of them passing in the halls of Texas Instruments saying, "We should get together and start a business someday." When that day finally came, they had no idea what they wanted to do. They sat down at Murto's dining room table to see if they could come up with something.

To get things rolling, they decided to compile a list of three items that each would like to get out of their future venture. Jim Harris recalls: "The interesting thing is that we all had the same three things written down, in the exact same order. Number one, we wanted to do something creative where we could control our own destiny and have fun doing it. What we were actually looking for was fun. Number two was a team working environment. We wanted a situation where the people joining us, who would also be very accomplished, would also enjoy that good feeling and have the fun of being in a successful company. The first two, then, had to do with the fun aspect. And the third was that, if we had accomplished the fun, it would be nice if the business was successful enough to give us some financial rewards, so that we could improve our lifestyles."

Now that they knew what they wanted to get out of their business, they started some good old-fashioned brainstorming, jotting down any and all ideas, no matter how crazy they seemed. The three went through about fifteen different areas and may have logged fifty to one hundred ideas for each area. Canion estimates they probably discussed a thousand ideas in a month. They ranged from a Murto/Harris Mexican restaurant to a Computerland franchise. The best concepts made a rotating Top 10 list, which changed as promising new entries appeared.

After a few months of conceptualizing, they narrowed the prospects down to one—an add-on Winchester disk product. But the idea was turned down by venture capitalists. A month later in January 1982 Rod Canion was sitting at home "going down a path of logic" about portable computers when he started musing about whether it was possible to build a "full function" portable computer with the same capabilities as a larger fixed unit. He almost dismissed the idea because there were hundreds of companies building computers at the time and it seemed impossible to get the right software to match another new brand. What made him not discard the idea was that he remembered that the first IBM PC was coming out in a few months and he had a hunch that it would set an industry standard for software. He called up Harris and Murto and the three agreed. They finally had their idea: the Compaq portable computer.

By sheer logic they had hit on the essential starting point for any entrepreneur. You have to figure out what you like to do and what you want to do. Consult your own interests, your likes and dislikes. Examine what it is you want to achieve. If it's power, you may not be content with running a restaurant. If it's creativity, you may not find satisfaction starting your own janitorial supply company. If it's money, you won't get rich opening a giftshop. It's pretty much common sense, but you should pick an area that's suitable to your goals, temperament, and taste. An introspective type may not get a kick out of the glad-handing garment trade, just as a party animal might find the insurance industry a little on the restrictive side.

The methodical, calculating approach to entrepreneurship seems to be prevalent wherever change and new industries converge. It may be called "systematic innovation" today, but it's really just classic opportunism. Observant types see new realms like hi-tech, video, health care, or telecommunications opening up, and they hatch plans to get in on the action. While there are enormous opportunities where tremendous change and innovation is taking place, there are also many hazards. One of them is timing.

GOOD TIMING

Timing is one of the main ingredients for any entrepreneur, but for someone trying to capitalize on a vortex of innovation the launch must be clocked to the split-second. There's the possibility of being too early and getting to the market before it's ready for your product. Many biotech ventures, for instance, have bitten the dust because commercial perception has yet to catch up with the technology.

"You don't want to spend 20 years of your life pioneering something people don't know they need," says Compaq's Rod Canion. You have to make sure you have a product that solves a current consumer problem, something people can use right this minute.

The bigger problem is getting there too late. Human nature being what it is, the herd instinct usually makes people wait to act until every other person on the block is talking about hi-tech. When everyone's got the same idea, it's time to stand back and get out of the way of the stampede. For instance, a year or two after Bill Tillson got into satellite transmission it was already too far along to get on the bandwagon. Shakeouts in his industry and hi-tech have left a trail of modern day '49ers reeling from overmined veins.

Helpful Hints

1. THE TIME TO MOVE IS WHEN NOBODY ELSE DOES.

2. IF MORE THAN THREE PEOPLE TELL YOU SOMETHING IS THE LATEST THING, IT ISN'T. Three's a crowd.

3. TODAY'S BOOM IS TOMORROW'S BUST. Success is a long-term market.

PLUGGING THE POTHOLES OF LIFE

Far and away, most successful entrepreneurs find their opportunities by following up chances provided uneventfully every day. They seize on little inconsistencies, incongruities, and exasperations of life, and find that something is missing. Karl Friburg, for instance, encountered difficulties when trying to wallpaper his house. He went to a couple of wallpaper stores in town and was treated rudely, overcharged, and sold an entirely inappropriate wallpaper for his kitchen. "I was trying to learn how to hang the wallpaper," he says, "and ripping the rolls in half. My wife and I got so frustrated we said, 'Larchmont needs a good wallpaper shop.'" That was the beginning of one of the nation's foremost wallpaper design firms, Motif Designs.

What was missing for two MIT students was a way to get on the college tennis courts. The only way to get a court reserved was to call a single phone after twelve noon the day you wanted to play. The phone was off the hook before that, and everybody on campus was dialing the number at noon. By the time Frank Manning got through on his rotary phone it was 12:25 and all the courts were booked for the day. "The problem was that busy tennis court number," notes Manning. "And the answer was the Demon Dialer." The gadget he and his friend developed to get on the courts became an indispensable feature of modern telephones and led his company, Zoom Telephonics, to sales of $6 million.

Successful entrepreneurs find the gaps, the potholes of human existence that need to be filled in for a smoother ride. When you learn to spot gaps, you will spot opportunity. You have to train yourself to be on the lookout for things that don't add up, for glaring and not so obvious displays of differences between what people want and what people get, between what's being offered and what could be offered.

Gaps are a tipoff that something's wrong and needs to be changed, the very same 'change' that is synonymous with innovation and opportunity. Every entrepreneurial idea can be traced back to the discovery of some apparent gap.

Here are the main kinds to look for:

The Frustration Gap

This is probably the easiest one to spot if you can see fortune through misfortune. The inventor of the vacuum cleaner was a janitor who got fed up with dust kicked up by his brooms and mops. The concept for Holiday Inn came from a bad vacation. After staying at a bunch of fleabag roadside motels on a trip with his family in 1951, Kemmons Wilson was convinced that Americans would flock to a clean, family-oriented, reasonably priced motor hotel.

Dal La Magna was inspired by a hide full of slivers he got while sunbathing on a rooftop. As he tried removing a hundred or so pieces of timber from his rear end with a hopeless, blunt-end tweezer, he found his calling—Tweezerman, purveyor of fine-point tweezers and beauty aids. Sometimes the creative impulse is as near as the thorn, or sliver, in your side.

The Efficiency Gap

Can something be done better, easier than it's being done? Alan Rypinski plugged the cracks in leather upholstery with a splash of Armor All. Compaq Computer answered the portability gap. We're all basically lazy and love to be pampered. Anything that can do it faster, longer, more attentively, take up less space, travel with us, or demonstrate an improvement in the leisure and quality quotient is an item that closes a certifiable gap in efficiency.

The Competition Gap

When a single producer is unchallenged in its market, you can bet that there's a hole big enough to drive a Brinks truck through. Philip Hwang's chance came when he stumbled on the fact that Motorola was the only maker of television monitors for the video game industry. Management was rude and their product overpriced. Hwang's Televideo stepped in with a vastly cheaper screen and made a bundle.

Rick Scoville noticed the same gulf between Perrier and nonexistent American competition in the sparkling water market. The Texas entrepreneur developed a lower-priced, home-grown alternative, Artesia Waters, now a favorite throughout the southwestern U.S. The bigger and more unchallenged the competition is, the greater the opportunity for a cost-cutting, quality-conscious entrepreneur.

The Transfer Gap

Sometimes the gap is one of availability or adaptation. The entrepreneur discovers already existing ideas successful in a given locality or field and expands the concept, transferring the successful technique to places where it's not available.

Much of innovation is improvising on an already existing theme. It's a form of borrowing, taking a piece from here and one from there and assembling a new consumer value. "Everybody's constantly borrowing," says Wichita State professor Fran Jabara. "We see things we can change and do better. Sure there are people who come up with new products. But it didn't start with their conception."

Some of America's most conspicuous entrepreneurial successes, like McDonald's Ray Kroc, Wendy's David Thomas, and TGI Friday's Dan Scoggin were alerted to opportunity by small-time successes that they simply bought and expanded. If a concept is working on a small scale, the underutilized success can be turned into a monumental one with proper marketing and distribution.

The Variety Gap

This gap in the market is created by many companies all doing the same thing. This is an outgrowth of the bottom-line pressure on big corporations to go for the largest audience with the most homogenized product. When there's a three-dimensional need and only a one-dimensional product, it's a sign that a possibly lucrative segment of the market is not being addressed. Lane Nemeth smelled something rotten in the toy shop when all she could find were war toys and dolls and nothing in between. Her Discovery Toys filled a $40 million gap in educational playthings.

The Identity Gap

This is the most frequent indicator of opportunity and one that involves insight into changing consumer attitudes and social behavior. The rise of the independent-minded consumer, concerned with self-expression and individuality, has triggered vast opportunities in fields from health products to fitness. The gap between how out-of-touch producers view consumers and how consumers see themselves leaves entrepreneurs lots of room to maneuver as changing views in taste, aesthetics, and personal image create new needs to be satisfied.

If you can create a new taste, literally, as in the case of California Cooler, or anticipate one by watching for emerging trends, there is a chance you may hit on the new item people are looking for to relieve consumer routine and boredom. Even more than most opportunity sources, the Identity Gap relies on gut instincts, usually gathered from common conversation, about what it is people really want. Mike Malone of Audio Environments thought the pop-music generation wanted more than old-fogey background Muzak in its restaurants and gathering places. He asked a few restaurant owners and they agreed. "Foreground" contemporary music was his answer to the problem of environmental music out of step with the tastes of its listeners.

The manipulations of Madison Avenue or Paris couturiers don't dictate the tastes of the masses as they used to. Today taste tends to be more consumer-driven, and that means opportunities for start-from-scratch entrepreneurs to spot and set the trends. With "cool" coming from the bottom instead of the top now, someone closer to the action may have a better chance than the big-time marketer.

Fashion is the most obvious exploiter of changing tastes, and every year there are shrewd entrepreneurs who figure out where preferences are going next. That direction might even be anti-fashion, if you are canny enough to discern it in your neighbors. Remember the story of Mel and Patricia Ziegler. They noticed that there was room for classic, unchanging, unhip clothes on the market. Banana Republic tapped a taste for sensible clothes in an adventure fantasy format.

Changing demographic and social trends are further sources of opportunity within the Identity Gap. You can follow your own nose to sniff out new attitudes, as Boyd and Felice Willat of Harper House did. Their Day Runner time-management books answered the organizational needs of a growing population of young professionals.

You can also make a more concerted effort to track down the marketing prospects afforded by changing population patterns by researching the trends in publications like *Demographics* magazine and studying the findings of public opinion polls.

Judi Sheppard Missett uncovered a massive social awakening in her dance classes in the early seventies. As more and more people enrolled, it became obvious that the chasm between old-style exercise classes and a new-age route to fitness was huge; she jumped in with Jazzercise.

Changes in taste, lifestyle, social behavior, and perceptions of self-image are constant and volatile. People will always be looking for a new appearance, a new style, improvements in self-worth and self-expression. Those who can anticipate the distant groundswell will find the Identity Gap fertile territory for opportunity.

THE ENVIRONMENT OF IDEAS

Now that you know where to look, how do you go about it? Probably the worst way is to sit down and rack your brain for inspiration. For some reason these things just can't be forced. Maybe it's because the super-calculating mind is too logical to see things in the illogical light that's required by entrepreneurship, which is, essentially, a vision that contradicts the immediate facts.

Ideas seem to pop up when the mind is relaxed enough to suspend the facts and tolerate wild and un-routine thinking, the "what if" approach.

Basic Principles

1. TWO PEOPLE ARE BETTER THAN ONE.

2. TWO PEOPLE IN A BAR OR RESTAURANT ARE BETTER THAN TWO PEOPLE IN AN OFFICE.

The give-and-take offered by a companion or two can do wonders for unclogging brain cells jammed with unrelated bits of information. Tossing around ideas with other people can help amplify, provoke, or streamline raw, directionless thoughts. This can take the form of classic brainstorming, where someone takes notes and everyone empties their cerebellums on a given topic, as the Compaq Computer guys did. Or it can be a much more informal conversation over dinner or drinks.

It's amazing how productive rambling conversation can be. Meandering along a casual, unpressured thought path with others often results in outrageous flights of fancy and suggestions of how things "should be," "could be," or "would be" if someone could only do such-and-such. This is when things loosen up, and ideas that have been germinating in the last row of the brain's balcony start moving closer to the stage.

Pizza and beer did the trick for Jim Jenks. An afternoon of shooting the breeze at a local pizza joint helped Jenks spot an Identity Gap that would catapult him from a sales rep who called on small surf shops to the head of one of the biggest apparel companies in the world, Ocean Pacific Sunwear, with sales of $300 million annually. His story illustrates that when we lay our frustrations and aggravations on the table in a relaxed, unpressured setting, profitable solutions may develop. The lesson to be learned: trust instincts, and act on them.

SIGHTING THE BIG SWELL
Jim Jenks/Ocean Pacific Sunwear

The pizza joint was Felipe's, a hangout in Encinitas, California, frequented by Jenks and his surfer buddies after a hard day making, selling, or riding surfboards. Jenks had just put in an exasperating day on the surf products trail. As a sales rep for a two-man company he owned with surf legend Don Hansen, he called on small surfboard retailers in Southern California, trying to sell them Hansen surfboards, as well as swim trunks, wetsuits, and car racks.

Jenks was disgusted with the quality of product he was getting from manufacturers. There were two basic problems: one, the swim trunks fell apart; two, the styles were uncool, nowhere near the hip duds that he and his friends knew had the real surf feel. Rambling on between slices of his favorite Felipe's pizza washed down with the local brew, Jenks complained about the returns he was getting on the latest faulty line of swimwear.

"Shit, I ought to make trunks myself," he blurted out. "At least I'd know they'd stay together." As a couple surf friends nodded, Jenks looked down at what was staring him in the face. "Shit, look at this tablecloth. This tablecloth print would make a neat pair of trunks."

That's when all the months of repping products he knew weren't right for his market finally came to a head. The tablecloth was the turning point, but there had been a long preamble that preceded it. The path to Felipe's had been signposted with disgruntled customers and Jenks's growing feeling that something definitely was missing. He was beginning to spy the outlines of a huge hole in the market, a first-class Identity Gap between what he, as an ace surfer and practicing member of the surf lifestyle knew to be the authentic surfer look, and what landlocked, "ho-dad" manufacturers like Hang Ten and Kennington imagined surfing was all about. He had spotted a big swell on an uninhabited beach and he was in position to catch the ride of his life.

Like any subculture, surf society dictates that the right uniform, the right language, the right attitude be present for membership in the fraternity. In the early seventies the right look wasn't available in the stores. Surfers had to customize walk shorts by cutting off corduroy jeans. As Jenks explains, "I had the custom trunks; I had the bitchen surfboard; I had the really hot wetsuits, I had all the trick equipment. But I couldn't get that kind of merchandise out of my suppliers because they wanted the mass market.

"God knows I couldn't get anybody to make walk shorts. Nobody knew what that was. A walk short to them was something an old man wore in Palm Springs. They didn't understand that you gotta get out of a pair of wet trunks in the fall and get into something that feels warm, but still is a badge, still has an identification with it, that still lets people know you're a surfer when you walk down the street."

Jenks had made surfboards for years with Don Hansen. "I thought, Christ, if I can make a surfboard, I can certainly make a pair of trunks."

Independence was the key for Jim Jenks. "I had to be able to live my lifestyle, had to get in the water," he says. When he was nineteen he dropped out of San Diego State, where he was an art major, and got a job making surfboards for Don Hansen. But after ten years of making and selling surfboards, he felt it was time for a change.

He took his plan to make a couple pair of trunks and walk shorts to his boss, Don Hansen, who talked it over with his financial partner, Bob Driver, a wealthy entrepreneur who had helped several young bucks get businesses started. Driver and Hansen noted that Jenks always had had good ideas, and they thought this one sounded interesting. Driver gave Jenks his first big shore break and extended him a $50,000 line of credit that capitalized the company. Hansen, Jenks, and a high school friend, Chuck Buttner, kicked in $5,000 each and Ocean Pacific Sunwear was on the map. It was 1972.

The plan was modest, "no big deal." Jenks had no thoughts of not making surfboards for the rest of his life. He just saw the obvious need and decided to do something about it, adding to the Hansen line in the process.

The major problems with the old trunks were in construction (rough surf would usually rip them right off), comfort (the material didn't dry fast enough and it fit badly), and style (hopelessly square). He knew what had to be done, but how to do it was something else. Jenks had never sewed in his life. He had no idea how to size things, or what the heck seam allowances were, or which fabrics worked and which didn't.

And so began the tragic-comic search for knowledge that every novice entrepreneur must embark on. Who knew anything about making clothes? Where do you buy fabric? How do you make a pattern? The Yellow Pages were consulted. Trade journals were tracked down and libraries were visited. There were countless trips to L.A.'s garment district, where the twenty-nine-year-old surfer knocked on doors trying to find out who the sewing contractors were and how he could get them to acknowledge him.

For the T-shirt and jean-clad surfer, the world of big-time garment manufacturing was quite a spectacle. "It was like going into General Motors where they're making Chevys and everything looks alike. I was going into these rigid, fixed places with hundreds and hundreds of sewing machines running in these rows of production, and if you put another zipper in or if you sewed a pocket on the left side instead of the right, it threw the whole thing into chaos. And that's what I was asking them to do."

Jenks's biggest problem was that since he had no prior experience and no big bucks he couldn't get access to the people who could make things happen for him. "I couldn't figure out how things worked." He developed a knack for sweet-talking secretaries.

"Behind every successful businessman is a super-strong secretary who knows his every move. You just go in and charm 'em. 'Goddammit, I'm a little guy and you gotta help me get going. Without you, I'm living in the back of my van with my wife and two kids.'"

Finally, he got his first break when a trade veteran, George Aftergood, took him under his wing, and waived the standard minimum order of 200 dozen. He let Jenks get by with runs of 25 dozen. Even that seemed like epic volume to Jenks, who was hoping he could sell three pairs of trunks to each surf shop.

Ocean Pacific Sunwear had two employees, Jenks and Buttner. Buttner was a gardener with nothing in particular on the horizon when Jenks suggested they make trunks together. "Here's how we're going to do it," said Jenks. "You're going to sell them because you were always the best salesman I ever knew. And you're gonna type up all the invoices because you were a clerk typist in the army. I'm gonna design them and make them."

Buttner said "okay," and before he knew it he had scrounged a job with another clothing company so he could get a cram course on the garment trade. Buttner had to do some hard initial selling to surf retailers, who were used to stocking surfboards and wetsuits, not shorts. But once the product got to the customers, the reluctance changed to reorders. O. P. had the right look and surfers knew it.

"We were adapting this business around a lifestyle," says Jenks, "which was our lifestyle."

The corduroy walk short quickly became a huge hit—and the O. P. trademark. Sales for the first year were $350,000 and over $700,000 the next.

O. P. solidified its hold on surfers as the bona fide badge of wave warriors, and started crossing over into the nonsurfer market. When the authentic surf fashions hit the streets the word traveled fast. Department stores wanted O. P.

Then things really took off, sales doubling every year for the next four years. The next big breakthrough for O. P. was the introduction of the baggy, 1940s-style silky shirt. Once again, Jenks found his inspiration in the careful observation of people around him. He started noticing more and more surfers wearing antique silk shirts, a cross between the Hawaiian print and a bowling shirt. The "silky" was the next big O. P. hit.

Thousands of other items were added to the O. P. line over the years and by 1986 it had mushroomed to a $300 million business. The California look was taking in $23 million a year in foreign sales and over 8,000 American retailers carried the label.

Today ex-gardener/surfer Chuck Buttner lives in regal splendor in the south of France. Jenks still finds time to squeeze in a little designing, but he's also working on a new sailing venture, Innovator Boats, and spending more time sailing his $3 million deep-sea fishing boat or playing with one of his two dozen classic cars.

Jenks doesn't believe his success is due to genius. "I think that anybody who's going to be successful has to have two things going for him. He's got to be able to see where the need is and pray that the timing is right. The guy who sees the need for something and says 'but the timing's not right' and waits for the timing loses the whole thing. You gotta get on it and hope that the timing is right.

"A real entrepreneur can't let the obstacles get in his way. I see so many guys who come up with beautiful, dynamite ideas, but they let things like no capitalization, or families, or the job they're in now, the security—all these things—get in the way and muddy it up. The true entrepreneur sees something, sees a hole, and says 'I'm gonna plug that hole no matter what.'"

Plugging the gap has been Jenks's motivation since the beginning. "I just wanted to build a better mousetrap. I wasn't in it for the money. It was a creative thing. I'm a maker. I like to make things. I think I want to go down in history as making the best walk short in the world."

*   *   *

Once you have begun thinking like an entrepreneur, once, like Jenks and Norm Pattiz and Bill Tillson, you have coaxed a few ideas from their hiding places it's time to figure out if they might work. It's time to leave the theoretical stage and enter the next phase: Testing.

4

Basic Training

LOOK BEFORE YOU LEAP

The bright yellow banner boldly announced to the world, "Grand Opening, The Hottest Videos!" The small store sparkled with attractive display fixtures and an eye-catching neon logo in the front window. Another entrepreneur had summoned all his confidence, and finances, proclaiming his wares to the world. The only problem was the world didn't want a fourth video store within six blocks. And if it did, it couldn't find this one if it wanted to.

Tucked into a space that could not be seen from the busy boulevard, in a mini-mall with only a handful of parking spots, the video store was struggling to stay alive four months into its grand opening. The owner had taken to jumping up and down on the sidewalk in a gorilla costume to get the attention of speeding motorists. No one slowed down. The store was empty.

The cruel fact is that the world is not waiting with open arms for the offerings of entrepreneurs, even those with a needed product. The owner of the store could have saved himself a lot of heartache by putting his idea to the simplest tests of logic and research detailed in this chapter. A drive through the neighborhood would have revealed too much competition in the vicinity. Anyone living in a car-mad city like Los Angeles should have known that a shop not visible to drivers is the kiss of death, and, if that is not enough, having no place to park certainly is the final straw.

Either the entrepreneur didn't do his homework, or, worse, knew about the drawbacks and went ahead anyway.

First-time entrepreneurs often think that because it's their idea, and they've worked hard on it, and because they're nice people, that other people will like their product as much as they do. Discovery Toys' Lane Nemeth was shocked when, as a new wholesale customer, she sent out requests to 250 toy companies for catalogs and got zip for response. "Maybe it was entrepreneur's ego, but I thought that everyone couldn't wait for me to tell them I was going into business. I thought they would be just so excited. And nobody responded at all."

DO YOUR HOMEWORK

Use strategy to survive the mercilessness of the marketplace. Examine your idea. What problem is your idea solving? What gap is your product/service shoring up in the everyday lives of your potential customers? What enhancement in someone's quality of life are you providing?

Once you have your rudimentary idea, you must do all you can to establish its desirability to the public. This means "research" or "homework," as most entrepreneurs think of it. The advance work falls into two broad categories: acquisition of functional business knowledge, and analysis of the opportunity.

Beginners can conquer the basics of business without a business degree or prior experience—but not without a crash course of some kind. The concept of commerce is easy enough. You have to sell something that people want at a price that covers your costs and makes a profit. But making it work requires some advance acquaintance with the facts of pricing, distribution, paying employees, bookkeeping, planning, and collecting payment from your customers. You should read up on these essential mechanics of business before getting underway. Any library or bookstore has plenty of manuals to choose from.

To develop a better working knowledge of business, you might try a practice run, maybe buying a product and selling it at a local flea market, or taking a job with a company that would expose you to the business knowledge or industry details you need to know. Chuck Buttner, a gardener, went to work as a salesman for a sportswear firm so he could learn about selling clothes, information that he needed to operate his fledgling Ocean Pacific Sunwear.

One entrepreneur who had never been in business before came up with an ingenious way to give himself a business primer. Philip Hwang, an engineer with a lot of product ideas, wanted to start a company, but felt he lacked business skills, so he and his wife bought a 7-Eleven franchise. The Southland Corp. then taught Hwang all the basics of running a small company, and in six months behind the counter of his 7-Eleven, he gained the knowledge that today runs his $165 million computer firm, Televideo.

For many people the idea of studying up on an opportunity seems to take all the fun out of it. It flies in the face of the romantic image of the entrepreneur as an impulsive primitive guided by pure gut instinct. True, millions have been made by people who didn't have a scrap of training to go on except their own internal homing device. But they are few and far between, and getting fewer everyday in an increasingly competitive marketplace. The vast majority of successful entrepreneurs succeeded because they were willing to learn the basics first.

The problem is that the same qualities that make someone a good entrepreneur—courage, spontaneity, decisiveness, initiative—can make a bad one if the impulsive, energetic side isn't tempered with a little detail work up front. A little knowledge can go a long way. A study at MIT, for instance, found that for first-time entrepreneurs who were exposed to some basic business practices and advice, the standard failure rate of 70 percent for new businesses was dramatically cut to only 30 percent.

A raw, unresearched idea is like a map with no directions. You have to find out where your idea is headed and to whom, and what the level of potential interest is. The place to start is by finding the answers to four strategic questions:

1. WHO PRECISELY ARE YOUR CUSTOMERS?

2. WHAT IS THE NEED? DO THEY WANT, OR CAN THEY BE MADE TO WANT, YOUR CONCEPT?

3. WHO IS THE COMPETITION? IS YOUR IDEA BETTER, DIFFERENT, OR DISTINCT FROM THAT OF THE COMPETITION?

4. CAN YOUR IDEA MAKE MONEY? IS IT PROFITABLE?

Testing your idea is a 3-D process. You need to *define* the appeal of your idea; *devise* a plan and business strategy; and *deploy* your product or service in a small way.

DEFINING COMPETITIVE APPEAL

There are plenty of opportunities in the world, but few hold truly commercial promise. Add up the numbers of your business before you jump in. How profitable are similar businesses? If you have an idea for a new kind of health club, investigate current ones to see what kind of profits they're making. Make sure your hard work can pay off with a reasonable profit margin.

If the money is there, you have to determine why people should be giving it you. Before you open your hypothetical health club, go around to other gyms and see what they're doing. Study the market and its trends. Find the gaps that will allow you to satisfy needs nobody else can. You can't just say your product or service will be better. You have to define in advance the element(s) that make that crucial difference apparent.

Studying the competition is one of the most important first steps in defining your concept. If you don't know what competitors are doing, you could be wasting a lot of time and energy. Some people spend years inventing things that are already on the market in one form or other. Richard Buskirk, head of USC's Entrepreneur Program, sees cases like that all the time.

"We had a guy come by with a device for mouth-to-mouth re-suscitation. He spent all his money on a patent, but he didn't do his homework. There were already lots of those things on the market."

You have to scour your potential industry for similar products. Quiz people in the field, compiling a list of all possible rivals. Determine the distinguishing factors that will make yours stand out from the crowd.

If there are others in the market, how well are they doing? Kevin Jenkins saved himself from the wrong enterprise—computer retailing—when he took a hard look at how the competition was faring. After visiting several stores and asking the right questions, he found out the market was glutted and changed his plans. He looked for a new opportunity and found a much more lucrative one, Hercules Computer, a $35 million maker of computer graphics devices.

THE VIABILITY CHECKLIST

A good idea is one that can stand up to scrutiny. Go to the library, read the trade journals, talk to people in the industry, and to potential customers. Make absolutely certain you have something new to offer, something different from what's out there, and something people will want to pay precious dollars for.

Many entrepreneurs get so carried away with their ideas that they forget to ask the most basic questions, like "Is It Affordable?" Buskirk again: "One entrepreneur had an elaborate idea for a pack that goes on a bicycle. It looked great, but it cost him $142 to make it. That means by the time it gets to retail it has to sell for $500. Who's going to pay that kind of money for it?"

The couple of days or weeks it takes to do some basic investigating can prevent you from squandering your time and money on a product that has no consumer appeal or profit potential.

The U.S. Patent Office has floors full of patents for products that have no commercial prospects. Such items as the Automatic Hat Remover, Motion Pictures with Synchronized Odor Emission, and a toilet paper holder that plays music make a strong case for the distinction between invention and commercial opportunity.

The smart entrepreneur submits each promising idea to a viability checklist to see how it stacks up against the commercial realities. One of the most savvy examples of this technique is the criteria California Cooler's Stuart Bewley developed to measure his concepts with. He started his preparation far earlier than most entrepreneurs. He knew back in college that he wanted to have a business of his own someday, so during summer vacations he sought out successful businessmen to find out their secrets.

He pieced together a list that he calls his "Five Truisms," an outstanding collection of guidelines for any entrepreneur:

1. NOT EVERYTHING'S BEEN THOUGHT OF YET. "People say if it's a good idea then somebody's already thought of it, and if you came up with it it's probably no good. That's based on the fact that most people don't have a lot of confidence in themselves."

2. THE PRODUCT SHOULD BE LOW CAPITAL-INTENSIVE. "Because entrepreneurs can't raise that much capital."

3. IT SHOULD BE LOW COMPETITION OR NO COMPETITION. "An entrepreneur faces tremendous difficulties starting a company anyway. To go against heavy, well-established competition doesn't allow you to get on your feet and running."

4. IT'S GOT TO HAVE A GOOD PROFIT MARGIN. "Because if you're going to be successful, you're going to need the capital and dollars to be able to expand your business."

5. IT'S GOT TO HAVE POTENTIAL. "If you're selling pencils on

the street, or if you're running a wine cooler company that's selling $200 million worth of product, it's still going to take all day and all your time. You might as well do the one that has potential."

TALK TO THE CUSTOMER

The main reason for new product failure is the absence of a consumer-responsive idea behind it. Get to know some of your potential customers, find out how they think and act. See where your concept fits into their buying patterns. There's nothing more important to any business, entrepreneurial or corporate, than knowing and understanding the bankroller, the consumer.

Sometimes entrepreneurs and their customers are one and the same thing. Their businesses grow out of personal passions that they determine must be shared by others as well. O. P.'s Jim Jenks and Mel and Patricia Ziegler of Banana Republic were their own best customers. It's a major advantage to have that kind of affinity with your audience. But it's also a big mistake for anyone starting out to assume the rest of the world is on the same wavelength as you. You still have to make sure that the perceived shared "interest" is also a shared "need," or intense "like."

The best way to learn what the customers think is to get out and talk to them. Ask them. If your product is different, see if they're willing to buy that difference.

Michael Crete knew people loved his wine cooler because they'd been demanding it at parties for six years before he decided to market it. But that wasn't enough proof for him. He went to a local college and tested students for their reactions on everything from the tartness of the drink to the price they might be willing to pay for it. Total cost of the test: $30 for paper cups. (Colleges are a great source of information for the entrepreneur. Instructors are usually happy to answer questions and offer advice for enterprising members of the community. Marketing professors are only too glad to bring real world product introductions before their classes, providing you with valuable free testing.)

To determine whether there was a bona fide need for his product, Mike Malone jumped into his VW van and drove cross-country interviewing prospective customers. His fact-finding mission produced all the proof he needed that his idea had a solid market behind it. So he started Audio Environments, Inc., which would become an $18 million company, supplying restaurants, hotels, and boutiques with contemporary "foreground" music tapes. His methodical approach, sounding out the market before diving in, planning for contingencies, shows how you can verify your idea and increase your odds of it working through basic research, without suffering any reduction in swashbuckling spontaneity.

PROGRAMMED FOR SUCCESS
Mike Malone/Audio Environments, Inc.

Mike Malone got his idea for success one night at a friend's Seattle restaurant. The 8-track stereo had conked out again, leaving the hangout devoid of decent music. "You should really put all the music on reel-to-reel tapes," Malone suggested to the restaurateur, "then you wouldn't have to worry about that machine breaking down all the time." He knew someone who could put some tapes together for him for a small fee.

Malone was a twenty-five-year-old securities analyst who was between jobs. His company's Seattle office had just closed down, and his options were to relocate to New York or Boston, or quit and find a new job in Seattle. He decided he'd rather live in Seattle. He was looking for a new line of work when the restaurant music concept popped up.

The restaurant owner had four other establishments that could be livened up considerably by some good rock 'n' roll. Malone got to wondering how many other restaurants might be able to use a musical facelift.

At his old job, which involved researching new companies

and industries for stock salesmen, he had run across data on an emerging trend in the restaurant business—a move to casual-themed, young adult-oriented restaurants. Music combined with new dining trends might make a potent combination.

"My observation," says Malone, "was simply to take the music that they enjoyed at home and in their cars and put it in a public place. It was a natural idea. It was an opportunity to develop a better mousetrap. It wasn't my knowledge, or interest, or awareness of music, and certainly not my knowledge of electronics. It was more an appreciation of the business and marketing aspects of what a contemporary foreground music service could offer to retailers."

Lifestyle changes had brought about a new kind of watering hole. It was 1970 and droves of single baby-boomers were gravitating toward the salad bar, with its nonplastic plants and food, as an informal meeting ground. There was one thing missing in the concept, though, the very ingredient that defined the generation hanging out at these new chain restaurants: rock 'n' roll.

To see if he really had something, though, Malone decided to take his idea on the road and find out if there really were enough customers for it. Touring the country in his van, he was amazed to find "that there was no commercial music service company offering contemporary, familiar music to these emerging restaurant chains."

In fact, all the restaurant operators had the same problem his friend had. They had consumer machines that were always broken. Some restaurant chains even had waitresses doubling as deejays, playing records on their way back from serving tables. "When I asked these people," he recalls, "what if there was a service available where you got programmed music on a machine that didn't break, the reaction was always, 'Where the hell have you been?'"

Seeing the need firsthand was the final piece of logic Malone needed to induce him to take the plunge. He bet the $20,000 in his savings, and Audio Environments was formed.

Malone discovered on his trip that his only competition was Muzak and 3M, and they weren't competition at all. Theirs was "background music," the barely audible, celestial static that dogged shoppers and elevator riders and was the antithesis of the music his generation had grown up with. He had a brand-new concept: "foreground music," contemporary songs by the original artists intended to be heard and enjoyed on a high-quality sound system.

He wanted to develop a product that had some staying power, one that someone couldn't come along and easily duplicate. He recognized a desirable ingredient for any start-up company: the "proprietary" product, something made exclusively by his company.

Recording tapes for restaurants was definitely not it. That would put him in direct competition with the major record companies in sales of recorded music. CBS and Warner Bros. were never going to give this little guy in Seattle permission to duplicate their product, and if they did, they could easily put him out of business at any moment since they controlled his commodity.

He decided that the only way he could protect his investment from encroachment down the road, and establish his concept as something substantial, a new category or industry, not just a new company, was to make his own playback machines. None of the consumer devices worked anyway or ran tapes as long as his customers needed. Piecing together odds and ends from the radio and broadcast industry, he assembled a machine that could play four-hour tapes and that his market could buy nowhere else.

By thinking things through ahead of time and making his own label playback equipment, Malone increased his chances for success immensely.

Audio Environments, Inc. offered restaurants six four-hour continuous loop tapes, and one new tape each month, plus playback recorder, amplifiers, and speakers, for $1,500. Malone started the company with a partner, who recorded the tapes.

But after they had 20 accounts around Seattle, the two had a falling-out and suddenly became competitors, the partner starting his own foreground music business. Malone had to start all over again. The former securities analyst set up shop in a stairwell, five feet wide and thirty feet deep, next to a recording studio that helped him with his programming.

One of the daunting problems that would occur to anyone contemplating a business like Malone's is the legal can of worms of dealing with performance rights, publisher's clearances, and royalty sticklers. The legal bureaucracy was so staggering, in fact, that it had caused CBS Records to shelve a foreground music plan that they had spent hundreds of thousands of dollars on. Malone was told by the person at CBS who tried to get it off the ground that the alphabet soup of music monitors, the American Federation of Musicians, and the TV union, AFTRA, would never give him the clearances to use the original songs.

Another entrepreneur had been advised his task was impossible. Malone's approach was to build his company slowly and establish his proprietary product first and bother with clearances later. His product was in a gray legal area, where there was no definitive ruling, but he was confident that when the pressure eventually came for legalities, that he would be prepared to accommodate them. He had those possible contingencies and extra costs built into his business plan.

Record companies wouldn't return his calls anyway in the early days. "It took us years to be taken seriously," he says. So he would wait for them to call him. After all, his service complimented the promotional efforts of record companies and gave their music public exposure. They eventually did come around and all the legal agreements were signed.

Malone got his big break about four years out, when he used a classic sales tactic, playing competitors off against one another, to reel in two major restaurant chains. Sitting in the offices of Victoria Station, he told management that an arch rival, The Cork and Cleaver, was starting to use his foreground music. The room buzzed, and everybody said, "Hey, the Cork's using it, let's go with it." That evening he got on a plane and the next day was meeting with Cork executives in Denver, telling them that Victoria Station had decided to use his service. Eyes lit up. "The Station's going with it? Let's do it." In one fell swoop two of the nation's largest restaurant chains were on board.

"One thing that the entrepreneur has is the confidence of quantum leap," he explains. "Even if he stretches a bit, he doesn't do it to deceive. He does it with the confidence of knowing that he'll make it good. A deceiver is not successful. You can only deceive people so long before you get into trouble."

As the sound of foreground pop music began to serenade more and more diners across the land, not everyone was happy. The hard-driving beat of Audio Environments, Inc. had awakened the sleeping giants, Muzak and 3M, from the background. Not only was this upstart company making their product obsolete, AEI was using some of their own salesmen to do it. With lucrative incentives and commissions, Malone was able to get many independent Muzak and 3M distributors to rep his product too. Malone's giant competitors tried to slow his progress by initiating several major copyright suits against him, but he won in the courts, as he was doing in the market.

Seven long years after it was started, foreground music was beginning to catch on as a potent marketing tool for businesses outside the restaurant world. Department stores and fashion outlets found that customers liked to shop to their favorite hit songs. The right music, demographically arranged by AEI, could set the right customer mood, give the store the right image, and make a customer feel part of an event, playing the cameo role of shopper to a blaring soundtrack.

The accounts grew, and now range from trendy fashion outlets like The Limited, where the music is the latest in new-wave pop, to upscale restaurants, where the mix is atmospheric new age music. Malone's eleven full-time programmers, ex-deejays, make four-hour tapes for every every conceivable taste—

pop, rock, jazz, soul, classical, country, oldies but goodies, Latin—and for every mood subdivision within those.

By 1986 AEI's 20,000 accounts included just about every major restaurant chain in the country, Houlihan's, the Charthouse, Chi Chi's, Flakey Jake's, Marie Callender's Pie Shops, Steak and Ale, even fast-food places like Burger King and Pizza Hut. There were hotel clients—Ramada Inn, Sheraton, Hilton, Holiday Inn—and plenty of music in the air, literally, with in-flight programming for 22 airlines from Continental to Japan Air. Incredibly, a Dental Division was pumping out chairside tunes to drown out the dentist's drill team.

Malone believes his success is in large part due to planning. "You have to give a lot of thought to your business, your concept, your idea before you commit too much human energy and financial resources. What is it within your concept that's proprietary? Is there a copyright, a patent, a licensing agreement? If not, you stand the chance of having a good idea being recognized by someone with greater financial resources, leaving you in the dust with only the knowledge that you had the idea first."

Now the owner of a top hotel in Seattle, the Sorrento, a restaurant in San Diego, an air-taxi service and a couple of his own planes, in addition to his thriving music firm, Malone has boiled his prescription for success into a five-point plan.

1. The business shouldn't be capital-intensive and require a lot of initial start-up cash.

2. There's no relationship between more employees and more sales. Keep internal sales staffs to a minimum and rely on outside independents.

3. Keep contact between ownership and employees direct and unions out.

4. Find an idea with minimal government regulations.

5. Offer a product whose profit margins increase with volume. The more you make the more you make.

Anyone who's observant and does their homework has a chance to achieve what he has, thinks Malone. "I'm not a music nut, and I don't know much about electronics. I just recognized the opportunity. It wasn't hiding underneath a rock. It was available to anybody else."

CREATING THE NEED

Discovering a pent-up demand as Mike Malone did, where the idea is immediately recognized and solves a readily apparent consumer need, is the dream of every entrepreneur. Unfortunately, not every new concept meets with the same initial approval. When you are fixing something that the market knows is broken, like those run-down tape machines, it is easy for customers to see where your product fits in. Many times, though, the entrepreneur's role is one of fixing something that people don't know is broken. This is a much harder sell. Here you have to create the need for your product, not just point it out.

This involves changing old habits and ways of thinking. Change is something everyone is in favor of, but no one likes to be the first to endorse. Since change is the calling card of the entrepreneur, as you make the first rounds of friends and advisers and potential customers, you are naturally going to run into resistance.

If it's a brand-new product or service, most people don't know they need it until they see it in action. People weren't knocking down Henry Ford's barn door telling him to get those horseless carriages on the road or else. Life could have gone on without cars. But not after the early auto entrepreneurs created a new perception about people's transportation needs. Once the wonders of the car were demonstrated, people quickly had a new perceived need, and forgot that four out of five of them earlier had questioned his sanity.

So expect some flak for your new idea. The nay-sayers only know what's happened before. You have an inkling of what's going to happen. To get a reliable reading on your product, you have to find a way to show how valuable it is. A sample, a prototype, or a brochure can help out here, or an example of a similar venture or product. If your idea is too sophisticated or expensive to make a lifesize sample of, a scale model or even a sketch can get the point across and cut your explanation time in half.

Some of you may be wondering just how talkative you should be, and with whom. After all, there are unscrupulous types who like to eavesdrop on free opportunities. Here are some guiding principles.

Rules of Secrecy

1. Protect yourself if possible with a trademark or patent. You can't patent an idea or suggestion. It has to be a "new and useful process, machine, manufacture, or composition of matter, or any new and useful improvements thereof." It costs $170 to file for a patent, but you can pay thousands of dollars for all the appropriate territorial rights once it's granted. Jerry Wilson of Soloflex, for example, paid $2,000 and got off cheap for his home gym device. It can take two years to get a patent—if your item is ruled patentable.

   Trademarks can protect words, names, or symbols that are used to indicate the source and distinction of the product. These take a long time to get, and you have to be already engaged in the business of selling the item before you are eligible to apply for one. Contact the U.S. Patent and Trademark Office in Washington, D.C., for details, or consult the nearest library.

2. If your idea can't be officially protected, other protection includes sending yourself registered copies of your idea, sketches, plans, prototypes through the U.S. mail, keeping

the packages sealed for any future contingency. Ads called Fictitious Name Statements, which can be taken in any local newspaper, place an indisputable date on when your idea started.

3. Very few ideas can be decisively protected anyway. Even patented products are routinely evaded by slight alterations.

4. Keep in mind that undue paranoia has defeated many an entrepreneur. If you keep your idea a secret, it's never going to get to the marketplace.

5. Use common sense. Don't tip off potential competitors to your idea, but don't overdo the undercover gambit. Very seldom do ideas get appropriated in the concept stage.

6. Your idea is most vulnerable to knockoffs once it's on the market. Most people will take your idea for what it is for the moment, hot air, until it is a physical, and successful, reality.

TRYING IT OUT

The best way to test an idea, of course, is to try it out. You can satisfy yourself that the product can be profitable, and that no one else is doing it, but the only conclusive way to figure out if people really want to buy a Pet Rock or high-quality tweezer is to put a few of them on the market on a trial basis. To minimize risk, it's a good policy to operate the test as a sideline business while you continue to hold down your regular job. It's amazing how many of the most successful entrepreneurs started out this modest way, at first just picking up a few extra bucks on the side, getting familiar with business, and then gradually building it into a full-time hit.

Ron Rice, you will remember, kept his high school teaching job for three years while he built up Hawaiian Tropic tanning oil. Boyd Willat kept his job as a set decorator for two years until he felt his Day Runner appointment book was profitable enough to support his efforts full-time.

If there's no other way to launch your venture than to go at it full-time, you still should start with a small, gradual test of the idea. Smart entrepreneurs try not to risk so much that they can't recover if it falls through.

The realities of the beginner mandate a measured pace. As O.P.'s Jim Jenks says, "You gotta crawl before you can walk." Newly christened entrepreneurs can only get their legs under them by first taking a few ungainly, teetering steps. With great pinwheeling of arms and probing of limbs, they place one foot in front of the other in a determined trial to see where their new ability will take them.

Boyd and Felice Willat were self-described "babes in the woods" when they started. Their story illustrates that beginners can make it if they follow the only sensible course open to them—measured experimentation. The Willats' path was one of progressive plots on the learning curve until they had a $25 million company on their hands. Their firm, the Culver City, California-based Harper House, put the time management/personal organizer on the map.

One Day at a Time
Boyd and Felice Willat/Harper House

Like many ventures, Harper House was the end-result of an organic process that started with a simple sideline foray. Both Willats were working in the movie business, Boyd as a set decorator and art director on films like *Ordinary People* and *Raise the Titanic*, and Felice as a director's assistant. Between filmings there are long periods of time off, known in the trade as hiatus. To give herself something to do during one layoff Felice took a course in intensive journal writing. She hoped she could get better in touch with her true thoughts and objectives by putting it down on paper and organizing her mind's congested clutter.

This was a very natural thing for her to do. Both Felice and her husband are quintessential products of the soul-searching, identity-questing sixties. Boyd had sampled thirty different jobs by 1980. He sold candles, worked at an advertising agency, spent time as a cowboy, a coal miner, carpenter, and sales clerk.

"I wasn't a typical entrepreneur," says Felice, "although I'm the perfect companion to one because I'm really open for challenge and expanding my horizons. I do have a creative strain in me; I love to explore. I really like to daydream, and I was never really good at a routine-type job. I used to work at the Arthritis Foundation, and they called me The Daydreamer, because I really liked going into other realms of information, like science or metaphysics."

Felice found the journal process "magical" and decided to create a new kind of diary. The old ones with the blank pages didn't provide enough suggestions to encourage people to write things down, so she came up with an item called the "Keeping Track Journalog." A cross between a personal diary and an appointment book, the small volume was sold to a San Francisco publisher. "We were amazed that a company picked it up and paid us a royalty," says Felice.

When it actually started selling, the Willats were suddenly in the middle of their first market test. Though it had all been unplanned, they interpreted the data like marketing pros. Some 15,000 people bought it, that must mean there was something to it. They had confirmed a customer need and it hadn't cost them a dime.

Their reaction wasn't to jump into production with checkbooks blazing. Instead they studied ways they could make the next version of the journal even better. If they defined it further, and gave it a more attractive cover, maybe they could sell even more. Boyd put his design talents (and the Yellow Pages) to work and discovered a small factory in downtown L.A. that made colorful, patent vinyl covers. It was there that a shop foreman from Thailand introduced him to the raw materials and processes that would make the mass marketing of Felice's journal a possibility. Out of that little 12-by-40-foot factory came the ideas for brightly colored vinyl covers and a three-ring binder instead of a book format.

Now they had something truly different. The presentation was unmistakable with shiny wild pink, chartreuse, yellow, and purple vinyl covers, and inside the Journalog had been modified to an all-encompassing datebook and personal organizer. But how could they go about selling it on their own?

The next step was one that has helped get many low-budget entrepreneurs off the ground: a visit to the local merchandise mart. Located in most of the major cities—New York, Miami, Boston, Atlanta, San Francisco, Dallas, Chicago, Philadelphia, Minneapolis, Denver—these centers display the gift/stationery/furniture wares of thousands of manufacturers, large and small, in showrooms operated by independent sales reps. Inside are loads of sales representatives, whose whole livelihood depends on spotting hot new trends. Their business of selling manufacturers' products to retailers survives on newness, so any rep caught at trade shows without new merchandise can develop an image of being out-of-step very quickly.

For anyone with a promising new product like the Willats, the sales mart can be a great way to start a business. All you need are a few samples of your product and your rep can start making sales for you. The Willats' shiny organizers caught the eye of a rep at the L.A. Mart who then went out to stores and got them some initial orders. Only then did they have to plunk down their $12,000 in start-up capital and go into production. Getting customers before you dive in is just another way to minimize risk and ensure that the venture starts off on some semblance of financial footing.

That year Harper House, named after the Willats' home/office on Harper Avenue, did only $80,000 in sales, but broke even, a good performance for a first year. Felice ran the business while Boyd helped support the start-up with his full-time film job. They still had a lot to learn in the university of the marketplace. On the production front, they had problems with the Velcro flap of vinyl that wrapped around and closed the appointment book. It was breaking off with repeated use and had to be fixed. In the sales area, most buyers were typically resistant to a brand-new concept.

But Felice saw positive signs in the rejections. They would always say, she recalls, "'There's no way I could sell this fancy phonebook, but I'll take one, I think it's kind of cute.' Then their partner would want one. Then they would order two, then six."

These same buyers who rejected the product in the early days "came back three years later and shook our hands," adds Boyd.

Gradually, they picked up sales reps in other parts of the country and sales began to creep upward. Even though they weren't making much money at it yet, Boyd was hooked. "I loved working with color and new ideas. It was exciting having products people bought. It took me out of the consumer position and into a creative position. For the first time in my life I got to do what I wanted to do."

The Willats continued refining their product until their original calendar/journal had become "The Day Runner," a sophisticated time-management tool for business professionals. It had taken two and a half years in the market and the Journalog experiment before that to reach the point where the outside world, unaware of the process, could greet the mature idea as a natural, overnight stroke of genius.

The Day Runner is the information age's loose-leaf answer to the computer. It files, organizes, never forgets, and processes words and thoughts into usable data. "People today have so many roles and responsibilities," explains Boyd, "that it has become impossible for anyone to instantly remember and keep track of everything they need to know as they race from one place to the next." Each 7½-by-9-inch binder has a raft of features, from a checkbook holder, to an event calendar for birthdays and anniversaries, designer notepad, calculator pocket, a goal and project planning system, daily planner, in short, anything "necessary for people to get things done, to run their own lives."

At first the stores that carried The Day Runner were small gift shops or office-supply outlets. After about three years of trying, they finally got a large chain deparment store, Bullock's, to take a chance. This was the big break that got them off the minor-league treadmill and into volume sales.

With sales moving up to $450,000 in the third year, Boyd finally felt there was enough evidence this crazy organizer business was going to make it that he quit his other job and joined the growing operations in the Willats' home, which would eventually house up to 55 employees.

The Willats were proving once again that with a little bit of homework, and the proper incentive, amateurs could crack the inner sanctum of business. After five years of measured, step-by-step growth, by 1986 The Day Runner was a fixture in almost every gift and stationery store in the country. Harper House sales were at $15 million annually. There were also foreign-language versions in Europe in French, Italian, and German.

Boyd remembers a time in his life when he was "haunted by companies who improperly stole my ideas and capitalized on them before I could because they were stronger than I was." Now that he's a successful entrepreneur he is in control of his ideas, his objectives, his destiny, the search for which had taken him down so many different roads in the sixties. Like many of his generation he had found the self-expression he was looking for in the independence of enterprise. "Business is the great frontier," says the animated Willat. "Business is the opportunity to make a contribution, to break open things, to make what never existed before and to feel the light of history come down on you just once."

THE RIGHT TIME

The Willats had a great idea, passion, persistence, and a sane approach to growth. But they also had something else on their side, an ingredient that often spells the difference between success and failure. Timing. Their Day Runners hit the market at the same time droves of upwardly mobile baby-boomers were hitting full professional stride, at a time when the accelerating demands of life in the information age were reaching a chaotic crescendo, and needed some sorting out. Their idea would have been just as useful to people ten or fifteen years earlier, but it wouldn't have sold because the right demographic and psychic conditions didn't exist then. It took the raw numbers of baby-boomers entering the professional ranks, particularly women (80 percent of the initial buyers of The Day Runner were women), plus that generation's special inclination to getting itself together to provide the Willats with their opportunity.

"We created something that was based on the needs of the baby-boomers," notes Felice. "It's a tool for them to be in touch with what they wanted for themselves. It just happened to be the right time at the right place creating the space for them to answer some questions for themselves."

Anyone starting a business has to seriously consider the exigencies of the moment, as near as they can be figured out. Timing is the most instinctual and prophetic side of entrepreneurship, but even so, one should try to gather as many favorable signals beforehand as possible.

Spotting a hole in the marketplace does not always mean the time is right for its exploitation. For instance, the Advent Corporation, first on the market with large-projection-screen TV in 1974, found its Advent screens to be ahead of the times by about a decade. It predated the public demand for large-screen technology that would accompany the VCR revolution. It wound up going bankrupt. Its founder licensed manufacturing rights to his process to Japan's NEC (no American companies were interested). With characteristic patience, the Japanese waited for the right moment and now dominate the market in projection TV.

The question you have to ask is: Are consumers ready for my idea? Are they over-ready? Am I too early or too late, (like our friend with the video store)? American palates weren't ready for spicy food in 1970, but in 1985 they made hot Cajun and curry fare big favorites on the restaurant circuit. Those who deciphered the moment of change and better-traveled, more adventurous tastes were able to capitalize on right timing.

Who would have thought the time would be right in 1986 for clunky, one-speed bikes in a world of fancy ten-speeds? Yet these were the hottest wheels on the market. Vanguard teenagers in California beach towns had taken to riding fat-tired, big-seat, no-frills bikes in a reverse-status symbol move in the early eighties. Bike makers who spotted the trendsetters discovered it was time to reintroduce the humble one-speed, or, as it's now dubbed in its hep form, the cruiser.

If you can identify vanguard consumers for your product, the ones who would be the first to buy it, and see what their reaction is to your item, you may be able to get a valuable appraisal as to whether you have the right timing.

While research can provide some evidence, in the end timing is essentially a "gut" call.

DEVISING A PLAN

Once you've gotten a feel for your idea and are reasonably confident about market acceptance, it's time to devise a plan to implement it. The business plan for most entrepreneurs is like spinach for kids. They know it's good for them, but they'll do anything to avoid it and its dreaded jargon—"cash flow," "balance sheet," etc.

But there's no substitute for planning out the numbers of your venture. You need to know not just how much money you need to open your doors, but also how much you need to stay open. How long can you last if sales are slow for the first six months, or year, or couple of years it takes to get public awareness up for your product? What are your sales targets for the next few years? What will your personnel needs be? How are you going to promote, advertise, and market your product? How long will it take from the time you make the sale to when you collect payment from your customer? How conservative can you afford to be in ordering supplies and carrying inventory as you nurse your precious start-up capital in the early months?

Projecting cash flow over several years for a company that doesn't as yet exist and a product that has never been sold may seem absurd but it has to be done to provide direction, and contingencies for what can, and often does, go wrong. Beginners shouldn't be intimidated by the numbers. Have a good accountant, a professor, or a business student at a local college help you prepare the figures. Or take in partners who are more experienced in the financial area. Remember, not everyone knows everything, or has to, to be a successful entrepreneur.

Besides the mathematical calculations, it's also useful to condense your concept briefly on paper. Pinpoint its promise with the all-important summation: the selling proposition. Again, make it simple and logical. Get across (1) what problem your product solves and (2) what it does that no other product can. Your message is as simple as three letters: PSD—Problem, Solution, Distinction.

Specific strategies for establishing a winning product with consumers and outdoing the competition depend on the particulars of the field in question, and are outlined in thousands of marketing and management books. However, there is one main precept that every entrepreneur should bear in mind when devising a plan of attack. Create a small success first and build from there.

Over and over the story of successful entrepreneurs is one of starting out not to conquer the world but one small town or region first. The key to the spectacular success of California Cooler was the tactic of the small success. Once the product was made a hit in its home territory of central California, that success was used to persuade distributors to take on the product in northern California. After northern Californian distributors were happy and prosperous selling Cooler, then that success in turn was enough to convince southern Californian distributors to enthusiastically sell the product. And so it went, one little victory leading to the next, across the U.S., and then across the world.

WEIGHING THE RISKS

Quantifying your idea with a plan of attack or even a trial run is the final step in your risk-evaluation process. It's now time to weigh the evidence in favor of your venture against the attendant risks. If the information confirms a bona fide market opportunity, you've reached the fateful moment. Should you, or shouldn't you, plunge in?

Chances are, if you've gotten this far and have done your homework, going ahead shouldn't seem risky, but simply the next logical move in your plan to take control of your destiny. That's not to say, though, that turning in your notice to the boss or plunking down your life's savings is without risks. No matter how favorable the odds look, there are no guarantees. When you start a business, you take a risk. Risk is the central element of entrepreneurship, and before we move ahead, you need to fully understand its critical role in the entrepreneurial process.

The dictionary defines an entrepreneur as "one who assumes the liability" for a business endeavor. If an entrepreneur doesn't have something on the line, then, is not risking money, house, reputation, or career, he's not really a true entrepreneur.

It's basic human nature to avoid risk-taking. People fear the loss that might come from an unknown route. Englewood, Colorado, psychologist Mark Held, who specializes in the study of entrepreneurial behavior, says that "most people are not big risk takers because they want to be that way, but because the fear immobilizes them. The risk taker is willing to act despite the fear."

A common prod to risk-taking for today's entrepreneurs is the fear of standing still. The fear of landing on your butt is less than the thought of sitting on it in perpetuity in a boring or unfulfilling job.

"It's lack of motion," says Gymboree's Joan Barnes, "and standing on the dock that drives me crazy. I want to jump off the dock and make waves, be in there swimming. I'll weather the conditions when I feel them. The thing is to keep moving at all costs."

Banana Republic's Mel Ziegler concurs: "I don't think I'd get up in the morning, if I knew what was going to happen all day long."

In weighing the risk of your venture, then, measure the potential loss against your current predicament. If you're bored and stuck in your present job, how long can you take staying that way? Can you tolerate doing the same thing five, ten, or fifteen years from now? Can you live with yourself later in life, knowing you passed up a golden opportunity?

Regret can be a very effective spur for the achievement-oriented. When TGI Friday's Dan Scoggin worries that if he doesn't "get off the dime and do something" he's going to be an old man in his rocking chair talking about what he could have done, his fear of later regret easily overwhelms the uncertainty of a risky present. If you have high expectations for yourself, and want to get as much out of life as possible, you are a prime candidate for an active regret mechanism. Use it—or you'll regret it.

Ralph Keyes, who interviewed hundreds of risk takers, from firewalkers, to topless dancers, to entrepreneurs, in *Chancing It,* found lots of regret, but never over chances taken, only for those passed up. "Over and over again," he told *People,* "I heard people mourning the risks they wished they had taken, yet hadn't. But I never once heard anyone who took a substantial risk that they fully understood—whether they won or lost—ever say they regretted it."

The best way to overcome a fear of risk-taking is to simply ask yourself, "What's the worst thing that could happen if I fail?" For most people the answer is simply that they have to get another job. And what have you really lost by replacing one dime-a-dozen job for another?

Once you've reached the conclusion that success is a probable outcome from a venture, or that the rewards are considerable enough to be worth the effort, your attention will be focused more on potential opportunity than the risks involved. When you decide to go ahead, like many entrepreneurs, you probably won't think what you're doing is risky.

As Celestial Seasonings' Mo Siegel explains, "I take a risk, but don't see it as risk. If there's something that I'm doing that

I believe will work and even if everyone tells me that it won't work, I'm not overly concerned. To me it's not high-risk. When I started the tea company, I gave it a ninety-nine percent chance of succeeding."

J. Paul Getty, in describing the role risk played in his career, put it this way: "There is always an element of chance and you must be willing to live with that element. If you insist on perfect certainty, you will never be able to make any decision at all."

So it comes down, finally, to the thing that movie sets and new ventures were made for: action. There's no other way to find out if your idea has what it takes to make it. However small the first step may be, you have to take it: There's no next step without it. As the German writer Goethe wrote, "Whatever you can do or dream you can do, begin it. Boldness has genius, power, and magic in it."

DEPLOYMENT: DIVING IN

The first steps in deploying your venture should be approached with feet-on-the-ground pragmatism and the recognition that companies, like people, are not born fully grown. Too many entrepreneurs are defeated by the go-for-broke, Charge-of-the-Light-Brigade mentality, believing that because they think big that they can be big right away.

Entrepreneurs must reckon with the paradox of the dream deferred. The grand vision can only be acquired on the installment plan, one payment at a time. "You've got to start really small and work up," says Richard Thalheimer, founder of The Sharper Image. "The people who think that you start big are sadly mistaken because they don't realize that you make a lot of mistakes. So you've got to start small so that you can start again if you blow it the first time."

Thalheimer has practiced what he preaches to perfection. As I mentioned earlier, his motto of "Start Small, Think Big" made him a multimillionaire by the time he was in his early thirties. It turned a humble office supply company into the household name for the latest, and splashiest, in toys for grown-ups. The Sharper Image today sells $100 million worth every year of hi-tech gadgets, from portable car alarms to miniature spy cameras to electronic flea collars for pets. Thalheimer's story is vivid proof of the spectacular results that can come from the unspectacular route of due course, of piling one small success on top of another.

Start Small, Think Big
Richard Thalheimer/The Sharper Image

It begins with a high school lad from Little Rock, Arkansas, shoveling gravel for the state on a summer job with a road crew. Though he had helped out at his father's small department store, working in the toy department at Christmastime, this was his first exposure to the working world, and the young Thalheimer found something lacking in the fixed-salary concept.

The next summer, when he was sixteen, he took a job selling *Encyclopaedia Britannica*, where commissions determined the amount of money he could make. But Thalheimer wasn't any good at it. He couldn't make a sale. Thoroughly frustrated, he was taken out on some sales calls by his boss, who showed him the proper technique.

"He used the *Britannica* presentation book to the letter," Thalheimer remembers. "There's a tremendous strength in using something simple properly. That principle runs through many successful businesses, whether it's McDonald's or The Sharper Image. Keep it very simple, and execute it perfectly. Most people in life try to make it more complicated. You're more successful if you stick to a simpler approach but do it better."

Thalheimer stuck to it so well he became one of the company's top salesmen. When he went away to college at Yale, he picked up where he left off, selling *Britannica*s in New Haven to support himself. He figures he was the only Yale student who instead of doing homework at night was out pushing ency-clopedias. Yet he was able to sell as many as three sets a night and by the end of his freshman year had made enough money to buy himself the Porsche that his classmates got for high school graduation presents.

The years of sitting in customers' homes, patiently listening and feeling them out, learning how to "make it make sense to them," was another valuable step in the greening of the entre-preneur. It was to be the groundwork for one of his main max-ims, "Listen to the customer."

After graduation (with a degree in sociology) he moved to San Francisco in 1971 to study law, which he thought would be handy in complicated business deals. He had made up his mind he was going to have his own business. It didn't take long. The second day in town he was already at work on his door-to-door office-supply business, cold-calling businesses in the financial district. His start-up costs were $25 for business cards and $300 for supplies. And from that humble start he was able to work his way through Hastings Law School on a com-fortable $25,000 a year selling copier supplies.

After graduation he practiced law for a year and added re-placement IBM typewriter ribbons to his business, which he continued to expand on the side. He changed the name of his company from Thalheimer Paper Systems to The Sharper Im-age, after his copier products. It was catchier and broad enough to take in any other items he might want to sell.

While working for a law firm, he noticed that lawyers go through a lot of ribbons on self-correcting IBMs. Law firms were extremely picky about their correspondence, much more so than industrial companies. Thalheimer had isolated his first target market. Because there weren't enough lawyers to make ribbon sales profitable in San Francisco alone, he came up with the idea of selling them by mail to lawyers across the country.

Mail order was a routine step in selling more office sup-plies. But it was also another unposted landmark on the long and winding road of the entrepreneurial process. By sticking his nose in the business of selling by mail, trying it out, seeing what it did, he was prepared to seize an opportunity that cropped up a couple of years later.

Thalheimer, an avid runner, bought himself a $29 stopwatch in 1977, so he could do what runners like to do—measure his fitness by the clock. The watch was a hit with friends, who all wanted one but couldn't seem to find it in the stores. Enter opportunity. If people want the watch but it's not available, why not make it available? He tracked down the Japanese manufacturer and made a licensing deal to sell the watch by mail.

Leave it to the outsider to spot the hole. The watch manufacturer was concentrating its advertising and marketing on retail sporting goods stores. It had never thought to sell directly to consumers. It advertised its product in the running magazines (that's where Thalheimer spotted it), but didn't give runners any idea where they could buy it. Thalheimer fixed that by taking out a 1/12th-page ad in *Runner's World* for $200. He made $300 with each ad and ran it four more times. It wasn't great money. But it was a start.

His curiosity piqued by the mail-order business, he went out looking for a more lucrative product to advertise. He found it at the Consumer Electronics Show in Las Vegas in 1978. It was a waterproof stainless-steel watch that could retail for $69, yet had all the features of the Seiko model which sold for $260. He made a deal with the manufacturer, and took out a full-page ad—this time for $1,000.

"I had the confidence from doing that $200 ad that I wouldn't come out too badly," he says. "I broke even on the first one, so how badly can I do on this one? That kind of logic is my type of logic, I guess. You take an analogous situation and make a deduction from that. I didn't lose any money on the first one. This is a better product, therefore I won't lose any money on this one."

The headline of the ad read: "Own the Genius of a $250 Chronograph for $69." It was pure genius. Orders flooded in and Thalheimer was suddenly selling 1,000 watches a month, grossing $30 on each one. By the end of the year, he had made $300,000.

From there it was just another simple evolution to advertise several products at once in a mail-order catalog. He did a little research first. He took a $129 course in mail-order selling and got the fundamentals down. He consulted with a few ad agencies, but the information was too expensive and not as accurate as going directly to the customers.

Since his *Britannica* days, Thalheimer had been convinced that nothing was a better gauge of what people wanted than a public face-to-face. "I'm a great believer in going out and asking people who you think are the target customers what they think of either the ad or the placement of the ad, or what magazines they subscribe to."

According to Thalheimer, "The whole secret to my career is simply that I really try and understand what the other person's feelings and thoughts are and therefore I change my product or business to make it so that a customer appreciates what we're doing. It's nothing more complicated than listening to the customer."

When customers called in to order watches, Thalheimer would get them to recite a list of other publications they read. By the time he started his catalog he knew exactly what magazine lists he should buy, and he had 60,000 names of his own to work with.

With $20,000 in funds from his watch profits, he sent out 50,000 copies of the first issue of The Sharper Image catalog in the fall of 1979. It was a modest effort, twelve slick ads bound together, featuring his popular watch, some fancy telephones and other hi-tech trinkets. He didn't make any money from the project, but, as a veteran observer of the process, he knew these things take time. Since he hadn't lost anything and broke even, why not try it again?

With each issue of the catalog he honed his formula further until he had made his presentation and niche unmistakable: hi-tech, high-ticket gadgets and toys for upscale professionals, like himself. The look of the catalog, with quality photographs and lively, well-written copy, made it stand out in drab mailboxes. The attention to competitive detail, and aiming for the highest standards began to pay off. By his second year he started to see some profits.

As The Sharper Image catalog evolved, he found that his customer was a dead-ringer for himself, a man fascinated by toys and gadgets but who doesn't like to shop for them. There were a whole bunch of these young executive types who wanted to indulge themselves in hipper leisure pursuits than backgammon and pipe-smoking. It was a classic Identity Gap. In 1981 The Sharper Image racked up $27 million in sales and had 110 employees, up from 8 in the days of his first watch ad. By 1982 the sales had reached an astounding $56 million, with $1.1 million in profits.

Most of his gadgets, from $2,000 motorized surfboards to $500 exercise equipment to $100 pogo sticks, found an audience. But he made mistakes, too. He tried to translate his knowledge of the male gift market to women with a female-oriented catalog. But The Sharper Image woman could not be found. He had violated one of his most sacrosanct principles: Know Thy Customer. He didn't know the female market, and some $2 million went down the drain.

The Sharper Image survived to post sales of $100 million and take another major step in the entrepreneurial growth process—going retail. With the mail-order market near the saturation point, Thalheimer was facing the obstacle that drives entrepreneurs crazy—blocked forward movement. So he embarked on his biggest gamble yet. By the end of 1986 he had opened thirty Sharper Image stores around the U.S. Would those busy executives who don't like to shop now frequent his stores? Yes, says Thalheimer. Things were moving along well enough that by 1986 Thalheimer was plotting his next big move, Sharper Image resorts, hi-tech escapist hangouts where execs can get away from it all.

It seems incredible, but Thalheimer likes to demystify the accomplishments with an analogy of business to marathon running. "Everyone says, God, how'd you do it? There's nothing to it. I'm not even very fast. I just manage to keep putting one foot in front of the other for twenty-six miles. The trick is to run a business like you're going to be doing it for a long time and not to sprint and burn yourself out before the finish."

The problem for most people, though, is that they "can't keep the discipline going day after day, year after year. I started when I was twenty-two and it wasn't until 1982 that the catalog really hit its stride. That was 11 years. The whole time to me was one long continuum, one long responsibility, one period of very short vacations. And that daily rut can wear you down."

His advice for entrepreneurs looking to implement an idea is to focus on "something people want and then advertise it in a small way. Once it's profitable then do it in a big way. Most people only do the last step."

5

Capital Offense

* Phase I *
# The Informal Circuit

*I*BM FOUNDER Thomas Watson once said, "They say money isn't everything, but it is a great big something when you are trying to get started in the world and haven't anything."

Just the thought of the cash requirements needed to start a company keeps most people from even bothering. No doubt about it, raising money you don't have is a daunting affair.

But it's a big mistake to take yourself out of an opportunity simply for financial reasons. If the idea is good enough, and you're resourceful and persistent enough, and have an achievable goal in mind, in most instances you can dredge up the dollars.

START-UP STAKES

How much start-up capital you need depends on the nature of your venture. Many of the new service businesses, say, travel tour operations, cleaning services, or research and consultant firms, can be started on less than $15,000. When your commodity is service, and not a manufactured item, there are no major capital expenses like production equipment to worry about. The lower the capital requirements, the easier it's going to be to get your company off the ground.

Judi Sheppard Missett only needed a week's worth of leotards to launch Jazzercise. Customers at her aerobic workouts paid for the rented halls where she conducted her classes.

Joan Barnes got her children's fitness company, Gymboree, going on $3,000, enough for some toys and mailers.

Launching a manufacturing firm that needs research and production facilities, or starting a retail operation that has to stock huge inventories, is going to take a lot more money and fund-raising. You may have to amass between $75,000 and $1 million or more to get these kinds of operations rolling.

Whatever your venture, there are basically two sources for the start-up stake, your own (savings, equity, properties) and somebody else's (outside loans, credit, or investment in your company).

Most ventures, artful predictions that they are, are going to be difficult to translate into the quantitative logic necessary to get financing from a bank or an investor. Even though your product or service may pinpoint a vital niche in the market, few people are going to believe your personal vision until they see it proven in the marketplace. If you're like most entrepreneurs, chances are you don't have the establishment's concept of bankable "credentials"—the right résumé, connections, business experience—required to loosen up reluctant purse strings.

So, in the beginning, your best bet to raise money is to thoroughly plow the *informal* finance network. This includes self-financing, family and friends, future customers, trade financing, and angels, wealthy individuals who can be persuaded to look beyond the objective facts of your case to your vision and its possibilities.

THE PERSONAL INVENTORY

Since it's so hard to translate your view of the future to someone's else pocketbook, it's not surprising that personal resources are the most common means of financing a new business. In fact, even in the hi-tech Silicon Valley, where we're led to believe every entrepreneur got started by big-time venture capital, 90 percent of the companies were financed personally by the founders.

The usual approach is Nest Egg Financing, dipping into

personal savings, or that of relatives or friends. This is entrepreneurship in its most defining form, an undertaking at great personal risk and financial liability. Unlike the risks of venture-capital investment, the funds for which come from mostly institutional sources (pension funds, corporations), and can be written off as bad debt on the ledger, mistakes made by people who have the Egg on the line can take a long time to recover from.

When you risk your personal assets, the cardinal rule, especially for first-time entrepreneurs, is not to bet the entire farm. "A clever entrepreneur avoids the disaster of putting too much of his money in up front to where he's wiped out if he fails," says USC's Richard Buskirk.

Always leave something in reserve because in the trial-and-error process of starting a business not everything goes right. Try out your idea in a small way first. If it proves out, then sink in your rainy-day funds or the kids' college tuition.

When you hunt for money, your object should not be merely to get your company off the ground; you want to make sure your efforts are worthwhile, that you will own and control as much of the company as possible. This means tapping as much of your own resources as you can before going out to bring in others.

Places To Start Looking

1. Savings, stocks, bonds.

2. Company credit unions. Before you quit your job, pay a visit to the credit union and take out a "home improvement" or working "vacation" loan. It shouldn't be difficult to obtain $3,000–$5,000 this way.

3. A second job. A few months of extra earnings might be enough to fill the opening coffers.

4. Cashing in other assets. Trading in a new car for an old one or selling useless heirlooms might pick up an extra $5,000.

5. Credit cards. This can be an easy way to raise as much as $10,000 by pooling cash advances from a number of different credit cards. The average person gets a steady stream of credit card applications in the mail. All you have to do is sign up, and, like one recent pitch for a "High Credit" Visa or MasterCard, you can get an immediate $1500 with a credit line of up to $10,000. Dal La Magna of Tweezerman used 20 credit cards to back his ventures.

6. Swapping a start-up stake. Sometimes you can get the money to start by simply starting in a very small way. For $500 to $2,000 of your savings or vacation money, you might be able to buy or assemble a small amount of your commodity and start making money from it by selling it at a swap meet. Mel and Patricia Ziegler, you will remember, started Banana Republic when they bought up $1,500 of Spanish army surplus shirts and started selling them at a swap meet. That gave them enough money over a few weekends to pay the rent on a small storefront, and one thing led to another. A $63 million Southern California off-price clothing retailer, Clothestime, "shoestrung" its way to the top with sales from a van at swap meets.

7. Your house. As collateral for a secured bank loan, or refinanced with a second mortgage to get the equity you may have built up on the property, your home can be a valuable source of start-up capital. Jerry Wilson found that owning a home with its ever-increasing property valuation gave him $60,000 in equity and borrowing power to bankroll his home gym startup, Soloflex. Putting up your house is also a considerable risk, so it's best to do as Wilson did and get confirmation that your idea works before betting your home. Wilson used $20,000 in savings to test his concept in the market. Once the orders started coming in, then the house, his small plane, his cars, everything he'd been saving for fifteen years—even his patent—went for collateral.

Wilson's money advice for anyone who is thinking about someday becoming an entrepreneur is to start building the savings, the credit rating, the equity, that will most likely be your prime source of funding for a future project. Like a modern-day Ben Franklin, Wilson cautions frugality first, then boldness. "Don't piss away your money. Stow it up, save it."

He continues: "There's an old quotation that solvency is entirely a matter of temperament and not of income. Most people spend a little more than what they have. They're a little bit in debt and have just a little bit of savings. If you really want to bet on yourself sometime in the future, and give yourself a shot at the American Dream, you have to play the game. Incur debt, bet on yourself, and then pay it off."

ALL IN THE FAMILY

Once you've exhausted your own assets, the first place to turn for outside capital is to people who may have common interests, beliefs, or a personal stake in your success—typically, family, friends, and contacts. Parents, and not wealthy ones either, are probably the most reliable source. When all is said and done, Mom and Dad will believe in their kids, if not necessarily their projects, when nobody else will. Loans or investments in the $5,000 to $20,000 range are conceivable here.

Loans are easier to extract than investments, and have the added advantage of not requiring you to give up big pieces of the company. But keep in mind that it's not Monopoly funny money if things don't work out, you're liable. Failure to live up to your bargain could result in family strife and broken friendships at the time you can least afford it.

After your immediate family, friends are the next choice, and can be good for contributions in the $5,000 to $10,000 range. If they're close friends and can bring needed skills to the table, it might be worthwhile taking them on as partners, either as silent investors or active, hands-on associates.

Another way friends can help you get started is by lending

services, deferring payment until you have the money, or in return for a piece of the company. T. C. Swartz got a big boost from a friend in the graphics business, who printed and designed the mailers that got Society Expeditions its first customers but told Swartz he didn't have to pay him until he had the money.

Friends and family can also lend their good name, and/or credit history to your cause. Their personal assets and reputations can be enough to get banks to cough up loans the entrepreneur could never qualify for. Jim Jenks was able to launch Ocean Pacific Sunwear on a $50,000 line of credit signed for by an affluent friend. Mo Siegel sold shares in his tea company to enthusiastic friends, but when it wasn't enough to put Celestial Seasonings on the map, one of his partners' mother went to bat for them.

"I can understand the reluctance of banks now," says Siegel, recalling his first attempts to get a loan as a 22-year-old, long-haired entrepreneur. "Here's this guy with a Tupperware container of tea saying 'We're gonna start a major food corporation, and the first product's called Red Zinger.'" When his partner's mom co-signed a loan for their first $5,000, the idea didn't seem crazy at all to the bank.

An entrepreneur quickly learns that, however ruggedly individualistic and self-driven you are, getting your hands on the money is usually a collaborative affair. Those starting with minimal holdings have to pool all possible reserves and interpersonal connections.

That's how John Todd, a $23,000-a-year product engineer for GAF Corporation, was able to make his company, Guest Supply, Inc., now a $35 million marketer of hotel amenities, materialize out of thin air. His story shows how with careful marshaling of the most modest assets a beginner can graduate up the ladder of capitalization, from backing a company with a credit card to financing it with a public offering on Wall Street four years later.

CAPITALIZING ON ALL YOUR RESOURCES
John Todd/Guest Supply, Inc.

The second of eight children, John Todd grew up in a distinctly unentrepreneurial environment, in the coal town of Scranton, Pennsylvania. His father, representative of his generation, worked for one employer his whole life, putting in 40 years as a warehouse superintendent. The Todd children would have more options, though, because they all would go to college, and would come into their prime at a time when new attitudes and opportunities would open the door to career independence.

At Kean College of New Jersey, John Todd studied Biology. "I saw myself being a crackpot biologist," says Todd, "looking to get a Nobel Prize in Biology, creating a new drug to cure cancer. I guess I had visions of being great."

Entrepreneurship, though, never occurred to him. After graduation he got a job working as a glue salesman for a chemicals company. Later, he switched his chemicals trade to the cosmetic field and joined GAF's toiletry division as a product engineer. Here he sold some of the base ingredients that went into the toiletry products of Revlon and Gillette.

Much like the way another glue salesman, Artesia Waters' Rick Scoville, came upon his bright idea, Todd picked up the glimmerings of his notion in an article in a trade journal. It described how cosmetic giant S. C. Johnson spent $30 million to introduce Agree Shampoo to consumers, spending $1 a unit to send samples to houses around the country. One of the bottles came to Todd's mailbox. He figured it only cost about 10 cents to produce the sample. There seemed to be an inordinate gap between that 10 cents and the dollar S. C. Johnson wound up spending by the time it was in a customer's hand.

Todd spent a lot of time on the road for GAF and he always forgot to bring shampoo along. One morning on the road at a Hyatt Hotel in Chicago, Todd was washing his hair with soap for the umpteenth time, when he flashed back to the article he read on the high cost of introducing new shampoos to the public. "Since I was so involved with shampoos," he recalls, "it just dawned on me that morning that there had to be a better way to sample a product, like in hotels. Why couldn't hotels offer sample shampoos to guests like they did with soap?

"The idea was only to get a couple hundred extra dollars at the end of the month," he explains, "maybe to buy a new car. It was just something to do on the side. I could go to the shampoo companies and they could pay me two cents a sample packet, instead of the 90 cents they paid the direct-mail people, and I would try to get hotels to put it in their rooms. I never really thought about it as a national thing."

What did he know about running a business? Not much. As a marketing type he was completely green on the nuts and bolts of purchasing, operations, finance. "I didn't even know what an invoice was."

He had a lot of homework to do. He found out at the library there were 50,000 hotels. Each had hundreds of rooms filled with hundreds of scalps crying out for proper hair tonic. The next step was to try to convince shampoo manufacturers that he could get their promotional products in front of the public for a fraction of the dollar charged by direct-mail marketers. But manufacturers didn't bite. There was no market research on whether people who tried products in hotel bathrooms would then be likely to purchase them at the store. Plus, hotel customers in 1978 were 90 percent male, not a major buying influence on the shampoo market.

Changing tactics with entrepreneurial versatility, Todd bypassed the nay-sayers and went directly to hotels with his pitch. He bought some bulk Ultramax shampoo packets from one of Gillette's packagers (headquarters wouldn't deal with a "nonentity" like Todd) and sent out a mailer to hotels advertising his cheap sample shampoos.

The idea was simple. The hotel could offer its guests a little something extra and create goodwill. The guests could go home with a free packet that bore the hotel's insignia on one side and the manufacturer's on the other. For a company like Gillette, the cost was one-tenth of a direct-mail promotion. Everybody benefitted.

Todd tried to interest GAF in his idea. He wanted to get into the new products area of the company, and out of chemicals, and thought his concept might open some doors for him. It didn't. When he found he was "running into a brick wall," he decided to quit his job and make his idea work himself. He quit GAF and got a job with a food flavorings company, while he built his suds on the side.

His mailing had produced some orders. The first was an invoice for 10 cases (1,000 packets) at 10 cents each from the MGM Grand Hotel in Reno. Now that he had to ship product, suddenly he had to figure out how he was going to pay for it. To dabble on the side was one thing, but to start dispensing a mounting volume of lather was quite another. He had no cash to spare. Zero. His solution was to tap personal contacts, who as a team might be able to pool just enough money together to get things going.

Todd didn't go after just any friends, either. Since he knew nothing about finance and money-dealings, he went to the family accountant, Ray Romano, whose wife was a cousin of Todd's wife. The other friend he persuaded to join him was a salesman who knew something about putting a sales force together. The three friends each put up $2,000 to capitalize Guest Supply, Inc. Todd's $2,000 was a cash advance from his Diners Club card.

He set up operations in the dining room of his East Brunswick, New Jersey, home. His wife, a schoolteacher, was pregnant with their second child, so she was the company receptionist. A younger brother helped pack boxes.

Naturally, $6,000 doesn't go very far in a new business, so Todd had to come up with some creative ways to make ends meet. "For several months there was no income in the company, and I had to use whatever I had in savings to buy food," says Todd. "We got the packagers of these little packets of shampoo to give us extended credit terms, 90 days, 120 days to pay, and we collected from our customers within 10 to 30 days. We paid no salary, and, of course, we had no overhead because we were operating out of my house." Todd's sales for the first year amounted to $67,000.

The next step, though, making the leap from a part-time, mail-order cottage affair to a full-time manufacturing concern, was going to require the kind of cash that Todd and his partners could hardly even conceive of. After 14 months of dining-room growth, Guest Supply was on the verge of its first break, an order that could propel it from a shoestring hopeful to a serious business contender. It was bidding with three amenity industry titans, Procter & Gamble, Armour-Dial, and Helene Curtis for a contract to provide shampoos to the 100-plus-unit Marriott Hotel chain. If Todd got the deal he would need $100,000 for production tooling to make custom Marriott shampoo bottles. That was exactly $100,000 more than Guest Supply had to its name.

Guest Supply did win the Marriott account, by out-creating, out-hustling, even outspending its giant competitors. It won the day by offering Marriott its own custom-designed soaps and a tear-shaped shampoo bottle with the Marriott logo emblazoned on it.

The amenity business was only a tangential, rote-budget operation for Procter & Gamble and Armour-Dial. It was Todd's whole business—and life. So despite their multibillion-dollar operations, they weren't willing to spend as much as a guy working out of his house.

With a purchase order from Marriott for over $1 million Todd thought it would be no sweat getting a loan to cover production expenses. But he quickly ran into "a brick wall of bankers."

Bank after bank turned them down, worried that since Guest Supply had never manufactured anything before, it might not be able to get the bottles made according to the Marriott contract. Now what? It was time for break number two. Accountant and partner Ray Romano called up a friend who had a connection at the Small Business Administration. The SBA seldom gets involved in start-ups, but the friend prevailed. "I don't know that we would have been able to get an SBA loan if we hadn't had Ray's contact," says Todd.

Romano's financial background made the SBA feel comfortable and they loaned Guest Supply $150,000 "in dribs and drabs," payable at $3,500 a month over five years. "We all had to sign over our houses, our first-born, our cars," notes Todd. "Every asset we had we had to turn over to the bank."

The average person takes a product on the shelf at face value, but the entrepreneur is painfully aware of all the details that go into something as mundane as a one-ounce shampoo bottle. Production was as difficult as the money for Todd. Getting the mold made for the bottle, the right plastic combination, the right cap and printing for it, and contracting out a place to fill it gave him some sleepless nights because "if we messed up we'd not only lose the money, we'd lose the opportunity to stay in business and we'd have to pay back $150,000."

Luckily, Marriott got their amenity package as described and Guest Supply had a great corporate reference. "Back in 1981 when we got the Marriott contract, that really shaped the company because we had something different and unique. No one ever saw a bottle that looked like that. Marriott was the first major chain that made it a standard. Then we could go to the Hiltons that were in the same cities as the Marriotts and try to sell them the Hilton programs, and the same with Holiday Inns. It snowballed from there."

The decision to manufacture custom amenities instead of simply pass out promotional giveaways was a huge gamble for the young company. But it was the kind of risk struggling companies need to take to rise beyond a certain survival treadmill. The custom concept gave Guest Supply the important proprietary product, changing its role from that of run-of-the-mill shampoo middleman to exclusive marketer of its own products.

By 1983 Guest Supply was growing so fast it had to raise a substantial amount of money to finance the production of mushrooming orders. Thus began the next phase in the nonstop money-raising saga of a new business. Banks were telling Todd that he should slow down his growth, that he was getting over-extended, and that he should stretch vendors further and collect sooner, rather than take out a loan. The advice was so discouraging that he thought of selling out to a larger company to get the needed infusion of cash. But Guest Supply got a lucky break. It was 1983, the Year of The Initial Public Offering. Wall Street was snatching up new companies left and right and even something as way-out as amenities found ready stockholders. Guest Supply went public and raised $3 million by selling 50 percent of the company. In 1985 another offering raised $10 million. An additional offering in 1986 produced another $18 million.

By 1986 Guest Supply controlled over half of the $50 million amenity business. Of the 13 major hotel chains with corporate amenity programs, Guest Supply supplied 11 of them, including Ramada Inn, Hyatt, Hilton, Sheraton, Best Western—a total of over one million rooms among the majors alone.

For the lack of a bottle of shampoo those many years ago, Todd has made sure the world will never be wanting for suds again. His company turns out 100 million one-ounce bottles of shampoo each year. And that's not all. There are bath gels, hand lotions, finishing rinses, sewing kits, shower caps, vanity kits, colognes, toothbrushes, and a whole range of soaps.

The man who had no money and didn't know what an invoice was now has a company on the stock exchange, is personally worth over $4 million, and owns a two-and-a-half acre, $1 million estate. What's his suggestion on how to raise money?

"There is a hungry banker out there somewhere," he says. "He's going to be very hard to flush out. But it's better than going to a venture capitalist. They're in it for the quick pop, for you to go public or cash out. They're not in it for the long haul. And if that's what you're in it for as an entrepreneur, banks are the better solution.

"I would also recommend looking for partners. I see too

many people trying it on their own and becoming disheartened or frustrated. I was very fortunate that one of my partners was a CPA. He was able to carry that ball for me. If I was left on my own I probably would have spent more than I should have and would have had a tougher time getting off the ground."

He advises entrepreneurs "not to have stars in your eyes. Take care of what's happening today versus what's going to happen tomorrow. Perseverance is critical, and, if your instinct is different from what everybody else says, stick with it. Follow your gut."

THE BUSINESS PLAN

When you've gone through all your assets and those of people you know, and you still don't have enough to get started, you'll have to reel in some outsiders. Before any of them (or many friends, too) will take your idea seriously, your venture has to be fleshed out in a comprehensive professional business plan. This document, ranging from 20 to 50 pages in length, is the road map for your business. It tells you how much money you need, what you need it for, and how your company will operate. You'll need to project cash flow for the first three years of operation, anticipate contingencies—such as customers not paying you promptly—and lay out an expected rate of growth.

A plan gives you a direction to go in, targets to shoot at; otherwise you'll just be flailing about wildly. So it's as important an operational tool as it is one for raising money.

If you can write, are a good researcher, and can get comfortable with the numbers, you may be able to put the plan together yourself. If not, you'll have to spend some bucks, but when it's the difference between a company that works and one that doesn't, it's a small price to pay. You may be able to get by with a basic plan for $2,000 prepared by an up-and-coming accountant. For a pro job you should expect to pay in the $5,000 to $10,000 range. However, there are ways to keep costs down. If your idea is hot enough, and offers obvious profit potential, you might be able to get your plan prepared in exchange for a piece of your company. Some large accounting firms produce prospectuses for free in return for future business. College business departments may also be able to direct you to an inexpensive proposal writer.

One of the biggest misconceptions about the plan is that it is merely a 20-page synopsis of how great your idea is. Frank Kilpatrick, a specialist in new venture planning, sees far too many plans that "don't describe the operation of the company. Entrepreneurs a lot of times are too in love with their products. They don't talk about cash flow, when you put the product on the market, contingency plans, the boring stuff."

Another Los Angeles business consultant, Steve Harvey, agrees. "Idea guys are a dime a dozen. If you're looking for a substantial amount of dollars, you have to show you have the horsepower to support those dollars."

No investor is going to give you money unless he or she is completely convinced you have considered all the details of implementation of your idea, from marketing to operations to financial strategies. You have to demonstrate that you have the skills to spot a viable market niche, expedite the product to fill it, manage staff, solve problems—and make money.

Most investors require previous experience in the field, or some track record of success. But what if you're like most entrepreneurs and haven't made all the right moves to date? Is it going to be the old résumé lock-out once again? Do you have a chance of breaking out of the pack on the strength of vision and desire? The answer is yes, if the idea is potent enough and you can indicate uncommon expertise on the subject, plus supplement your weak points with partners who are strong in those areas. You might find the strong résumé you need in your investor. If you have no background in sales and marketing, find an investor skilled in those areas who could solve the sticking point himself.

Producing prototypes, going out and getting some advance sales and customer interest, and starting your venture in a small way, can help make up for lack of experience and show the investor that you can follow through and operate a business.

The résumé issue depends entirely on who your backer is. If it's someone you know, background can be offset by personal factors like drive, creativity, decisiveness, and resourcefulness that are obscured by stock employment résumés. Successful entrepreneur/investors will also overlook textbook qualifications because many of them started in the same boat. Angels—wealthy private individuals who contribute seed money for start-ups—will want to see a professional plan, but they, too, often demonstrate a maverick streak that can gauge promise beyond the facts and figures. However, if you don't have the right corporate credits, there's no way you're going to get backing from venture capitalists. That's a complete write-off.

Business plans should be as long as is necessary to tell your story, but not more than fifty pages or it will start to bore. The style should be succinct, no-nonsense. For a complete description of what should go into the document, consult some of the many handbooks on the subject at your local library.

TRADE FINANCING

What's good for your business is usually good for somebody else's. Before you start shopping your plan around the formal investment circuit you should explore your industry for potential interest. If you are truly onto a good thing, there are suppliers and customers who stand to make a lot of money off you once you're operational. Your product taking off could mean a significant new source of revenue for vendors or subcontractors.

Linda Enke started her $10 million New York–based sales and promotion company, Anne Rothschild & Co., by "working on other people's credit." She and a partner had only $10,000 between them, nowhere near the amount needed to get her apparel promotion business off the ground. To sell promotional nightgowns, pajamas, and lingerie to big corporate clients required the wherewithal to finance the production of major orders. "There was no way that I, Linda Enke, newly declared entrepreneur, was in a position to go out and finance $500,000 worth of piece goods," she relates.

Numbers that juicy, though, can make suppliers salivate, and Enke knew it. She understood that manufacturing operations don't like to turn away business and sometimes rely heavily on outside salespeople to bring in customers.

She went into partnership with the factory that would be producing her $500,000 order for custom pajamas for a Fabergé promotion. It didn't take much out-of-pocket expense for the manufacturer. All he had to do was put up a modest amount of administrative capital for Enke's one-person operation, and then with his credit he could get credit from all the other suppliers involved in the transaction, from fabric houses to packagers.

Enke's experience shows that the low-budget entrepreneur does have some leverage. It's a question of finding the source who needs what your product offers. She brought in $7 million of business to her factory partner in her first year of business.

CUSTOMER SUPPORT

Other than having the money yourself, getting your customers to subsidize your venture is probably the best way there is to raise capital. You may have to give them a good price, but not a *piece* of the company. If you have a working prototype, you can visit major accounts or exhibit at trade shows and get enough advance orders to loosen up a loan from an enterprising bank or credit terms from entrepreneurial suppliers.

Every industry has several major trade fairs annually where wholesale and retail buyers converge to order the latest wares of exhibiting manufacturers. Chances are you might not have enough money or clout to get your own booth at one of these events, but with a little initiative you can usually bargain your way into somebody else's booth for anywhere from $300 to $1,000, depending on how much space your product takes up.

If your display and product is attractive enough, it can bring extra buyers and business into the booth, a fair exchange for any vendor.

If your product has enough immediate appeal, you may get orders from the show for anywhere from $2,000 to $30,000 or more. In addition, you will meet many sales reps and distributors from around the country who may offer to rep your product in their districts and add to your advance sales.

You can then take your purchase orders from the buyers to suppliers and try to work out credit terms, explaining that you're good for the money because these particular reputable customers will be paying for their orders. Not all vendors will go for it, since there's nothing binding about a purchase order. But if their out-of-pocket costs are minimal (mostly time and labor), and you're convincing enough, you could get 30-day credit terms based on your orders.

Banks seldom will grant loans based on purchase orders. But it does happen. With a convincing stack of invoices from blue-chip customers, and a hot product, a financially savvy entrepreneur can coax modest sums from an aggressive, entrepreneurial bank.

Sometimes you can even get financing from the customer who placed the order. That's what happened to Philip Hwang, a Korean-born engineer, who got his big initial order but then couldn't find banks, vendors, or anyone else willing to lend money or credit against his order. He was able to parlay $13,000 into a $165 million company, Televideo Systems, on the basis of credit from a customer. The amazing tale of his search for capital shows that the immense difficulties of raising money can be overcome if you can improvise, be a human jack-in-the-box, and just keep bouncing back until you have the cash.

THERE'S NO DIRECT FLIGHT TO FORTUNE
Philip Hwang/Televideo Systems

The entrepreneurial bug first hit Philip Hwang when he was working for National Cash Register in Dayton, Ohio, in the early seventies. A graduate of Utah State University with a degree in electronics engineering, he had an idea that applied emerging computer technology to typewriters. With $350 in spare parts, he and a friend designed a prototype. But he was too early. The technology didn't exist to run his "smart" typewriter. It required the miniaturized power pack of the microprocessor, which would be developed later to run a much smarter typewriter—the personal computer.

He moved out west to California, to a place where engineers like himself were starting to flock like swallows to Capistrano. Hwang got a job with a San Jose video game company, where, in the creative cauldron of the mid-seventies Silicon Valley, his thoughts soon turned to starting a venture of his own. His opportunity came sooner than he expected when his company went bust and he was suddenly out of a job.

Like the best entrepreneurs, he used this setback as a spur for independent ambitions. He didn't want to work for some corporation anyway. He had always thought he was going to do something on his own, run his own business. But comfortable salaries had been holding him back. "I couldn't break out from the job," he says. "When the game machine company fired me, I said this is my moment. Wow! I'm free now."

But before he could go into action on his idea for a computerized video game machine, he had to build a prototype, and he had to figure out something about running a business. To pick up the knowledge he needed he attended one of the more underrated business schools, the University of 7-Eleven. He invested the family savings of $7,000 in a 7-Eleven franchise, which he staffed 16 hours a day, seven days a week for six months.

Between Slurpees and nabbing shoplifting kids, he learned

about the ways of purchasing, inventory control, and cash flow. One day a customer buying some milk asked Hwang about the ring he was wearing. "That's my college ring," noted Hwang. "You went to college?" the customer asked incredulously. "As a matter of fact," smiled the man behind the cash register, "I've got a Master's degree in electrical engineering." Hwang knew what all entrepreneurs know: that sometimes you have to take a step backward to take a step forward.

After learning the ropes, he asked his wife to take over the 7-Eleven while he and two friends worked on the game machine prototype in his Cupertino garage. About $9,000 later, Hwang had a product, but no one would finance it. Banks said he was crazy. Venture capitalists said it was interesting, but hit him with the usual refrain: No management experience.

The dead-end on the money front forced him to reconsider things. He looked around and decided he probably couldn't compete with big-time game manufacturers like Atari anyway. But in the course of building his prototype he had stumbled across an interesting observation. Reasonably priced monitors, the TV-like screens that played video games, seemed to be in short supply. There was only one company that produced monitors, Motorola, so consequently prices were high, and the service team arrogant. Hwang was provoked into this realization by a rude encounter with a Motorola salesman. The man not only would not give Hwang credit terms to buy the monitors he needed, but he also refused to accept COD. It had to be cash up front.

"I decided I'm not gonna buy from this guy, he's so mean," recalls Hwang. "I'm gonna make my own."

He knew that black-and-white television monitors only cost $60, while Motorola's screens were $200. If he could convert black-and-white televisions into video monitors, he could cut the price in half. There was no way he could do this project himself, though, so he came up with a plan to get a low-cost Korean television manufacturer to do the job. He flew to Korea and made the rounds of factories. A half dozen companies showed him the door. He managed to come up with one possibility—but he had to be able to give them more orders than the 200 to 300 a month he was projecting.

The irrepressible Hwang came back to the Silicon Valley and started shopping his sample monitor around to video game companies. He showed it to Atari's chief engineer, who pointed out numerous flaws. Hwang was undeterred. He'd go to Korea and get it fixed tomorrow. "You're going to Korea tomorrow?" asked the engineer.

The Pacific Ocean wasn't going to get in Hwang's way. He was on the plane for Asia the next day. He spent all day and night at the Korean TV factory ironing out the monitor's problems, and two days later was back in the office of the Atari engineer. "I thought you were going to Korea," said the Atari man. "I already did. It's fixed," Hwang replied.

The amazed engineer ran some tests on the monitor, but found that the changes had caused some other problems. It wasn't acceptable. No problem, said Hwang. He'd fix it. When? He'd go to Korea tomorrow.

By this time, Hwang's cash reserves were on empty. To save money on his Korean shuttles, he took bargain, no-frills flights that were half-price but twice as long, going to Seoul via Manila and Hong Kong, and taking twenty-five hours instead of the direct eleven-hour route. How low was his low budget? The $2.50 taxi ride from the airport was too expensive, so Hwang would shuffle two miles with his suitcase and sample monitor to catch a ten-cent bus ride into Seoul.

All they could do at Atari was shake their heads. "God, he's back again." The bleary-eyed entrepreneur presented his new and improved monitor one more time. For the third time it fell short of the mark. He repeated his standard line. No problem, I'll get it fixed.

As he climbed on board the flight to Seoul, he knew this would be his last trip. There was no more cash. Beyond that, his normally inexhaustible spirit was flickering out. Hwang had one saving grace, though. He knew that however bad things got, he had survived worse. In a bombed-out northern city during the Korean War, he and his family went for days without food. Some American GIs took him in as a houseboy and he wound up supporting himself and his parents and brothers and sisters on C-rations. When the Chinese army invaded, he escaped by stowing away in a U.S. Army truck, hiding underneath a load of maps. Separated from his family, he survived in South Korea by working as a shoeshine boy. He sold pencils. Several years later, in a story that deserves a book in itself, Hwang was reunited with his family in the south.

Hwang came to the U.S. to go to college with $50 to his name. He paid for his studies by working as dishwasher, a busboy, waiter, two jobs during summer vacations.

With these reminders of where he had been, Hwang faced Atari for the fourth time with high anxiety, yet the knowledge that starting over at some electronics firm was not as bad as it could get. The monitor was tested again. There was still a kink or two, but, finally, it was usable. "After all your effort," said the engineer, "I'm convinced." Atari placed an order for $150,000 worth of monitors. Hwang had his first break.

"I couldn't believe it," Hwang says. "After all that flying back and forth, the airports, and I had no money left, I got it. I got the order!"

Hwang's ecstasy didn't last very long. He needed a letter of credit, a bank document that guaranteed payment to the Korean manufacturer, to get production rolling. He thought that with his purchase order from Atari as collateral, he could get a bank to float him the letter of credit. But all the banks turned him down. To get the $25,000 letter of credit, he had to have $25,000 to secure it. He borrowed money from every friend he could think of. His wife produced $3,000 from a secret emergency fund. But the $13,000 he scrounged wasn't enough.

To break the impasse, he decided to improvise. He would go back to Atari and see if they would guarantee their own order. As an enticement, he offered a five percent discount on the order. It was a bold move, admitting his precarious financial state to a client he was trying to impress with his wherewithal. But start-from-scratch entrepreneurs can't afford to stand on ceremony. Hwang laid it all out there, and Atari went for it. Finally, in 1975 Hwang's Televideo Systems was funded, on a customer's credit.

For the first two years, he took no salary, and had no secretary. By the end of his second year his quality monitors, priced 30 percent below Motorola's, had hit $1 million in sales. An animated fellow with an infectious laugh, Hwang recalls the million-dollar moment as his greatest thrill. "It was just an incredible experience to think that I, from where I came from, had that much money. Wow! A million-dollar company!"

One of the cardinal features of a successful entrepreneur is the ability to improvise on a dime, to sense changing market conditions and scrap strategies on a moment's notice. Hwang was a master at it. By 1978 the black-and-white monitor business was tailing off with the video game business. The growth area was personal computers. He decided to switch from monitors to the related field of computer terminals, the computer screens being just a more sophisticated version of what he was already doing.

Most of the terminals on the market then were so-called dumb terminals, which can report information but whose data can't be edited or changed by the user. They offered usually only upper-case letters and had a limited memory. A "smart" terminal, where text could be revised and played around with, cost twice as much as the "dumb" variety. Hwang figured out a way to make "smart" terminals for the same price as "dumb" ones. He stopped production of monitors and sunk $120,000 into tooling at his Korean plant to produce attractive injection-molded plastic cases for his terminals.

A production snafu delayed shipment of the cases, though, and put Hwang on the brink of bankruptcy. With no monitors being sold, and everything riding on payment from delivery of orders for his "smart" cathode-ray terminals (CRTs), there was no money coming in. His staff left, and he had to mortgage his house to pay bills. He was a week from going out of business when the cases arrived from Korea.

The dice rolled his way. Within three years, by 1981, Tele-video had gone from nothing to $90 million in sales. It had become the world's largest independent supplier of smart termi-nals, and was number one even in Japan. In 1982 it passed IBM in market share of display terminals. The secret of success? Hwang cut costs without sacrificing quality. His incessant im-provising resulted in cheaper ways to do things down the line of the production process, and he subcontracted labor-intensive work to Korea. He had used the Japanese technique of deliver-ing a superior product at low cost.

His next lower-cost product came with a series of small business computers that allow up to sixteen people in an office to be on line at the same time. His price range of from $3,995 to $19,995 was a fraction of the going $100,000 rate for sim-ilar systems.

To raise money for this venture, he took his company pub-lic in 1983 and Wall Street went nuts. Though he sold only 30 percent of Televideo, stock was bought up so wildly that his share was briefly worth one *billion* dollars on paper. After a few years of the computer wars, Televideo stock prices readjusted and Hwang's net worth went down to a mere $150 million by 1984. It was still enough to get him included in the hallowed ranks of the Forbes 400, making the former destitute Korean war orphan and insolvent entrepreneur one of the 400 richest people in America.

No more chasing after investors. By 1986 he was running a $165 million company with 750 employees in a complex spread out over 340,000 square feet of an industrial park in San Jose. In his gigantic parquet-floored office/conference room, as big as a roller rink, he reflects often on the road to success. The details are still very fresh in his mind.

"I never thought to do this to make a lot of money. I never dreamed I would be a millionaire. I was just going to accomplish my idea. A lot of people say, 'Hey, you're a multi-millionaire, why are you working so hard.' It's not because I'm trying to make more money, but because I enjoy seeing and proving progress, carrying out daily progress. I enjoy that more than going on a vacation.

"What I learned is if you have an idea, you have to have confidence. If you don't have confidence in your idea, don't do it. Don't give up easily. The Bible says God helps those who help themselves. I really believe that."

ON THE WINGS OF ANGELS

After self-funding and family/friend financing, the most frequent source of start-up capital comes from an invisible legion of princely benefactors commonly known as "angels." These are wealthy individuals who take promising business plans, and entrepreneurs, under their wings, helping start-ups to fly with seed investments of from $20,000 to $200,000 or more.

As mentioned earlier, Bill Tillson got his satellite company, Netcom, on the air and transmitting with the aid of a $15,000 investment from an angel. Dan Scoggin found several angels through business associates to help finance the $100,000 needed to get TGI Friday's restaurants cooking. California Cooler's celestial backer was a multimillionaire commodities trader.

Angels fill a critical void in entrepreneurial finance, providing risk capital for ventures that need start-up money in the $50,000 to $500,000 range, a zone beyond the self-financing capacity of the entrepreneur, yet still too minor league for the venture capitalist. Since most new businesses fall into this category of financial need, your best bet for capitalization may be to hook up with your friendly, neighborhood angel.

The glamorous, mega-buck world of venture capital may get all the fanfare, but it's these freelance investors doing their good deeds in private who really fuel our era of enterprise. The venture capital community finances less than one percent of all start-ups. Angels fund twenty times that amount in the estimation of William Wetzel, a University of New Hampshire business professor and author of one of the few studies on the hidden world of private investment.

Businesses with no potential beyond $1 million or $2 million in sales and twenty employees are too small to interest angels. However, for middle-market companies with prospects in the $2-million to $10-million range, angels, unlike venture capitalists, judge investments with an eye on more than financial gain.

"They don't look necessarily for the next Apple or Lotus or Federal Express," says Wetzel. "They derive a kind of psychic income from the role they play in helping establish new ventures that succeed. Sometimes these motivators are reflective, too, of what I would call a sense of social responsibility. If the system has helped them to succeed and make a bundle, they often are anxious to make it possible for other entrepreneurs to succeed. But the overriding nonfinancial motivator is just the personal satisfaction derived from helping a venture get going and succeed."

The big question, naturally, is how in the world does someone go about latching onto an angel? The answer, unfortunately, is, "It ain't easy." Finding them, says consultant Steve Harvey, "is probably the single most difficult thing there is in launching a business. The only thing I've been able to come up with is you talk to everybody and anybody you know. You just broadcast to beat the world and try to network. That means your banker, your CPA, your attorney, everyone in the world you can think of. I've run across good contacts at parties, and even at church."

In his study on independent investors, Wetzel tried lists of Mercedes owners, college alumni, and entrepreneurial and small-business organizations. In the end, though, the thing that worked best is what Wetzel calls the "snowball" technique. One investor typically leads to four or five others, because "they tend to be linked by a loose network of friends and associates."

In an attempt to try to make the process more systematic, Wetzel began the Venture Capital Network in 1984. Using a computerized data base of 300 investors and 133 proposed ventures, VCN was able to generate over 800 face-to-face meetings between angels and entrepreneurs by early 1986. That's an average of six investors per proposal. Though the program doesn't have systematic contact with the parties once the introductions have been arranged, Wetzel is aware of at least five funded deals through the process, and probably more. This is a much better rate than the three out of 600 to 1,000 business plans financed per venture capital firm.

But given the informal, maverick nature of angels, who, like entrepreneurs, aren't inclined toward groups and organizations, and who tend to be more impulsive than methodical about their ventures, the hunt for private investors is likely to continue to be a case of networking and dogged detective skills. You're going to have to go through dozens, possibly hundreds of dead-ends, but you have to just keep pushing. As Wetzel says, "Keep the faith, do your homework and you'll get the odds right sooner or later."

Guide to Angel Hunting

1. You have to have a business plan spelling out your market and how you intend to capture it.

2. You need a top accountant/CPA to help you with your plan and drum up angel leads. (A good banker or lawyer doesn't hurt either, but make sure these professionals are committed to the project and have the contacts or your money's going down the drain.)

3. Angels want to keep an active hand in your business, so they want it to be nearby. Concentrate on investors within a 50-mile radius, no further than a day's drive away.

4. Don't do wholesale mailings of your proposal. Try to select candidates who have some potential affinity with your pro-

ject. Angels tend to be interested in things they know something about and can make a contribution to.

5. The lower the investment unit, the easier it is to find. But too many investors can gum up the works and give you a smaller piece of the pie. The fewer investors the better.

6. Describe the actual deal you're looking for in the plan. Is it a 50% for sweat, 50% for money deal?

7. Ask for the money. Many people are afraid to explicitly ask for the cash for fear of maybe alienating someone or being told no.

Watch Out for Bad Angels

As in any business, there are a few fast-talking hucksters who prey on the uninitiated. Stay clear of super-self-promoting wheelers and dealers who may be scam artists or money launderers for illegal operations.

The people you have who prepare your plan, whether accountants or consultants, are perfectly legitimate in charging you for their professional services. However, those who take your plan, to make the introductions and actual deals with investors don't require cash up front. If a venture capital deal is a good one, there won't be charges for legal fees, or miscellaneous "services." The customary practice is that the venture capital organizer will be paid out of the deal that's struck with the investors.

Another important point: You don't have a deal until the money's in the bank. Don't start spending money in anticipation of funds that might never arrive.

Venture Capital Clubs

Another attempt to try to organize the scattershot capitalization process is the venture capital club. For an annual membership fee of $200 to $400, isolated entrepreneurs can come in out of the cold and rub elbows with the formal investment network. At home gatherings, or hotel banquet rooms, entrepreneurs get a chance to make their pitch before an assembled cast of fellow entrepreneurs, investment bankers, accountants, headhunters—and hopefully, a potential investor or two.

Venture capital clubs are springing up all over the country. In 1986 there were some fifty clubs with close to 3,000 members. While they address a dire need of solitary entrepreneurs to connect up with other enterprising minds, the clubs seldom come through with deals. For one thing, most investors are secretive characters who don't relish the thought of being accosted by droves of sad-faced entrepreneurs. Number two, people with bucks don't need to go out looking for places to spend them. Opportunities are brought to them by every acquaintance on a daily basis.

However, the venture capital club is a good place to commiserate with fellow entrepreneurs, swap stories about the deal that got away, learn start-up tips, find an accountant, a lawyer, and make contacts with leading members of the community. You never know where some of the connections might lead.

Just as video dating will never rival the personal encounter, organized money matches are no threat to unseat the traditional haphazard hunt for cash. Venture capital clubs add to your knowledge, but not to your coffers.

6

Capital Offense

Formal Financing

S TART-UP FUNDS may be sought from conventional finance
sources. Success on the institutional lender/investor front,
though, depends on knowing which organization to approach, how to approach them, and on certain eligibility factors
ranging from personal assets to the growth potential of your
venture.

INSTITUTIONALIZING YOURSELF

The going gets tougher as you move into the formal arena. For
the commercial lending outfits you need assets; the venture capitalists want the background. This puts most entrepreneurs in a
hard place, between a bankbook and a résumé. If you can scrape
some collateral together or locate a sympathetic loan officer, or
if you do have management skills and savvy, with a little luck
you might make some headway. Here's the lowdown:

Banks/Finance Companies. The pin-striped bottom line at financial institutions has nothing to do with dreams or drive; it's
dollars, and you need 'em to get 'em. First-time entrepreneurs
are always shocked to discover when they go to banks that have
lent billions to penniless Third World countries that they can't
borrow $25,000 unless they have $25,000 in collateral. "If I

had the money, I wouldn't be here," is the chorus of entrepreneurs learning the song of secured loans.

Banks want to see either collateral (a house, property, boat) or assets (stocks, bonds, savings) equal to the amount of the loan. The general rule of thumb is: Banks won't touch start-ups.

If you need a small stake of $10,000 to $15,000 to get going, don't even bother telling anyone that it's for a business. A personal or home-improvement loan won't arouse suspicion. It takes a track record of two to three years before banks will even start considering business loans. However, the hard-and-fast dictates of the large banks are sometimes waived at small, entrepreneurial banks.

If you are on friendly terms with any banker, the connection might be able to use his personal influence to get your loan approved. Rick Scoville of Artesia Waters got his first break this way. His advice: "Don't stay with your bank, stay with your banker, because he's the guy who knows your payment history." He followed his banker, Carl Clemons, to four different banks, taking out personal loans and paying them back promptly.

When Scoville told his banker about the idea for his bottled water company, Clemons thought it was great, but reminded him that banks don't fund ideas. Because he knew Scoville, though, he gave him a $10,000 signature loan, which got him up and running. When Scoville got in a jam and needed $15,000 more, the banker came through again.

The best way to increase your odds of getting loans from banks is to build up your assets—save your money—and prepare the financial side of your plan thoroughly. According to First Interstate's Tim Hodgins in Los Angeles, "Most small entrepreneurs don't have much of a background in finance, so they really don't know what a bank wants to look at. They'll show us a lot of sales and profit numbers, but never think about a balance sheet, or what it's going to take after they buy the equipment to make the widget. What's it going to take to carry the inventory and receivables?

"You should have a well-defined business plan with a lot of financial data, not just projected sales and earnings. We look to cash flow and balance sheet proportions."

Try calling bankers ahead of time to find out exactly what it's going to take to get your loan. Then give them what they want. In negotiating a loan you're going to have to satisfy the bank: not only do you have the ability to pay it back, but you can also make payments if something goes wrong. If you can find a hungry banker, and your plan and experience stamp you as a potential business client, you may get the money.

The Small Business Administration. The SBA is a source for people with more marginal credit, who may have just missed the means cutoff at banks. The SBA guarantees loans through banks up to 90 percent, to a maximum amount of $500,000. The payoff period usually is five to seven years. The average SBA loan is around $175,000.

Like banks, the SBA rarely gets involved with start-ups. The SBA is most often resorted to by companies with cash flow emergencies during the first few years of business, and for later expansion.

Be aware that the SBA, as a federal bureaucracy, has no concept of time as we who pay bills know it. More than one company has gone under waiting for an SBA loan to be approved. Allow for at least three months for the money to come through.

The SBA requires the same solid business plan and evidence that you can run a business as a bank does.

Small Business Investment Companies. These are privately owned venture capital companies that are chartered and regulated by the SBA. SBICs must get their initial capital from private sources, but once operational the SBA provides leverage financing. Government loans can make up as much as 75 percent of an SBIC's capital base.

Once a major force in the venture area, SBICs, with

limitations of funding, government regulations, and loan schedules that capital-intensive, sales-weak start-ups can't meet, have been supplanted by the large number of independent venture capital firms.

SBICs might still be the place to look for funding if you have a minority enterprise, a venture that might bring jobs to an underemployed region, and for non-hi-tech projects that still require high capital costs to get started.

State Financing. To attract business and jobs many states have begun venture capital programs of their own. Most of the funds go to helping existing businesses grow and expand, but some money is available to entrepreneurs with the right projects, usually those that have good potential for creating employment. The Massachusetts Community Finance Corporation, for instance, invests about 25 percent of its $2.5 million annually in start-ups.

VENTURE CAPITAL

The most well-known but least understood part of the funding picture is venture capital. Venture capitalists may seem like the perfect people to provide you the funds; after all, their sole job is to recognize the brilliance of better mousetraps like yours. Venture capital may seem like a philanthropic defender of the American Dream, where the best man/idea wins.

But ninety-nine out of a hundred entrepreneurs are barking up the wrong tree going after venture capital. Only a select breed of entrepreneurs and a tiny range of products ever find funding this way. Fewer than 1,000 businesses get venture capital out of the 650,000 new companies started annually. That's one-tenth of one percent of all start-ups! According to Venture Economics, an industry research firm, venture capitalists fund only 3 percent of the plans they see; *Venture* magazine puts the figure at 1 out of 100.

But it's not just the mathematical odds that make venture

capital an extreme longshot. These funds are really only available to a single, narrowly defined product sector—technology-related items in extremely fast-growth markets. Eighty percent of the companies financed by venture capitalists are hi-tech. One study of venture investments in the early 1980s measured the breakdown this way:

Computer-related	30–40%
Communications	10%
Other Electronics	12–14%
Medical	7–8%
Genetic Engineering	4%
Industrial Automation	3–4%

If your product doesn't involve technology and a lot of scientists or engineers, you're wasting your time sending proposals to all but a handful of venture capitalists.

The other item likely to disqualify most entrepreneurs from the venture race is the growth requirement. Venture capitalists back only companies with the potential for enormous profits, ones which can earn big without delay. A company must demonstrate the capacity to be at least a $10-million firm within five years, and to grow at a 20 percent rate thereafter, with after-tax profit margins of 10 percent. Venture capitalists scour the thousands of plans they receive each year for those few fast-track firms that can generate windfall returns via a public offering or a megabuck acquisition, usually within five to seven years.

The other reason you should forget about venture capital is that it's not really for start-ups anymore. Only a small portion of such financing goes to launches—just 14 percent in 1985. Venture capital has become more of a tool to finance the growth and expansion of new established companies rather than a midwife in the actual birth process. In fact, your odds of getting venture capital, though still slim, greatly increase once your product is selling in the marketplace.

With big-time venture capital concentrating on fewer,

larger deals and later-round financing, the only bright spot for entrepreneurs has been the emergence of a few smaller venture funds that cater to start-ups and capitalizations under $1 million. Several dozen "seed" funds, specializing in investments from $200,000 to $500,000 and comprising 3 percent of the total venture capital pie, tackle deals that are too small and risky for most venture firms.

A pioneer in the field, Paul Kelley, of Zero Stage Capital Equity Fund, Cambridge, Massachusetts, describes his business as "adventure" capital. "Seed investing," he explains, "is very different from venture investing in that it requires a great deal of intensive nurturing and hand-holding and assistance to help guide and work with the entrepreneur."

He sees his company's role as helping an entrepreneur develop a promising opportunity, getting a company up and running so it can demonstrate its value, and then attract follow-on funds from bigger venture firms.

Another development that may open venture capital up to a few more entrepreneurs has been the emergence of consumer funds that do no hi-tech at all. Early Stages, of Palo Alto, California, is one of only a half-dozen firms in the country to invest in entrepreneurs with consumer and retail products and services. Some of the companies it has backed include Ross Stores, a discount apparel retailer; Businessland; Pace Warehouse, a very successful home improvement club; and Thomas E. Wolf, a men's slacks firm started by four ex-Levi-Strauss employees. It prefers investments of $200,000 to $750,000 in companies that have gotten some initial footing in the market.

HOW TO PICK UP A VENTURE CAPITALIST

For those of you who remain undaunted, the process of obtaining venture capital is one of convincing someone who has heard every line in the book that your product is everything he has ever been looking for. This is going to be hard to do. The average venture capital firm receives from 600 to 1,000 business plans each year, making the average venture capitalist a very jaded individual. Only 10 percent of the hundreds of plans get a second reading. Most are knocked out of the running within the first page or two.

Venture capitalists, hit up constantly by smooth talkers, begin with a natural predisposition against your plan. They will look for quick excuses to give you the brush-off. An inexperienced management team, a product in a market that's already saturated, a product they don't handle (retail or service ideas are not going to go over with hi-tech investors), poor writing, writing that's too polished, requests for too much money or not enough to make a profit on, a market that will take too long to develop, all these things and more can get a plan tossed within the first two pages of the executive summary.

To understand what the venture capitalist wants you have to understand what his real profession is. It is not launching businesses; it is not that of talent scout/mentor in search of new protegés. It is investment banking. The venture capitalist, who is usually either a banker, successful entrepreneur, or former corporate marketing pro, is engaged in the business of investing money mostly from large institutions (like pension funds and endowments), corporations, and from foreign investors and wealthy individuals, in companies that can bring the biggest profits to those investors. Backing a plan is a financial transaction, not a beauty contest for the best-looking idea.

Funding depends entirely on the venture capitalist/investment banker's belief that a good idea can then be executed and deliver the dividends you say it will. Execution is the collateral of venture capital. The proven ability of the entrepreneurs to carry out the project is seen by venture capitalists as the only way to protect their investments.

The secret to getting venture capital begins and ends with your references.

The Approach. The only opening line that works with a venture capitalist is one that comes from somebody else. You need an introduction. Most venture firms say they read all the hundreds of plans that come into their offices each year, but like unsolicited movie scripts sent to Hollywood producers, the chances of getting anywhere without a connection or a recommendation is between zero and nil.

First make sure that the venture firms you approach fund your kind of business. Then find someone who can make an introductory call. Forget all gimmicks, bottles of wine, imaginative stunts; nothing convinces a venture capitalist except solid arithmetic and credentials.

Proposals should average twenty to thirty pages in length, and be crisp and succinct. Venture capitalists don't care about the graphic design of your report. Just the facts in loose-leaf form with all the words spelled right will do.

The Entrepreneur. For venture capitalists, those behind the company are as important as the business itself. The entrepreneur required here is not even remotely related to the usual breed of passionate beginners, hard-driving mavericks or visionary niche-finders. Even the garage-tech genius of Apple Computer days doesn't make it anymore. Instead, the darling of venture capitalists is the corporate manager, and not a single individual, but a fully staffed team of management pros.

Len Baker, a partner in the Palo Alto firm of Sutter Hill, which has backed such major hi-tech firms as Qume and Apollo Computer, echoes the importance of personnel credentials. "We spend more time evaluating the people than anything else. We look for people who have been outstanding successes at something previously in their careers."

Though Sutter Hill has funded entrepreneurs aged twenty-eight to sixty-five, Baker's ideal candidate would probably be around "thirty-five years old, a very bright person who has previous success in the field he's planning to enter, either as a general manager or a marketing VP, and who has a product that has economic advantages over what it replaces, so it's selling into a market already established."

The Product. Like any entrepreneur, venture capitalists look for a gap in a growing market that can be plugged with a proprietary product. They look for new technologies, new applications, new production or retailing concepts that are neither too innovative to be ahead of the market, or too imitative to be behind it. "We don't like to back things that are involved with too much pioneering," says Baker, "where you have to convince the customer he needs something he hasn't decided he needs."

Benjamin Rosen, whose venture group Sevin-Rosen Partners, has backed big winners like Lotus and Compaq Computer, described product timing in *The New Venturers,* "You want to catch technology at the right point on the wave. If you catch it too early—like artificial intelligence—you have a technology in search of a market. And if you catch it too late, you end up in a commodity business."

When three Texas Instruments employees—Rod Canion, Jim Harris, and Bill Murto—proposed that the wave was rolling in for smaller, faster, compact computers in 1982, Rosen hopped aboard with $1.5 million in venture capital and the four took off on a ride as perfect as anything Duke Kahanamoko ever laid eyes on. As discussed previously, Compaq Computer quickly racked up the largest first-year sales of any company in U.S. history—$111 million—and within three years had become the world's second-largest seller of personal computers for business, with 1985 sales of a boggling $505 million.

For anyone trying to crack into the venture capital vault, the Compaq story offers hope and instruction in the art of attracting venture financing. Its founders were first-time entrepreneurs, but their offering was anything but amateur. It was just the seasoned mix of market sensitivity and management savvy venture capitalists look for.

SUM OF THE PARTS
Rod Canion/Jim Harris/Bill Murto—Compaq Computer

In another era Messrs. Canion, Harris, and Murto would have faithfully served out their careers at a prestigious company like

Texas Instruments. They had good jobs, excellent salaries, and respect from their colleagues. For Canion and Harris, "TI" was the only employer they'd known since college. But after a dozen years moving up the ranks of the large organization, the forward movement had stopped, and a sense of automatic pilot had set in. The thrill was gone.

Rather than make peace with this natural evolution in corporate life, they began to get progressively more restless. In their late thirties, they weren't ready to plateau out. They had a lot more to do. The differences between what they wanted to accomplish and what they would be allowed to accomplish in senior management roles, were irreconcilable. They needed a corporate divorce, and in the America of the 1980s the split came not in the form of being fired or eased out or reshuffled later as malcontents, but as a voluntary act to determine a future course for themselves: entrepreneurship.

Anyone working in the midst of the hi-tech explosion of the seventies and eighties couldn't help but be affected by the entrepreneurial itch. Companies were being started right and left by people with a lot less experience than the TI trio. Murto, a sales manager, and Harris and Canion, engineers, worked together as a team in a PCC, a product customer center, one of many small "intrapreneurial" enclaves within TI charged with creating, developing, and marketing new products.

On one project involving a computer storage products business they were setting up for TI, they took a trip from Houston to California to visit suppliers in the nascent storage field. All the young firms were start-ups, and as the Texans met with entrepreneur after entrepreneur at new venture after new venture, the power of entrepreneurial suggestion began to be felt.

Murto recalls, "In meeting those people time and again, you'd see the lifestyle, get the feeling of their company, and in the back of your mind you're wondering 'Why don't I do this? It looks like they're having fun and that's different from what I've been doing. Why don't I just go try it?'"

Harris had a similar reaction to the entrepreneurial fever.

"We liked that environment. It seemed challenging and exciting. And then you compare that to the battle you may be fighting on the home front in a large organization. It seems refreshing, and you envy them because you know they're enjoying themselves, that they're really having fun."

After casual references in the hallways and at the water cooler that they "should do something together," one day "somebody said if we're serious about this we need to quit talking about it and do something," Harris remembers. They set a time and date and assembled at Murto's dining room table.

In idea sessions over several months they toyed with everything from a Mexican restaurant to a Computerland franchise, finally settling on a disk drive system that they envisioned would be an add-on device for the new IBM PC.

Since they didn't have the money to start their business, the plan was to raise venture capital. First, they had to figure out what venture capital was. "We didn't know anything about venture capital other than that some people had done it," admits Rod Canion. So they did some homework, reading up on the start-up process in entrepreneurs' manuals at the library, and poring over materials on venture capital—from how-to books to reports on venture capital conferences.

As key players at a top hi-tech firm already essentially running a business of their own within the TI PCC system, the three were just the type venture capitalists like to hear from, especially hungry venture capitalists. Through contacts in the Texas tech world, they sent their plan off to a new fund, a local start-up itself, the Sevin-Rosen group.

Ben Rosen was a top electronics industry analyst and L. J. Sevin, a former TI man, had just sold the semiconductor company he founded, Mostek, to United Technologies for $345 million. Sevin and Rosen were well connected to the insular world of hi-tech engineers, executives, and marketers that breeds venture deals.

The venture capitalists liked the Canion-Harris-Murto team. It had the background and methodical temperament to do the job. Canion and Harris felt good about their prospects for getting funded, so they turned in their two weeks' notice. Murto, who had a child in poor health, decided to stay on because of medical costs.

A week later they got the bad news that Sevin-Rosen wouldn't be backing the disk drive idea. It was too easy to duplicate and therefore wasn't the kind of hi-tech contribution on which major companies are built.

It was a critical moment for Canion and Harris. They hadn't yet left TI, and the company had asked them to stay on now that their project had fallen through. They could go back or face the great unknown of unemployment. They decided to take the risk. "It was something by this time," says Harris, "that I had to do. There's no way I could feel good about myself if I didn't. I would always question that decision. I didn't want to be an old man sitting around regretting that I didn't take a chance."

Being good engineers, they had built in fault-tolerance, the contingency of failure, from the beginning. They figured each could survive on savings and credit cards for about six months before they'd have to call it quits and get another job. "We were very strict about each of us having enough money for six months," says Canion. "We didn't want to be forced into a bad decision because we ran out of money. But we were very confident that within six months we could find an idea, develop a business plan, and get funding somewhere."

They had quit TI in mid-December 1981. All through the holidays and into the new year, while the rest of the world was eating and drinking and making merry, Canion and Harris were anything but relaxed as they tore through product ideas by the hundreds in search of their future employment. Developing salable notions was something Texas Instruments, with its semi-autonomous product customer centers, had prepared them well for.

"We had learned to be very in tune with market needs," says Canion. "What we were doing was not just blue-skying, looking for technological breakthroughs, but really looking for needs in the marketplace that weren't being satisfied."

In less than a month Canion came up with something. He telephoned Harris and described his idea for a portable computer. At first they both thought it was just another concept to add to their rotating list of product prospects. It seemed kind of ambitious. "We hadn't necessarily been thinking that we were going to conquer the world," relates Canion. "We were thinking more of a nice, reasonably small business that we could do very well in. We knew the odds of a full-blown computer company surviving from a start-up weren't very high."

However, the more Canion thought about it, the more the engineering side seemed feasible. The technology was there to build a full-function portable computer, much more potent than anything on the market. The only problem was the software. With more than a hundred computer companies on the market, it would be impossible to get the proper software developed. But he had a hunch that an industry standard for software was imminent. He had talked to many software manufacturers who were gearing their programs to the new IBM PC set to come out in early 1982. All he had to do was to make his portable compatible with IBM and hitch his train to the big time.

After a week of trying, Canion finally got Ben Rosen on the line to tell him about the new idea. Apparently, his last idea had not worn out his welcome. When the new plan was ready, the venture capitalist would take a look.

The entrepreneurs put together a new proposal and contacted an industrial designer friend about doing a rendering of their portable. At a pie shop in Houston, Harris and Canion described to the designer how they wanted their computer to look. It was in this diner, in legendary hi-tech fashion, that the beginnings of a half-billion-dollar company were sketched on the back of a paper napkin.

Sevin and Rosen liked the idea. They cautioned the engineers about the massive scale of the project they were undertaking, starting a computer firm from scratch, but they admired their pluck. Sevin conferred his own Texas-style praise on the team. "You guys got big balls," he drawled.

After a couple of meetings in Houston, the entrepreneurs were sent out to San Francisco, where they met with one of the nation's top venture capital firms—Kleiner, Perkins, Caulfield, Byers. Venture capital firms usually don't take on all the risk of a major investment themselves. They bring on associates from the close-knit venture world to share the risk. An effective venture capitalist needs entrée to other powers in the business; Sevin-Rosen had it.

There was "a lot of pitching and presentations," says Canion, but finally a commitment came through for $1.5 million, under the $4 million they had projected in their plan, but reason enough to celebrate. They had pulled it off. And they were only out of work for a month and a half. In the deal struck, Sevin-Rosen put up $750,000, Kleiner Perkins advanced $500,000, and a Sevin connection in New York, $250,000. Canion, Murto, and Harris each bought $1,000 worth of shares in the company at a penny apiece. The venture capitalists took 55 percent of the company, the founders took half of what was left, with the balance of the equity to be used to attract key employees.

"We were elated," recalls Canion. "When we got the call that they were going to fund us, we knew we were on our way. It was a very, very exciting time."

What did it take—what does it take—to prevail in the venture capital world? Says Canion, "The bottom line is that it's all got to be there. They've got to believe in the people and in the idea. The people belief comes from your history, what you've been able to accomplish. But a lot of it just comes from the personal interviews. Do you have common sense? Do you understand the business you're talking about being in? The level of understanding is something a good venture capitalist can really dig out. He can tell if you're superficially knowledgeable or if you really have enough background in that particular marketplace to understand what's going on."

The project that lay ahead of them was a staggering engineering and production nightmare. The plan called for them to have a working prototype developed and ready within five months for the National Computer Convention, and product to be shipped within one year. That meant complicated design feats and unpredictable production scheduling had to operate by the stopwatch. They had to create a financial control system. This wasn't corporate funny money anymore; it was "real money out of a real bank," says Canion.

The critical event in the Compaq plan was getting a prototype operable for the National Computer Convention in Houston in 1982. Murto's sales team had been working on getting Sears Business Systems as one of Compaq's first customers. By landing an account as conservative and established as Sears, they could achieve instant legitimacy and overcome the start-up image.

They had been priming Sears for a demonstration of the Compaq portable at the trade show. The day before the unveiling, though, it still wasn't working. Harris' engineers sweated it out, laboring into the wee hours, before they got it running at 1:30 A.M. When Sears came by at 8 A.M. everything worked. At the big Comdex trade show in Las Vegas in November, Compaq was able to announce that Sears would be carrying its product.

With the precision of a Swiss train, the machine left the platform right on schedule. Eleven months after they started, product was shipped, and shipped again, at a startling rate. By the end of their first year they had achieved an American record for first-year sales—$111 million.

The big concern was what would happen if IBM decided to squash the flea and make its own portable. "The investment community told us we were dead if IBM came out with a portable," says Murto. "So up came the IBM portable, and guess what? It was different than the Compaq portable. It had lesser capabilities than we had, and the market clearly saw the difference. The market purchased ours instead of IBM's."

Then IBM decided to go after Compaq by lowering its prices, but that didn't work either. Murto describes the continual challenges and close shaves of the entrepreneurial contest as "an Indiana Jones environment. Will he make it? Are the blow-guns gonna get him this time? Is that boulder gonna roll down on him?" Compaq lived through that adventure, warding off the big invaders with a superior product. The invincible IBM wound up discontinuing their portable PC jr.

The next miracle they pulled off was to challenge IBM in the full-size, desktop computer market, a contest that was equivalent to the one between the Christians and the lions. But IBM's "super" PC was bedeviled by production problems and quality-control lapses and the Compaq Deskpro 286 won the day. It has since become one of the business world's top-selling models.

The success of Compaq has focused attention on a new kind of entrepreneur, a "smart team" of expert businessmen who, despite having the best-paying jobs in corporate America, feel the lure, as many others today, of attaining independence and self-achievement. It shows how deeply the spirit of enterprise now runs. No longer do people have to be "pushed" by unfortunate circumstances into taking things into their own hands.

Rod Canion's wife had tried to get him to do something on his own, but he continually told her he wasn't the entrepreneur type. He wasn't a compulsive competitor. He could enjoy the game just as much when he wasn't winning as when he was.

The lure of achievement proved too much for the comforts of security to contain, and as a result, Canion, Harris, and Murto are now multimillionaires. Their company is a force not just in the U.S. but all over the world. There is Compaq, England, and Compaq, Australia. In 1985—only their third year of operation—they hit a staggering $505 million in sales.

Canion, who was so uncomfortable in the spotlight that he used to dread speaking before large groups of people, believes it's possible for anybody to be an entrepreneur with "persistence, discipline, and thoroughness. You have to be knowledgeable, but not a genius."

GOING ON THE CAPITAL OFFENSIVE

Raising money, like making it, is not simple. Money comes with hardship and in small allotments. But the persistent entrepreneur is not awed or immobilized by the challenge. Unlike those who live their lives prisoners of the money god, hoping it shines down on them, helpless to influence its unfathomable ways, entrepreneurs know you can't wait around for fortune to anoint you.

You have to go on the capital offensive. It takes a concentrated effort, and strategy, to piece together a start-up stake. It may take an alteration in lifestyle, sacrifice, persuading others to join in, or a strategy to place yourself in the vicinity of people and events that may lead to sources of financing. But it can be done.

Even if you can't raise lots of money, a little bit may be enough to start gradually and build from there. Create a company small enough for your funds and then slowly increase your cash reserves or ability to attract investment by sales in the market. Or set a minimum target of start-up capital you can get by with, and if you get reasonably close to the amount, just go do it.

As Discovery Toys' Lane Nemeth says, "Once you have your concept and minimum capital, you may as well jump in. No one will give you a second look for financing until you're off the ground."

Money may talk, but the entrepreneur can get a little of it to say a lot. "You can always get the money," says Ocean Pacific's Jim Jenks. "There's always a way to skin a cat if you really want to do it."

7

The Real World

ACCIDENTS WILL HAPPEN

When your idea hits the real world of the marketplace, anything can happen—and usually does. The early days of taking control of your destiny can often look a lot more like anarchy. But it's all part of the risk of starting a venture, of believing you can tame an unknown, hostile environment, of casting your fate to the wind and trusting your own wits.

Heading into uncharted territory brings surprises, and not always entertaining ones. Unforeseen perils can range from customer shake-ups, to cartels, to criminal mischief. Norm Pattiz's syndicated radio company, Westwood One, was brought to the brink when the ad agency executive who booked advertising on Pattiz's shows for his top client was fired. Her replacement canceled all existing advertising commitments of Pattiz's main client, who contributed 90 percent of his revenue.

The oil crisis of the seventies dried up Ron Rice's supply of base-oil for his Hawaiian Tropic tanning oil and almost put him out of business. Air-Vend's Dave Bobert didn't have much time to celebrate getting his tire-inflator vending machines on the market. They were soon being destroyed by vandals.

Certain things are beyond the control of the entrepreneur in the real world; the best one can do in those circumstances is not panic, develop a strategy to limit the damage, and try to turn the negative into a positive, shoring up a weakness with a newfound strength.

Successful entrepreneurs seem to be especially good at countering these threats with decisive corrective measures. Norm Pattiz flew to New York from Los Angeles the very next day to salvage a new advertising deal with his top client. At the first whiff of an oil crisis, Ron Rice scrounged every corner of the country for extra petroleum, and wound up having just enough to ride out the oil scare. Dave Bobert turned his rebuilt, vandal-proof air vending machines into a selling point—a product so solidly built it's guaranteed against vandalism.

Coping with crises is a lifetime proposition for any company, but it's the first two or three years of business—the start-up years—when the brunt of the disasters strike. Some are cosmic or market events the entrepreneur can't do anything about ahead of time. But despite these dramatic interventions, most new businesses are undone by problems that could have been avoided. Inexperience, impatience, and ego are more likely to be the culprits in an early bankruptcy than flood or famine.

The start-up begins life in a very fragile state, low on capital, customers, experience. The margin for error is slim, so you can't afford to make too many major mistakes. Yet running a business for the first time, or marketing a product that's never been marketed before, is naturally going to involve some trial and error. There's no way to avoid mistakes altogether. What has to be avoided, though, is the life-threatening blunder that invariably winds up leaving bigger bills than can be paid.

CASH FLOW HAZARDS

Among the pitfalls that can bring down a new venture, the number one menace is undercapitalization. Meager budgets can vanish very quickly. The shoestring start-up has to be even more careful than the average business with its cash flow.

Cash flow is the oxygen of business life. It means you have enough money coming in to meet the payments going out. It means never having to say you're sorry you can't pay the bill. You can have lots of sales, but if you don't have the money in hand from them when the bills are due, sales don't mean a thing.

One of the quickest ways to sabotage your cash flow is

spending above your means on the accoutrements of business. Plush executive office chairs, excess travel and entertainment costs, location in a high-rent district—these kinds of frills spell disaster for entrepreneurs who assume the trappings of business before it exists. You may start out with a nice sum of $15,000 at your disposal, but it won't last long. Every penny you spend on items that aren't absolutely essential for the growth of your company helps to undermine your precarious financial position.

Successful entrepreneurs learn to become masters of making-do. They can get by with a second-hand desk, recycled file cabinets, or a less than prestigious address. Society Expeditions' T. C. Swartz advises: "If you don't have money, don't buy it. I follow the strategy that when you have the $300 that's when you buy the typewriter."

Alan Rypinski, the entrepreneur who founded Armor All, adds, "You don't need to live in the greatest apartment in the world. You don't need a highfalutin' accountant. Let your wife or girlfriend do the books, or do them yourself in your spare time."

Anyone who goes into business thinking they immediately can pay themselves a big salary is also making a big mistake. The key to start-up survival is keeping your overhead as low as possible, and anything but the most modest wage, if any, can put your cash reserves in jeopardy. There's no entrepreneur in this book who didn't take a big pay cut to start his or her own business. Most took no salary at all for the first couple years, taking only enough money to eat and pay the rent. Scrimping on your paycheck and personal expenses helps save cash for the only expenses that matter, those that make your business grow.

The usual way a start-up gets into cash flow trouble is by spending more on production (if it's a manufacturing business) or operations (if it's a service business) or promotion than its shaky initial sales can support. It takes a while to get sales and interest going, and if you don't have enough start-up capital to tide you over the costs of getting established, you won't make it.

Manufacturing ventures can get into cash binds easily because they have to produce commodities in large volumes (to get the best price per unit, and because the items may take a long time to produce), based on sales projections that may not come through. Consequently, they can be sitting on big inventories of unsold product, which hasn't brought in the revenue to pay the production bill.

Don't go into production until you've carefully researched what kind of sales you can expect. When you do place your order be conservative and don't manufacture more than your worst-case sales scenario can pay for.

One way to reduce the risks of the inventory gamble is a production schedule called Just-in-Time. This system involves purchasing parts and assembly in smaller quantities, and only as you have customer orders for the product. A technique perfected by some of the large Japanese firms, this allows for parts to go from your supplier to the manufacturer to a truck on its way to your customer without stacks of raw materials or finished inventory lying around unsold in your warehouse. If sales are steady and your timing is good, this can help you to turn inventory quickly. This is one of the methods California Cooler used to stretch its cash flow, limiting the number of unsold bottles on hand at any given time.

GETTING PAID

Another cash flow hazard is chasing after creditors. In your old employee days, your boss gave you your check and you had a steady source of revenue. In the real world of commerce, you get paid only after doggedly pursuing and badgering your customers long after the point of sale (unless you're a retailer, in which case you never know when customers are going to come into your store).

The system runs on credit. Everyone is onto the cash flow maneuver, trying to hold off spending dollars as long as they can. You're doing the same thing. While you're pushing customers for prompt payment, you're trying to get the longest credit terms possible from your suppliers.

While it may seem hopeless for a newcomer to get credit terms from suppliers, a persuasive pitch can work wonders. Cite references, any past successes, and try to make some personal connection with the vendor, arousing his interest in your product, and its long-term prospects for bringing him more business.

Air-Vend's Dave Bobert was able to wrangle credit terms by using business contacts he'd built up through the years as references. His approach went this way: "Here's what I'm gonna do; here's my track record with other companies I've worked for. I've never been a failure working for other people, and with the added incentive of having everything I own at stake, I don't see why I won't be successful at this. Why don't you give me credit?

"I was able to get nearly all the components for the tire inflator on credit. So in inventory to build the initial machines, I probably had $30,000 to $50,000 in what amounted to interest-free loans from the vendors, who were convinced enough in the viability of the project to say 'Okay, we'll go ahead and take a chance with you.'"

The other side of the cash flow game is that while you're pressing for credit, you have to be hard-nosed about giving any yourself. A new company can't afford to wait the standard 30 to 90 days for capital sustenance. You have to be aggressive and collect as much money up front as possible. This is the money that allows you to open your doors the next day. If you can't get customers to pay COD, lobby hard to get terms like thirty and ninety days reduced to fifteen days and thirty.

Aggressive credit and collection tactics allowed Kevin Jenkins to build Hercules Computer up to $35 million in sales in just three years without a single bank loan. "I sold to everybody COD," says Jenkins, "and my partner's wife, Tan Suwannukul, negotiated net sixty days with all our suppliers. If one guy wouldn't give it to us, we'd go to another who would. The suppliers would come in here and I'd look 'em in the eye and say, 'You give me these parts, I'll make the product and I'll sell 'em.' And that's exactly what happened."

Drive a hard bargain. You're a new company and you need the bread. They may laugh, but then again they may help out. Give discounts if you have to to get that capital you need now, not later.

When you extend credit terms most accounts are going to take it to the limit, which usually means several weeks to a month beyond the agreed upon terms. The longer it takes to collect from slow payers, the more it takes a bite out of your cash flow. After thirty days the money owed steadily decreases in value, as you spend time and money sending out "past due" notices and use money earmarked for other purposes to make up for the shortfall.

Entrepreneurs learn the hard way that the credit/collection area is one of the most underrated pitfalls of a new business. A new company eager to make sales often won't check out credit references of customers thoroughly enough, and before you know it, there's a big stack of delinquent accounts that have to be sent out to collection agencies. Always check trade and bank references before shipping your merchandise. A legit customer will be happy to oblige.

The key to accurate credit analysis is getting the most current information. Some of the big credit firms, including the country's largest, have credit reports that are months old, and contain company profiles and net worths composed by the very customer you're trying to investigate.

Try to see if there's a credit organization operating exclusively in your trade or industry. They're bound to have more accurate information. In the gift/stationery business, for instance, the Manufacturers Credit Coop, a firm started by a manufacturer who was tired of being burned by deadbeat giftshops, sends out a list every month of slow-pay (past sixty days) and no-pay delinquent accounts as reported by fellow manufacturers. This way you have the most up-to-date, unvarnished information. If you have an order from an account listed as suspect, you can save yourself a lot of time and money and either ship COD cash or not at all.

Also, never ship a reorder until the prior order is paid for. Some accounts which pay on time initially, may tail off after a while and ask for new orders while they still have payment outstanding. This is usually a tip-off that money may be getting scarce for that customer. Shut off the supply of goods, otherwise you could wind up holding the bag if that company goes bankrupt.

Be very wary of large orders in general. Even if you know an account has the money to cover a huge order, it can always cancel or reduce the order without explanation. More than one small company has gone bust either outstripping its production capacity to fill a major order, or having the business canceled at the last minute. One jeans firm bit the dust in just this manner when after receiving a monster invoice from one of the top retail chains, it doubled its production of jeans to meet the order, which the customer then canceled after the entrepreneur had incurred the fatal production costs.

PRODUCTION BOTTLENECKS

For manufacturing entrepreneurs, one of the biggest problems is getting your item produced—so that it is reasonably close in appearance and function to the product you want to sell. All the unpredictable, bizarre aspects of entrepreneurship are embodied in the production arena. This is the Real World at its finest, where everything takes twice as long, costs twice as much, and has to be redone umpteen times over.

Even something as simple as the Auto-Shade—just a piece of windshield-sized cardboard with a picture of sunglasses printed on it—can contain a Pandora's box of travail once the Real World gets hold of it. Avi Ruimi and Avi Fattal had to dump tens of thousands of defectively made Auto-Shades and more than $50,000 in production costs before they could get the item made right. Certain types of cardboard wouldn't bend properly, colors faded on others, and printers loused up the job left and right.

To help limit the damage, every entrepreneur should do three things before going into production for the first time:

1. A THOROUGH RESEARCH AND DEVELOPMENT JOB. Make sure you have the precise materials in the right configurations to make your product work the way it's supposed to.

2. A COMPLETE PACKAGE MOCKUP. Analyze how your package will look on product shelves, how it will sell your idea, and function as a protective (and shipping-proof) container. Redesigns after production can break the bank.

3. A TRIAL PRODUCTION RUN. Work out the kinks in the manufacturing system by trying a few sample runs before risking your money on tens of thousands of defective products.

Entering the world of factories and assembly lines, fabricators and printers for the first time, you may feel like a stranger in a very strange land, baffled by a foreign tongue of industrial jargon, boggled by the noise and complexity of the machinery, and usually bamboozled by fast-talking salesmen who promise the moon and deliver a clod of dirt. If you're to have any chance in this environment you have to learn as much as you can about the process.

Try using the technique California Cooler's Stuart Bewley developed of exposing your ignorance, asking all the questions you want of people you don't want to do business with anyway. Then when you have the knowledge you can go to other vendors and stand your ground confidently on prices and other matters.

It's important to get as many different bids on your job as possible, not only because prices usually vary widely, but also because there are vast differences in the quality of producers. Also, try to find ways to cut corners on the standard factory practices. You may not need every feature of a production process, and may be able to save vast amounts of money that can make the difference between getting off the ground or not.

Using good old entrepreneurial resourcefulness, Tweezerman's Dal La Magna was able to find a way around the expensive blister-packaging procedure he needed to get his hi-tech tweezers on the market. "They told me it was going to cost $1,500 for the tool to make the blister," he recounts, "and I had to print up a minimum of 10,000 cards, so my start-up costs were going to be $5,000. If you don't have $5,000, you're not going to put the product out. I went around to all these blister companies and found one that fit my product. I didn't have to buy the tooling. I was able to buy the blisters for a nickel apiece, 500 for $25. Then I went to a local printer and printed up cards. I figured there must be some glue I could use to glue blisters down to cards by hand. There was. I was able to get my product out on the streets with an investment of $25. Had it been $5,000, I never would have done the project."

When it comes to the factories producing your product, quality is not "job one" or even "job 54." They are in the volume business. Your job is just like any other to the people on the line, who are making minimum wage—and often less—and aren't being paid to notice problems or irregularities in your product. The only way you're going to get any semblance of quality control is to be there yourself or stay in constant contact to ride herd on output.

Conquering the demons and deadbeats of production requires constant vigilance, pressure, and a little imagination. Jerry Wilson used all three, plus a shotgun, to fight his way through sloppy work, mutinous crews, and missed deadlines to build his Soloflex home gym into a $20 million operation. The only way to beat production and other start-up disasters, his story reveals, is offensive, not defensive, strategy.

No Pain, No Gain
Jerry Wilson/Soloflex

Jerry Wilson had the ideal background for an entrepreneur. He was a fighter by instinct and training. Surrounded by strict disciplinarians at home and in military school, at an early age he got used to doing battle with people who told him he couldn't do the things he wanted. As sometimes happens when authority is applied indiscriminately and without apparent logic, Wilson developed an attitude that can be an early spur to entrepreneurship. He began to question authority.

It got him into nothing but trouble at the New Mexico Military Institute, where he was expelled one semester before graduation for running a still in a chemistry lab. It also got him into hot water repeatedly with the Air National Guard. In his six-year hitch he was busted down to buck private three times for infractions like not wearing his stripes or having a bad attitude. "I just pissed them off," he recalls. "They pissed me off for enslaving me. I was not the best soldier."

As Wilson saw it, the regimented seniority system produced the opposite of leaders; it produced followers. The motto of his military school, "duty, honor, achievement," was all wrong. The only true achievement was individual challenge on one's own terms, being your own boss, not somebody's factotum.

None of this endeared him to the brass, who barred him, though he'd passed all the tests, from doing what he came into the National Guard to do—fly jet fighters. But he didn't give up his dream of flying. He got a commercial pilot's license and for the next twelve years flew everything from crop dusters to mail planes to Lear charters.

Doing what he wanted to do was the career Wilson chose for himself. "I didn't want to work for a living in the conventional sense of the word. I wanted to find something I didn't consider work, so I could really get enthused about it. I was willing to accept low wages and hardship if I could do something I genuinely loved to do."

Those who persist in trying to make a living doing what they want are usually shoo-ins for the entrepreneurial trade. Wilson tried several ventures to support his aviation habit. He ran a flying school for a year without success. He also started a tiny commuter airline which shuttled between Roswell, New Mexico, and El Paso, Texas. His wife sold the tickets and he flew the plane. But his inattention to paperwork led to his certificate being revoked, his business being grounded, and a $5,000 debt owed to his father-in-law.

The setbacks didn't dampen his desire to blaze his own vapor trails, though. After becoming a pilot with a charter service out of Las Vegas, he continued to try to hatch new projects. He spent a year developing an ultralight plane he thought he could market, but he had to abandon the effort when it became obvious he didn't have the technical knowledge to pull off a workable design.

A few years later he had another idea. Wilson's flying career was in a holding pattern. Ferrying the likes of Bill Cosby, Glen Campbell, and Ronald Reagan around in a chartered Lear jet didn't get the juices flowing like the old crop dusters and mail planes used to do.

As he was taxiing out of LAX one day, his jet stocked with VIPs, the thirty-one-year-old pilot thought he saw something new on the horizon. He turned to his co-pilot and said, "If I could come up with a mousetrap that would let a guy do all those old-fashioned weight-lifting exercises, like on a Universal, but would fit in his house, I bet I could sell a million of them.

"I got consumed by the idea and for thirteen months I would come back from charter trips with reams of paper wadded up, napkins. I was always thinking about this notion. All I was looking for was something I would buy."

His pilot friends thought he was nuts for wanting to leave a good-paying job for some half-baked scheme he knew nothing about. It was the usual response: Everyone trumpets free enterprise, but most can't imagine anyone participating in it. For Wilson, though, freedom was more than putting the flag out on holidays.

To research his new field, Wilson infiltrated the bodybuilding world by joining a gym. There he quizzed bodybuilders on the fine points of creating muscle mass. He listened to the arguments of the free-weight advocates and the machine supporters and decided to employ the best of both camps in his new device.

"I just used as much common sense as I possibly could," says Wilson. "I wanted that design to do all the key weight-lifting exercises with the minimum number of parts, like reducing a fraction down to its lowest common denominator. It had to be a significant improvement over anything out there so that the concept could carry you, in spite of your not knowing how to run a factory, or not knowing how to advertise."

It was a radical engineering task. "I was a salesman having to learn how to be an inventor," he remembers. "I had to go through every conventional mode of thinking that had probably been tried and discounted."

After six months he was no further than when he started. Finally, though, he came up with the missing link by adapting some aircraft technology. He used rubber straps, or elastimers, commonly used on airplanes, in place of iron plates for weight resistance, and found a way to neutralize the pulling power of the elastimers with the mechanics of a device on his Lear jet, a variable geometry fuel controller.

The next stumbling block was the prototype. That required a crash course in welding. Wilson took a drawing of his device to a steel distributor, who he hoped would let him buy up some scrap to experiment with. The distributor did better than that. He liked Wilson's idea, and went so far as to set aside part of his warehouse for Wilson to work in. He taught him how to weld and everything he needed to know about machine work.

Arthur Curtis, the man of steel, was Wilson's first break. He provided that critical passage from the world outside to the inside tools needed to get in the hunt. "If I hadn't had this guy step out at this time and show me how to weld and use the iron workers, and become familiar with all the kinds of steel that are commonly produced, I wouldn't have made it," states Wilson. "He would also call me up after I'd gotten mad and cut the project in two with a blowtorch, and walked off thinking I was about to go crazy. He'd say, 'You better get back to work.' I could never pay that guy back. There would be no Soloflex if it weren't for Arthur Curtis."

After Wilson had built a couple of prototypes he took out an ad in a Las Vegas shopper newspaper, and about a dozen body-builders came by to check it out. As they went through the various lifting moves, the weightmen grew more and more impressed. "The 'goddamns' got more exaggerated," and Wilson knew he was onto something. Over the next few months he was able to sell each of the ten machines he built by hand. That was his market test.

Wilson's hunch about the market seemed right on target. Home gyms had staggering potential. Other than barbells, fitness machines had never been sold to the home market, only to gyms and health clubs. Even if fitness manufacturers had been sharp enough to see the void in the market (20,000 fitness institutions vs. 80 million homes) bulky Universal or Nautilus-style equipment cost thousands of dollars. Wilson's sleek device would enable people to do 24 iron-pumping and free-body exercises for only $400.

Wilson had decided that since he didn't have the resources to build a national sales network, he would sell his product by mail order through ads in national magazines. With his last $20,000 in savings he took out three ads in regional editions of *Playboy* magazine, installed telephones with an 800 number, and put a down payment on a small production run of one hundred machines with a furniture manufacturer in El Paso.

But the phones didn't ring when the first ad hit. In a classic entrepreneurial initiation, the phone company had given Wilson the ultimate wrong number, publishing the wrong digits.

With $3,500 down the drain on the ad, bills coming due from the manufacturer, overhead on unused phones and office, and four kids to feed, Wilson sweated out the next four weeks until the next edition of *Playboy*. This time the right phone number got printed and the phone began to ring. Wilson sent out brochures to those who called, and converted a sizable 10 percent of the respondents into customers.

Now that he had satisfied himself that the audience for his product existed, he laid it all on the line—house, motorcycles, cars, and his patent—for a $60,000 bank loan. The bulk of it went into setting up his own factory. He had decided the only way he could control his product and make it profitable enough was if he ran the whole show, including manufacturing. It wasn't easy.

"Setting up that factory was the most traumatic experience I've ever had," says Wilson. "It wasn't the physical part of it; it was the emotional part that was bad. Confronting people and demanding from them what you've just paid them for. I fired everybody in my factory on three separate occasions. They wouldn't tell me how many machines they were going to produce, what quality they'd be. They'd steal. That first year was absolute hell. And the next year wasn't much better."

Because he could only get eight machines a day out of his factory, not only was he unable to keep up with orders, but the costs of making each unit swelled to the point where he was losing money on each $400 sale. By the end of his first year he was $80,000 in the hole and in the middle of a crisis that could put him away for twenty years on mail fraud.

Anyone who advertises a product, accepts customer money, and then doesn't deliver within eight weeks is breaking the law. Wilson had orders that were ten weeks behind shipment because of the snail's pace of production at his factory. After he had called all his customers and offered to send them their money back (which none asked for), he decided it was time for a factory revolution.

It involved both carrot and stick. Workers were divided into teams and made accountable. They could go home early if they finished a certain daily output, and salaries were made contingent on production. The more they produced, the more they made. To underscore the new seriousness, he announced to all assembled that he would have twenty machines a day coming out of that factory or they were all fired. Then for emphasis he took the shotgun at his side and promptly blew the time clock off the wall. "Sometimes you have to illustrate," he says. "I've learned to animate to get my point across."

It seemed to do the trick. Suddenly there were forty-eight machines being assembled every day. But then his cash flow dried up. A new ad failed miserably to attract any new buyers. He had seventy-five machines in inventory and no prospects of selling them until his next ad, which he didn't have any money to pay for. Early in his second year Wilson thought "it was all gone. I didn't think there was any hope."

He repaired to the place that was always his refuge in times of complete "mental failure," the public library. There he found a small book by the most famous body-building salesman of all time, Charles Atlas. He discovered the Atlas mail-order technique, sending out nine separate mailings, each one offering the product at a cheaper price. What he needed was a mailing, and a sale on his remaining inventory. He sent out a mailer to the list of 3,300 people who had called his 800 number so far, and offered his product for a discount. He sold 220 machines.

Now he had enough money to take out a bigger ad in a larger edition of *Playboy*. He sold 500 machines. Then there was an ad in *Sports Illustrated*. By the end of his second year he had done $1.25 million in sales and Soloflex was finally on its way. He had his sales up, his labor producing, but there was one new wrinkle. He couldn't get his suppliers to deliver enough of the parts he needed. "We had to limit our production to what we could talk them into making," he explains.

Since he had only one vendor for each of his custom materials, they could dictate his volume, and his prices. He relocated his factory from tiny Roswell, New Mexico, to Hillsboro, Oregon, a suburb of Portland and slowly built up a more competitive vendor network.

From there the fortunes of Soloflex and Jerry Wilson steadily grew with the fitness boom of the early 1980s, sparked by his master stroke, the attention-getting Soloflex ads. The marketing problem Wilson faced was how to take weightlifting out of the grimy, grunting world of cretinesque body-builders and make it cool for the upwardly mobile. "It wasn't socially acceptable," he says. "People who had muscles that were too big were considered low class. How was I going to make pumping iron and getting your muscles bigger socially acceptable?"

"I knew I could make weightlifting a socially acceptable thing to do if I would go into the national magazines and get that respect and credibility, if I would not show great big hulks with veins popping out all over. Just show the beautiful male physique. Maybe just what a gymnast has."

It was a daring move at the time, because the taboo against depicting the male form in any overtly sexual way was still in force. But Wilson, who directed the advertising, like everything else, found the right presentation, showing an Adonis-like figure (former Hillsboro High gymnast Scott Madsen) working out on a Soloflex, stripped to the waist. It was a body that was accessible and artistic, not exaggerated and brutish.

"I didn't want to sell fitness," says Wilson. "I was selling cosmetics. I'm in the birthday suit business."

It took the weightlifting industry four years to figure out there was a home fitness business, and by that time Soloflex built up a sizable lead on the competition. By 1986, hordes of new and old companies were in the home gym market. Wilson was doing nicely at $17 million per year. He and his wife, who is chief operating officer of Soloflex, were taking home close to $1 million a year in salaries, sales bonuses, and his 3 percent royalty on each machine that's sold.

There was one setback. His second product, called the Armchair Quarterback, didn't connect. But he expects another invention, a computerized sparring partner for home boxers to send sales through the roof in 1987.

A classic American maverick, Wilson made it his way, the hard way, for there is no other. "Everything is birthed in a bloody painful mess and the odds of survival are pretty marginal. You grow with a great deal of inefficiency and waste and pain."

But those who don't give up on their cause can make it. His advice: "If you want to make a lot of money you pretty much have to do what you want to do exactly how you want to do it. Nobody's going to do it for you."

MANAGING TO GET BY

One of the biggest pitfalls for the entrepreneur is his or her own lack of management experience. Running all the facets of an organization, from production to sales to administration, covers a lot of ground, more than most entrepreneurs can handle. Or want to. Most are in it for the creative thrill, the adventure, and would just as soon not bother with mundane details like purchasing and bookkeeping. But you have to watch over it all like a hawk or you're courting disaster.

Lane Nemeth of Discovery Toys, for instance, took a lackadaisical approach to the numbers and it almost cost her her company. She didn't look at her financial statements for three months. "I was with a small local accounting firm," she recalls, "who weren't very good. I didn't do physical inventories. I didn't do anything. I didn't know I was in big trouble. Suddenly I put my bills together and found that I had $100,000 of payables and I didn't have a dime."

The experts all have their own pet management theories, and bookstores brim with their secrets. It's not our purpose here, though, to get into the various and sundry theories. Suffice it to say, managing a business is open to many different approaches that all have the same objective: to operate the business as efficiently as possible, maximize profits, and avert disasters.

Managing is an information gathering process. You need to have as much data as possible on what is currently happening with your business; what's selling, what's not, and in which localities; how much inventory you have on hand; which payables you can stretch; which receivables you have to send out for collection; what your sales weaknesses are; how you can outflank the competition; how can you conserve capital.

But the data management task that's even more important for the start-up manager is the projection of information. You need to do more than simply monitor what's going on, you need to be able to anticipate what's going to happen next if you're going to survive the onslaught of Real World emergencies.

You need to look months and perhaps years down the line to see when you're going to run out of money, when you'll need capital to expand and how you'll get it, what you should do if the competition lowers prices, or what trends indicate critical changes in the market.

Lack of financial planning and an inability to spot changing conditions are the Achilles' heels of many promising entrepreneurs. They take each battle as it comes and fail to see it as part of a larger war for which long-term strategy and tactics are needed. As that wise reggae philosopher, Bob Marley, once sang, "You think it's the end, but it's just the beginning." There's no such thing as final victory in business. Because the market is constantly changing, misfortune always lies just around the corner, whether it's a capital shortfall, or a saturated market, and you have to be ready with new sources of funds, or new products to meet the challenge.

Successful entrepreneurs manage their way through the crises of the early years by tracking things like frequency of customer inquiry, reorder patterns, pricing changes in competing products, changes in the availability or costs of materials, and then they use the assembled data to implement strategies to ward off potential trouble.

If you're like most entrepreneurs, good management will probably mean attracting good financial and sales people to help you out. That's because entrepreneurs like to act, not plan and organize. As Jim Cavanaugh, founder of the Jani-King cleaning chain, says, "Any of us who are entrepreneurs lack some form of management capability. We're generally not good entrepreneurs if we're good managers. The entrepreneurs who really put things together find a good quality manager along the way."

Don't try to do everything yourself. It's best to delegate some of the managerial load to staffers who are strong in the areas you're not. That's especially true in the financial area. If you don't have the capital to hire good management, try to find advisers or consultants who can lend a hand on a part-time basis.

LABOR BLUES

While you need complementary and diligent employees to help you realize your dream, finding them becomes yet another Real World minefield. Entrepreneurs in this book cited personnel difficulties as one of the most trying areas of the start-up years.

Mel Ziegler, of Banana Republic, recalls frustration he and his wife, Patricia, had trying to get their mail-order travel clothing sold and shipped with an understaffed, underpaid operation. "We'd spend about five percent of our time for creative endeavors and ninety-five percent of the time making computers work and getting employees to put the stuff in boxes. We were begging people to work for less than they would, so they'd accept our dream. But nobody accepts the dream until they see it."

Limited budgets and the turbulent swings of the entrepreneurial environment can make for a revolving door and worse for a new company. While mass firings have marked some companies' internal struggles (Discovery Toys, Guest Supply, Inc., Soloflex), walkouts are also a possibility in the stressful birth of enterprise. Audio Environments' Mike Malone had his staff bolt and set up a rival company.

There will always be a certain amount of employee conflict, but if you target labor relations early on as a potential hotspot, you may be able to prevent damaging flare-ups from occurring. Here are a few guidelines to help you on the personnel front:

1. To entice key players aboard with scarce funds, try offering a share of ownership in the company. Profit sharing for the whole staff can also help keep good people around.

2. Don't let entrepreneurial ego keep you from hiring someone as good as you are. Power derives not from an omniscient figure at the top, but from a vigorous bottom line.

3. If there's not enough money to hire the best in the field, consider taking promising people from other compatible fields and retraining them for your market.

4. Compensate for the lack of prestigious office and salary by giving your employees more input, responsibilities, and a more humane working atmosphere.

5. Suggestion boxes and company beef sessions can help air tensions before they reach the breaking point.

OVERDOING IT

Despite its image of risk-taking bravado, entrepreneurship is really a contest in the early years of seeing who can exercise the most restraint. Each day brings with it a host of spending temptations, but you have to hold off on all but those that are absolute necessities, or the most prudent means to growth.

It can be quite tempting when a major account dangles a huge order you know you don't have the funds to produce, to go out and overextend yourself anyway. The thought of upgrading your headquarters to an expensive, fancy office after a few good months of sales or after landing a big account can be very inviting. But you have to constantly resist the urge to place short-term considerations ahead of the long-term survival of your company.

Avoid temptations like:

1. LETTING THE GOOD TIMES ROLL. Success is not a single event in the life of a business. It has to be repeated over and over. Conserve your cash even in good times.

2. THE EAGER BEAVER SYNDROME. Entrepreneurs are optimistic to begin with, and so as sales pick up there's always the temptation to exaggerate momentary positive signals. Don't rush out and triple your production because the news looks good today. It might be a seasonal or temporary upturn that won't continue at the same pace. Be conservative with your production projections. Don't get stuck with a warehouse full of wishful inventory.

3. THE BIG SCORE. Spending all your time going after the Big Order can put you in a bad spot whether you get it or not. If you do, you may not have the resources to deliver it, and it may not last; if you don't, you won't have anything else to fall back on.

4. THE SUGAR DADDY COMPLEX. Ditto the above. If 90 percent of your revenue is coming from one customer, you're in a very precarious situation. Don't rest on your laurels. Broaden your base of customers and products before the bonanza ends.

5. THE BIG SPLASH. Don't squander precious dollars on one-shot splashy advertising. Whether it's to introduce your new product with a lot of fanfare, or prop up sagging sales, quick-fix advertising doesn't work and is very expensive. Start-ups can conserve their funds and get better promotional mileage out of a coordinated advertising plan that uses a mix of inexpensive publicity efforts and a few, well-placed ads repeated over a long period. One of the cheapest, most efficient ways of advertising is publicity. Get stories written up on your company and product in the media. When T. C. Swartz got stories in the media profiling his offbeat tour company it didn't cost him more than the time to write and mail a press release.

One other juicy apple that entrepreneurs sometimes can't resist biting into is the tendency to *go off on tangents* apart from their area of expertise. After some initial success it can be tempting to expand into operations over your head.

Richard Thalheimer, you will remember, found that out when he tried to duplicate his success marketing mail-order products to men by introducing a catalog for women. He discovered that while he knew The Sharper Image man inside and out, he didn't have a clue to what The Sharper Image woman wanted. The mistake cost him $2 million.

In Search of Excellence advised major corporations to avoid unprofitable tangents and "stick to the knitting." The advice applies equally to entrepreneurial companies. Don't wander off the main road; you might get lost. Celestial Seasonings' Mo Siegel became a believer in this philosophy when his company went off the track and almost got derailed. The experience taught him to stick to what he's good at, and also to have contingency plans ready in case the course goes wrong.

Beyond those lessons, Siegel's story also illustrates other facets of the survival start-up kit, from a bare-bones approach to overhead, to the economical use of independent distributors, to creative packaging as a substitute for nonexistent advertising dollars.

Make Sure It's Your Cup of Tea
Mo Siegel/Celestial Seasonings

Like a surprising number of entrepreneurs, Mo Siegel found his inspiration in a pastime, not a calculated search for market niches. It grew, literally, out of hikes he took in the mountains near his Boulder, Colorado, home. Planted right in his path on his treks were a host of wild herbs that it dawned on him were the ingredients for the very herb tea he sold in the health food store where he was working.

It wasn't long before he was making his own herb tea from plants gathered up along the mountain trails. Everyone who tasted it, from friends to customers at his store, thought Mo's natural tea had it over bland, generic tea by a longshot.

So he started to sound out distributors and people in the trade about the tea business. In his research he discovered that, unlike the U.S., where one brand, Lipton, controlled the tea market, in Europe a wide variety of herb teas were popular.

Siegel was building a textbook case for an exploitable gap in the marketplace. Except he didn't know he was doing anything of the kind. As an exceptionally inquisitive twenty-year-old coming of age in a time of runaway inquiring minds (it was 1969), he was merely exploring the world around him and a particular interest within it. He was demonstrating, though, the kind of insatiable curiosity that is such a key in the entrepreneurial process.

In fact, the route from curiosity to opportunity would be an easier step for Siegel than for most people because he had a sizable head start (in initiative, not financial means). While most kids his age were working at hamburger stands and starting college, an interest in art led him to start his own poster store on a few thousand borrowed dollars at the tender age of eighteen. It didn't make any money, so after five months he quit and went in with a friend in a health food store.

Health was more than an interest of Siegel's; it was an obsession. A bad case of asthma had plagued his childhood and forced him to sit on the sidelines while other kids were playing football and basketball. When the disease eventually subsided, he was determined to be a "health fanatic" the rest of his life. He found the health food business a good outlet for his preoccupation with health and fitness but a poor way to make money. He decided "the health food store was the way to make a small fortune. You start with a large one and it'll shrink."

Before starting any other ventures, though, he decided to see the world. Seized by the need for new experiences, new information, and new approaches to life that so characterized his generation, he took off for a year of traveling through Europe and the U.S.

When he got back home, he took a job demonstrating carrot juicers at health food stores. When he wasn't juicing he was out combing the landscape for wild herbs that could be brewed into new mixtures of tea. His custom blends were finding an enthusiastic audience among his friends. "I kept making tea for people," he recalls, "and the feedback was so good that I thought maybe I ought to do this as a business.

"I had a little house in the mountains. I got a bunch of old screen doors, cleaned them up, built legs underneath them, and sides around them, and turned them into drying vats, so the wind could blow through the screen. I'd go out during the day and pick tea. I even got some people to join me."

He and his friends spent two months roaming through the brush and backwoods picking a bumper crop of wild spearmint, chamomille, rose hips, and red clover blossoms. They dried nineteen bales of tea and wound up selling it to a large health food store. That done, Siegel's wanderlust struck again and he took off the winter of 1970–1971 to see what was going on in South America.

On his return he discovered that his tea was selling well all over Colorado. The original store he had sold it to had in turn sold it to other outlets, all of which were really moving that homemade stuff. A startled Siegel reviewed the situation and concluded, "Maybe I should do some more of this."

He did. In 1972 with a friend, John Hay, who contributed their total start-up capital of $500 (Siegel didn't have a dime to contribute) he formed his herbal tea company, which was named after Hay's brother's girlfriend, Celestial Seasonings.

It was a quintessential flower child image, long hair, peasant dresses, communing with nature through a branch of a favorite sixties medium, the herb. While the style of that time seems comical by today's sophisticated standards, nonetheless, its substance—self-reliance, control of your own destiny, the desire to live life on one's own terms, instead of by corporate or societal dictates—was the root of today's entrepreneurial era.

There was no way Siegel was going to hand his life over to

the whims of a corporation, and smother his potential in lower-rung bureaucracy. "I didn't want to work for anyone else," he says. "I wasn't cut out to be the fourth peg in a big corporate structure. I have to be at the top or I'm not interested."

Siegel's product was based on sixties' attitudes that have become cornerstones of the consumer society: quality and health-consciousness. "When we started," recalls Siegel, "no one really made herb tea in the U.S. for taste. My view was if I could make it taste good, I could trick people into good health. Instead of lecturing why they should have a healthy drink, I'll just make it taste great and they'll drink it. Then I'll market it with some pizzazz and it'll sell. I didn't want to spend my life doing something that wasn't good. I wanted to reach for excellence."

The struggling start-up had ideals and not much else. Any misallocation of its meager funds could be fatal. They scrimped and recycled and improvised to cut corners. They did everything themselves. They picked the tea, dried it, and then blended it, "the worst job I've ever had in my whole life," notes Siegel. It involved stirring up the dried herb leaves in a big vat with grain shovels. The purpose was to get the stems out. As they stirred a huge cloud of herb dust would fog up the windowless, run-down barn they worked in. "The stuff would fly in your eyes, in your mouth." The stirrers would have to hold their breaths as long as they could, then run outside to catch a deep breath, then run back in to stir again. Then in another room they would grind the pulverized leaves further and sift for particles, an experience Siegel describes as "total hell."

As usual, everybody told the entrepreneur that it wouldn't work. "You're doing what? You say you're going to start a major food company and your leading product is Red Zinger herb tea?" But he and his partners remained undaunted, if not impoverished.

The first year Celestial Seasonings had sales of $71,000. "We ate and didn't do anything else," he says, "unless it was for free. When you start something you have to be willing to put in long hours and work exceedingly hard. I had nothing. It was that simple. The first year I lived on $8,000, the second maybe $10,000 at the most."

He made up for lack of capital with entrepreneurial resourcefulness. He and his partner, their wives and friends, hand-stamped the label on the Celestial Seasonings boxes with a rubber stamp, and because they couldn't afford anything to close their five-inch bags of loose tea, they used scrap wire from Ma Bell. "In those big cables that they lay are fine little strands of copper that are coated in multicolor plastic. Multicolored plastic wires were used to close the packages until we eventually got enough money to get an automatic closer. Everything was just hand-to-mouth."

Although Siegel had no money or business training, he did have an instinct for marketing well beyond his means or background. He knew how to communicate the value of his product in the way successful entrepreneurs do—by creating a personality for his product, a personal connection with the consumer via friendly packaging, and most of all, through magical product names that cut through the clutter on store shelves.

The importance of a catchy name for a new product can't be overemphasized. When start-up dollars are unavailable for advertising or promotion, a charismatic name, along with attractive packaging, can be an effective, and free, promotion strategy, pushing your product where it really counts, on the store shelf.

"Red Zinger" filled the bill and then some. The splashy name gave it "cult hero potential," says Siegel. A bright red, hibiscus-based drink with a tart, citrus flavor, it was a hit from the moment it came out. The name described its nature in just the alternative, colloquial way needed to shove herbal tea into the spotlight for the first time. Siegel followed Red Zinger in 1973 with another winning title, Sleepytime, which would become Celestial Seasonings' leading seller. "Names are one of my strengths," admits Siegel. "I'm a born marketer. I like to name and market things."

Like most entrepreneurs with a new consumer product, Siegel had to sell his tea himself in the beginning. No distributors were going to take on a brand-new product. He recalls the rejections, "Forget it, kid, we're not going to sell this stuff." His tactic was to sell it to stores himself, make the product a success in a small area, and then entice a distributor with sales figures.

In the early seventies the health food industry was undergoing a transition. "It had been a bunch of pill shops," says Siegel. "That was the old line of health food distributors. All of a sudden there was a new wave of people, which I was a part of, who were more interested in the food end." Getting nowhere with the old-guard distributors, he tried to tie in with an upstart distributor, part of the health "underground" like Celestial Seasonings. "They believed in the same things we did, and said, 'We think you've got something here; we'll help you out.'" The distributor, called Air Wand, gave Siegel his first break.

Sales shot upward immediately, from $260,000 the second year to $1.3 million in 1974. But Celestial Seasonings didn't net anything out of the increase. It was, in fact, lucky to even be in business by the end of that year because of a disastrous decision to go off into farming.

Succumbing to the temptation to expand before he had the capability or revenue, and before he had carefully weighed all the options, Siegel sunk precious capital into peppermint farming in Wisconsin. He thought growing his own would give him more control over product and cut the costs of buying peppermint. But once the Real World intervened, Siegel discovered he had no control over anything.

"Nothing would work because the weather was so lousy," he remembers. "A big frost hit and we lost thirty-five percent of the crop in one night. We took the rest and stuck it into oil for chewing gum instead of tea. The loss was almost more than we could take. We had all our efforts diverted for many months. We were lucky to break even that year. We convinced the banks not to pull our loans, raised some more equity, and got back to the business basics, stopped fiddling around with peppermint and went back to selling tea. One of the things I've learned is stick to the knitting, and don't go off on tangents."

Siegel never got sidetracked again. He just kept blending and marketing tasty new herbal flavors. He was in perfect position to catch the wave of health-conscious, no-caffeine consumers of the seventies and early eighties. By 1984 Celestial Seasonings had created such a thriving herbal tea market that one of the country's major packaged food companies, Dart and Kraft, purchased the venture begun on $500 for $36 million. Flower power, indeed.

He had proven once again that the entrepreneur with enough tenacity, and who doesn't make too many mistakes, can reap a windfall in a market niche ignored by the big corporations. But you have to be willing to go to the wall to pull it off, Siegel believes. "You must be willing to sacrifice everything, and, boy, do you have to persist. I could have given up twenty times along the way, but you just have to keep going.

"There's no substitute for gut instinct and the willingness to go out on a limb and do something no one else has done. If you act like everyone else, you'll get to where everyone else gets to."

GROWING PAINS

One of the most critical periods in the life of a venture occurs three to five years out, after you've taken your sales as far as they can go with your bare-bones start-up operation. It's time for expansion, for leaping sales beyond the ceiling imposed by your limited resources. Expansion involves many risks, because the financial stakes are much higher than they were when you were a tiny garage outfit.

To make it you'll need new expertise. The entrepreneurial staff that got you this far may not have the managerial talent to exploit or administer your rapidly growing territory. Giving up seat-of-the-pants business for a more organized, orthodox system is something most entrepreneurs are reluctant to do. Don't wait until it's too late to make the transition.

The big problem is money. Stuck at a constant sales level, you have to somehow get an injection of funds that will allow you to produce enough goods to sell enough to achieve a level of sales worthy of your efforts—and to make a serious penetration of the market necessary for the long-term life of your company. Some start-ups can't attract the necessary capital and die stranded, while competitors who have the resources sweep in and take over the market.

One of the most common mistakes for those who can raise the money is misjudging the market, borrowing heavily against projected sales that don't come through. Entrepreneurs' hopes sometimes outweigh the current realities. It's best to plan for modest growth, and not quantum leaps.

A more realistic approach will make it easier for you to attract financing, too. Banks are the primary source of expansion capital and they love caution. As Guest Supply's John Todd found out in his battles for funding: "Entrepreneurs should present to banks a survival budget, as opposed to an aggressive spending or sales budget. These bankers don't believe anything but conservative survival plans."

Growing too fast can kill off even the most successful companies. People Express Airlines, for instance, one of the great success stories of modern times, ruined it all by getting too big for its britches and acquiring an operation it couldn't afford (Frontier Airlines).

Growth eats up cash. There's more overhead, more production, and possibly a long lapse before sales fill out the new dimensions of your company. You need bigger loans; inventory grows; more space must be leased; more employees hired. Things can get beyond the management ken of the entrepreneur.

Going from eight manageable children's fitness centers in Northern California to a national chain of over 320 brought considerable growing grief to Joan Barnes. She raised $2 million in venture capital to support her expansion. That kind of investment required a huge increase in staff and overhead to advertise, sell, and manage the franchising of Gymboree. With so much capital on the line, fluctuations in sales patterns put her company at severe risk.

"We had some periods," she says, "where we were selling franchises very rapidly and we made a whole plan based on those couple of months. Our plan didn't come anywhere near the actual results. We had some heavy times where we had to lay off half the staff, take big salary cuts. I was scared that maybe I had pushed the concept beyond its natural course."

A big threat to the young company is major competitors taking over the market with greater resources after the fledgling has paved the way. This is why it's so important to have a proprietary product that's either patentable or hard to duplicate; this buys you the time to get established in the market before the copycats move in. Entrepreneurs should develop a strategy ahead of time to deal with the prospects of competition.

California Cooler founders Michael Crete and Stuart Bewley knew that as soon as their wine cooler caught on, they could look forward to the Xeroxing of their invention by every major liquor firm under the sun. So they created a program of quiet, region-by-region expansion without hype and fanfare.

"Our feeling," says Crete, "was 'let's be as low-key as possible and kind of tiptoe from California into Arizona and Texas real quietly, and hopefully not wake some of these big giants out there, like the Seagrams and the Heubleins, and let's kind of quietly capture this whole market.'"

By the time the big boys did wake up, California Cooler had literally beaten them to the punch and was entrenched in almost every market in the country. Even with that, once the majors jumped in with knockoff coolers (over a hundred competitors in all), the superior ad bucks still posed a formidable challenge. To compete with the onslaught, California Cooler sold itself to the Brown-Forman distillery (makers of Jack Daniels and Southern Comfort) so it would have the cash reserves to match the ad dollars of the Gallos and Seagrams of the world.

KEEPING UP WITH YOUR MARKET

Because the market is constantly changing, another growth problem is simply keeping up with the evolving tastes of your audience. Just because something works in the beginning, it doesn't mean you can continue to do the same thing for the entire life of your company. Needs and demands change, and the market is always lusting for variety and improvement. To stay afloat you have to constantly monitor your customers for any alteration in their buying attitudes.

A study by the American Business Conference, reported in the *Wall Street Journal,* concluded that "one of the most essential traits of successful entrepreneurs is the ability to think like their customers." Top entrepreneurs are fanatics about staying in touch with their customers' fickle tastes. Mo Siegel credits the success of Celestial Seasonings to its undying devotion to the consumer. His cardinal rules: "Love of product, love of customer, and dignity of the individual."

Depending on your reading of the public, you may have to alter your product, the image of your company, or bring out new products because yours is headed for obsolescence. Remember when Televideo Systems' Philip Hwang saw his video monitor business leveling off at some point down the road, he exited the game before it was too late, and got into a new line, computer terminals, which offered high growth potential.

To survive in a world where nothing ever stands still requires the combined talents of secret agent, detective, survey taker, and manager in a nonstop intelligence-gathering mission. Reconaissance. Finding out what those infernal customers are up to. That's what saved Dan Scoggin and his TGI Friday's restaurant chain from succumbing to the bug that claims many businesses—and thirteen out of fourteen restaurants, in fact—customer apathy. The techniques he used to isolate the virus and develop a systematic cure point the way to a long life for entrepreneurs who get the message. You have to get inside your customers' heads and stay there.

THE RECIPE FOR SUCCESS IS AVOIDING IT
Dan Scoggin/TGI Friday's Restaurants

It had been building up inside of Dan Scoggin, like the Beach Boys said, for he didn't know how long, the feeling that his corporate life was all wrong. He'd spent thirteen years at the giant paper products company, Boise Cascade, fighting his way up the corporate ladder, but it didn't seem to matter anymore. At thirty-five, a senior manager of corrugated container operations, Scoggin felt—well—boxed in by boredom. He was looking for a way to do something on his own. He had investigated starting a concrete block company and a ski boot company, but neither was the right opportunity.

Seated with a friend in the TGI Friday's restaurant in Memphis, he banged his drink on the table in frustration. "If I don't get off the dime and do something," he said, "I'm going to be an old man sitting on the front porch of an old folks home rocking back and forth and talking about what I could have done. I'm going to do it. I don't care if it's something stupid like this." He gestured to the watering hole around him. Hey, why not?

TGI Friday's was more than a restaurant. Scoggin saw it as a "social phenomenon," the best of a new wave of bar-eateries catering to single-mingling. The pig-in-a-python baby boom demographic was in the process of being disgorged from campuses and rock concerts straight onto the nighttime streets of America, where the search for a constant companion, or at least a night's worth, led right in the front door of festive hangouts like Friday's.

The creator of Friday's, Alan Stillman, was content to operate his original outlet in New York City, licensing the name out to some people in Memphis who wanted to bring the big city-style dining excitement to provincial southern towns, like Jackson, Mississippi, and Little Rock, Arkansas. He didn't see the idea catching on in urban centers across America the way Scoggin did.

Scoggin, like Ray Kroc spotting the McDonald brothers' hamburger stand, recognized that opportunity doesn't always have to be invented. Something that works in one place has a pretty good chance of working in a lot of other places too. So he negotiated and got the rights to open a Friday's restaurant in eight big cities—Dallas, Houston, Kansas City, St. Louis, Chicago, Atlanta, and Indianapolis.

He went out and began talking up his concept. He attracted three partners to go in with him, one was a colleague from Boise Cascade, two were strictly financial partners who helped guarantee the $100,000 bank note that served as their start-up capital. The final partner came aboard as a result of a Real World encounter that almost ended things before they began.

They decided to open their first Friday's in Dallas, which had no comparable upscale liquor establishments and where their chances of success looked the best. They soon discovered, though, that the best-laid plans are often no match for government regulations. According to Texas law, no one could get a liquor license in the state without being a Texas resident. For two months Scoggin agonized through legal mumbo-jumbo to find a loophole.

"We came very close to abandoning the concept," he says. "At that point without stick-to-itiveness we could have missed the opportunity. Delay, the loss of momentum would have disenchanted our financial partners and could have led them to pull out."

He was finally able to persuade a Texas investor to join them and take out the liquor license in his name. The show could now go on. Scoggin had gotten his first break.

He and his partners found their lack of restaurant experience no handicap in building their eatery from scratch. "As we got into it, we discovered our lack of experience was an advantage because we weren't carrying the baggage of a lot of old precepts. Dallas and Houston restaurants prior to that had been 100-seat units, minimum investments. Stillman told me, 'You're putting too much money into it. Put up the red-and-white-striped awning, hang some Tiffany lamps, and go into business.' We said 'No! Standards must be raised.'"

Scoggin took the larger view: To address the new social freedom brought about by the sixties, it was necessary to make a more radical break from traditional dining. "Eating out for the single individual, and for the couple, was no longer an occasion. It was a way of life. They were looking for a casual, upscale, fun kind of experience. We intended to upgrade the food, upgrade the environment, and appeal to these people on a little higher level."

He figured the more detail work you did, the better the odds of connecting on a personal level with customers. Décor was an important part of the rapport, creating an "experience," not just a meal. Through his design Scoggin made sure that no one who wandered in to a Friday's could ever confuse it with any place else.

His theme of "elegant clutter" was developed on a collecting expedition across America while the first Friday's was under construction. Stopping at every barn and antique store from the Rockies to the Appalachians, he put on 100,000 miles in a VW van gathering up the antiques, old car parts, road signs, stuffed anteaters, and old phone booths that would give interior decorators heart attacks and Friday's customers endless amusement.

Scoggin worried that on opening day after a year of outfitting and planning he'd throw his party and no one would come. But the opposite happened. Friday's was a bigger hit than he could have imagined. By the end of the first week it had produced sales of $50,000, unheard of in the restaurant business in 1972. Year-end sales were a remarkable $2 million.

Within six months he and his partners bought out Friday's founder Stillman, and within two years he opened five more restaurants. Scoggin was ecstatic. The money was rolling in. Friday's was an industry phenomenon. It was also the hottest singles' place around, and the man behind it was having a field day. He had grown a beard and was reveling in his new independence and status.

"I was kind of enjoying the success," he says, "being single and strutting around Friday's. Sidling up to the girls telling them I own the place isn't all that bad. I wanted it to go on for a while."

The experts told him it couldn't last. It didn't. Restaurants have a well-defined life cycle that causes the vast majority of successful ones to peak out within three to five years. In 1974 it happened to Friday's. Sales dropped 50 percent. Scoggin was in the doghouse with landlords and his board of directors.

As an entrepreneur, Scoggin couldn't accept the alibis of "experts," and axiomatic theories about the limited lifespan of his business. As a trained manager, he needed information, the data that could explain what was going on. So he left his six restaurants in the hands of subordinates and took off on a sixty-day research tour into the heart of the dining experience. Incognito, he visited successful restaurant and bar operations around the country, which he divided into three stages of maturity—recently opened, "on their way to the moon," and those that had peaked out and were on the downward slide.

He was hoping to discover some common threads, and answers to what others had written off as an immutable rise-and-fall cycle. What he found was what he came to call the Success Syndrome. The service and attentiveness showered on customers on opening day slacks off with prolonged success. Over time "the owner is no longer worried about his bank note. Off goes the tie, and the first excess cash goes into some gold chains that go around his neck. The employees have figured out real quick that management is no longer concerned about the little nits that they were in the beginning. Even housekeeping—'we don't have to clean that up now.' The whole thing winds up that you as a customer are made to feel like you're lucky to be here."

Scoggin's probe uncovered more than a dozen "major things where we lost the feel of what the customer wanted." The popularity of the hamburger with multi-toppings had changed. The drinking habits of women had changed. He wrote all his entries down in a book he titled the "Four Walls Theory."

"There's nothing outside the four walls of your restaurant that affects your restaurant. Not the economy, not competition. If you execute to the standards of excellence inside the four walls, your volume will be there. After instituting this policy, within 90 days we had our volume back up."

His findings resulted in all the bartenders being fired from one of his branches when attitudes wouldn't change. He instituted an unannounced inspection policy, where a restaurant would be closed for twenty-four hours while it was cleaned from top to bottom. A goals and incentive system was devised to get employees to bring opening-day enthusiasm to every shift.

Scoggin's research pinpointed a malady widespread not only among restaurants but also among many entrepreneurial ventures in the growth years: product rigidity. No one likes to tamper with a formula that works, least of all an entrepreneur stuck on his or her wonderful creation. Yet it's constant regeneration of the product, a Darwinian ability to change and adapt to new conditions, that determines who or what survives in the marketplace. And the only way to find out about changes before it's too late is to continually monitor customers.

Whether it's sitting in one of his restaurants eavesdropping on customers' comments about the menu, surveying patrons himself, reports from employees about the most popular dishes, demographic and lifestyle information that may indicate new eating preferences, or computerized scrutiny of consumption patterns, Scoggin, from the moment he came up with his Four Walls Theory, has had the public palate wiretapped. This has given him the ability to anticipate new tastes and adjust his offerings accordingly.

This flexibility has been the key to Friday's survival and success in the marketplace. TGI Friday's has "changed dramatically over the years because our customers have," says Scoggin. "Pastas are more popular because people understand carbohydrates due to running and exercising. We never had fish items on our menus. Now we have quite a number of fish and chicken dishes."

Today Friday's is a long way from the singles' scene it used to be known for. In those days, Scoggin admits, "It was the best singles' place in the world. I had to get married to save my health."

Now he thinks it's the best at its current objective—providing meals, not introductions—and the sales figures bear him out. By 1986 there were 115 Friday's raking in $328 million annually. Scoggin was projecting $1 billion in sales by 1990. There was also a new restaurant venture called Dalt's, "a cross between a corner drugstore, the old pub, and an old diner," which he was hoping to expand to 150 locations by the decade's end.

Scoggin is now a very wealthy man, with each point in Friday's stock worth $1 million in holdings. He's also a very contented man, who thrives on the creativity and autonomy of being an entrepreneur. "I have almost zero day-to-day interference. I can make decisions quickly based on limited facts, without all the committees and baloney that goes on when you're working for a large company. I have the opportunity to excel, instead of being blended in with a homogenized batch of mediocrity."

It was all made possible because he took a risk, and then avoided the pitfall of losing touch with his audience. Dan Scoggin knows it pays to be a good listener. "If you follow what the customer says he wants, your lifeline can be limitless."

8

Down to Zero

LIVING WITH RISK

When we think of risk, most of us picture the momentary kind, little dramas that may be uncomfortable or terrifying but will be over by tomorrow morning. Risking money at the track, ego in a public speech, or your neck in a daredevil stunt puts us through a few anxious minutes at the most. Then the suspense is over in an instant—win or lose.

Risk confined to episodic events can be tolerable, if not thrilling, even for the most risk-averse person, because you know everything's going to be resolved within a certain time frame. However, when you don't know when the anxiety's going to end, when there's no lessening of tension in sight, you have to make way for a much more formidable kind of risk—the sustained kind.

It's this prolonged risk, not the heroic stunt that's over in a flash, that forms the basis of your entrepreneurial struggle. Contrary to its popular image, entrepreneurship is not an act of swashbuckling derring-do, but a much less exciting, unrelieved state of tension. The metaphors that describe entrepreneurs in feats of bravado—rolling the dice, "diving in"—are all wrong. The bet never ends; and the real aquatic analogy is something more drawn out—like Chinese water torture.

The cumulative risk of starting a business, facing down unglamorous challenges like uncertainty, rejection, humiliation, and deprivation, doesn't get a lot of attention, but it's this emotional and spiritual battlefield where victory is won or lost. You have to be able to withstand and operate cool-headedly under the constant pressure of imminent disaster on a host of fronts for an excruciatingly long time. You have to learn to live with risk.

THE STRATEGY OF SACRIFICE

One of the keys to co-existing with risk is the ability to sacrifice. You have to have the discipline and strength of will to give up some things for a while. The young and innocent days of disposable income and time on your hands will have to be replaced by a stretched pocketbook and fourteen-hour days. In a land of convenience, you will have to go cold-turkey on the basis of what constitutes life in America, that there's an easier, faster, more painless way to do something. For the entrepreneur there's no easy way.

Something this drastic is going to require an entirely new perspective on life. It starts with an understanding of the value of sacrifice. Giving up something to get something has to be seen not as cramping your style but as a means to increase it greatly later. Boxers have to get leaner before they can get meaner. Retreat is a time-honored strategy for marshaling eventual victory on the battlefield.

If you can focus on a future goal, instead of a present gain, giving up something, and going backwards, can be the best way forward. Don't let inertia or the fear of getting out of step with the pack leave you, like a mechanical toy, butting up against a wall with your battery running. A few steps backwards, a few to one side, then forward around the obstacle, could leave the wallbangers way behind.

Sacrifice is an investment in the future. Like any investor, you have to part with something to get a better return down the line. As an entrepreneur, you invest your money, time, and ego in yourself in return for a better day. You set aside a few years of toil for a career that's going to pay you dividends. Doctors invest six years of their lives in medical school; lawyers three years at law school. Entrepreneurship requires a post-graduate stint in the school of hard knocks to reap its professional rewards.

Before you move ahead on your project you have to weigh the sacrifices you're willing to make to see it through. "Make a list of sacrificial objectives for the first year," suggests Armor All's Alan Rypinski. "What am I willing to give up for this concept?"

The sacrifices in starting a business cover the gamut: financial, emotional, and even physical. One study, for instance, found that 57 percent of entrepreneurs interviewed had back problems, 57 percent suffered impaired digestion, 62 percent insomnia, and 64 percent headaches. Many of the ailments were helped along by the fact that 60 percent of the sufferers were working more than fifty hours a week, and 25 percent were putting in more than sixty hours weekly.

The top ten sacrifices cited by entrepreneurs were:

1. Personal sacrifice

2. Burden of responsibility

3. Dominance of professional life

4. Loss of psychological well-being

5. Lack of human resources

6. Uncontrollable forces

7. Isolation in problems

8. Friction with partners and employees

9. Commitment of personal finances for start-up

10. Difficulty of finding creative time

Despite all the problems, though, the entrepreneurs listed just as many benefits, including the freedom to make decisions, financial rewards, feeling of achievement, and accountability only to oneself. Only two out of 450 entrepreneurs didn't profess getting tremendous satisfaction and self-fulfillment from being their own boss.

Living with entrepreneurial stresses, both on-the-job and at home (divorce is a frequent companion of the entrepreneur) is a major part of the cumulative risk of enterprise. It requires you to give up peace of mind and security for a chronically unsettled, besieged state.

"When you're working for a company and making a good salary, you have to take the day-to-day stresses, but when it's over you can go home and you know the check has been put in the bank," explains Westwood One's Norm Pattiz. "When you're building a business, you give up those periods of well-being and relaxation where you can go off and be away from it all. You're always thinking about business. And I really believe if you're not, your chances of success are markedly decreased."

It's a tough adjustment, but it can be handled if you apply the entrepreneurial resourcefulness you use in business to your psyche as well. You can counter many of the ailments listed above by developing coping devices such as networking (to eliminate isolation), regular exercise programs, vacation time, more communication with subordinates, finding satisfaction outside work, and delegating some of your responsibilities.

Socially, you'll have to disappear from the calendar for a few seasons. Recreation will be a thing of the past. Linda Enke of Anne Rothschild & Co. describes her party-pooper circuit: "I consider myself a cultured person, but I haven't gone to the symphony once. I've barely gone to a movie. Seeing people is very difficult. Tomorrow morning I have a meeting at 7:30 and at night I'm working on a new project."

"You have to be prepared to devote all of your waking time to it," says The Sharper Image's Richard Thalheimer. "It goes on year after year after year. It's not like you can take a month off and forget about it. Once you start a business, you're totally committed to that responsibility, and you can never let it drop."

On the financial side of the risk scale, the sacrifices you may have to make can be even more severe. The plain truth is that you have to be prepared to go all the way, to go down to zero—and stay there—if that's what it takes to see a project through. If you are starting from nothing, it's virtually certain that you'll have to live with same for a long time.

Get ready for a plain-wrap world. Things of the past include entertainment, household items, and wardrobe (make sure your clothes are timeless enough—plain colors, durable—to withstand several generations of fashion you'll be missing). When cars and appliances break down you'll have to Band-Aid them because you won't have the money to fix them. You may wind up feeling like a heel at birthday parties and holidays. You won't be buying any gifts for a while. As for your eating habits, stock up on Mylanta. Your budget will be sack lunches and burgers.

Getting through it all takes determination as well as resourcefulness and a sense of humor. Jani-King's Jim Cavanaugh used up his limit on all three to survive his spartan saga. Like all undercapitalized entrepreneurs, Cavanaugh had no choice but to go down to zero, and reduce his overhead to the bare minimum. Unlike many, though, the deprivation never undercut his aspiration. He stuck it out and built his company into a $30-million firm with over 600 franchises nationwide. His story is a vivid testimony to the power of sacrifice and self-discipline.

SUCKING IT UP
Jim Cavanaugh/Jani-King International, Inc.

As the eldest of eight children in a family of very modest means, Jim Cavanaugh learned early on how to scrap and make do. To help the family pay bills he had paper routes, lawn jobs, and at age twelve was buying University of Oklahoma pennants for fifty cents and selling them for a dollar at the college football games in his hometown, Norman, Oklahoma.

Since he never had any, he was always looking for an angle

to make money. His curiosity about the ways dollars changed hands made him alert to opportunity buried even in the most bland utterings of small talk.

He was studying business in the daytime and working as a night auditor at the Holiday Inn in Norman, Oklahoma, when in the wee hours one morning he got into a casual conversation with the only other person awake on the premises, the night janitor. His voice echoing in the still of the vacant lobby, the janitor complained to Cavanaugh that with his evening hours it was hard to go out in the daytime to sign up new business.

Cavanaugh had some time during the day between classes. Maybe he could drum up some accounts for the janitor and then make a commission on the business he brought in. While the world slept, he had his own waking dream: "I thought there were probably people like the janitor all across the country who'd like to run a business and manage people and get the work done, but who don't like dressing up and making the polished presentations necessary to close sales."

Since he was a good talker and didn't mind putting on a suit, Cavanaugh thought he might pick up some extra income this way. He wound up running his own small janitorial account service, called Jani-King, which did the sales work for a number of independent cleaning contractors. He operated the business on the side while he attended college and held down his Holiday Inn job.

After four years in the cleaning world, Cavanaugh was more convinced than ever about its profit potential. He clearly saw a vacuum in the marketplace—with lucrative attachments. He envisioned an army of carpet-cleaning, mop-wielding franchisees keeping the corridors of commerce, like banks and office buildings, spic and span.

At twenty-eight years of age he sold his first five franchises in Oklahoma City. But he soon learned he had made a big mistake. He'd drawn up contracts that limited the number of franchisees in that territory to five. They had enough clients to keep them busy and wouldn't take anymore. Cavanaugh couldn't make any money off just five franchises, so he went to his franchisees and told them "if they didn't allow me to sell more franchises in the market or let me increase the royalties, that I would have to shut down my office and they'd have to run their companies on their own. And that's what they decided to do."

He moved to Tulsa and started all over again with just $500 to his name. He opened a small office, sold some new franchises, but it soon became clear that he still wasn't working on a livable profit margin.

"I revised the program a little bit, but I still didn't make the correct revisions," says Cavanaugh. "Seldom having had money, you just can't visualize things being worth a lot of money, so I sold my franchises way too cheap. I didn't have enough money for my apartment rent. It got down to where it was a choice between apartment rent and office rent. I decided that the office was more important than my apartment, so I started sleeping in my office."

He began living in his small office, which he got for free in exchange for cleaning the building. To clean himself up, since his office didn't come with a shower, he rented a room every other night at a motel. In a move that should go into the Entrepreneurial Hall of Fame for Best Resourcefulness/Solo Artist category, Cavanaugh figured out a way where he could shower and shave every day at the motel, but only have to pay for a room every two days.

As a former hotel worker himself, he knew that the night man at a motel doesn't like to add a guest arriving at six in the morning to the previous night's books—too much paperwork. So he checked into the motel at 6 A.M., could shower and shave, but not be on the official books until noon, spend the night, and shower the next morning. The following night he'd sleep on his office floor, and then he'd return at six the next morning to start it all over again.

"Things got worse when they repossessed my car. I couldn't make the payments, so they took it back and sold it. Can you imagine a salesman borrowing cars? But I did. I borrowed my secretary's car occasionally. A couple of franchisees liked me. I'd borrow their cars. I'd ride the bus. You can get to appointments riding the bus."

Despite it all, Cavanaugh remained undaunted. "I was going to build Jani-King and there was nothing that was going to stand in my way. We were going to have a national company."

Still, things in Tulsa didn't look too promising, so he thought he'd try somewhere else. He sold his Tulsa franchises for $5,000, $500 down and $4,500 over five years. With that $500 he talked one of his Tulsa franchisees into joining him and heading for greener pastures—in the new partner's car, of course. He would make his next stand in Dallas.

Like other amateurs playing the trial-and-error game, Cavanaugh could sense that his concept was right, even though his execution wasn't. He still believed in himself and his product. This is the unflagging vision that the entrepreneur projected from his orange Naugahyde booth at various Denny's restaurants. That's where he sold his first four Dallas franchises for $2,500 each. With no money or office, Cavanaugh improvised and came up with the local diner as the most cost-effective place to do business. He didn't have to worry about paying for any meals. He'd schedule his Denny's sessions at times when his potential customer couldn't possibly be hungry, 10:30 A.M. or 3 P.M., after breakfast or lunch. With unlimited coffee refills working for him, Cavanaugh could get clients hyped up for nothing.

Things weren't moving fast enough for his partner, so he left Dallas, taking the car with him. His father lent him a ten-year-old station wagon and he found another office to swap for janitorial services. He began to get a few contracts, and finally he seemed to be making some slow, steady progress. There were a lot of new office buildings in Dallas and with them new opportunities for a company like Jani-King. A rash of new high-rises meant good earnings if he could exploit the opportunity.

"Every time a building goes up," he explains, "someone has to clean it. I can put a vacuum cleaner in somebody's hand and in three minutes they can learn it as well as I can. The more I looked at it, the more I recognized that I could bring professionalism to this business and be able to provide a building owner with a franchisee who cares about the quality of service rendered to that building."

His timing was right and so was his idea: to apply modern organizational, marketing, and management methods to a basically unskilled industry. His business was appealing to a lot of people looking for a way to pick up some extra money. Anyone can operate a janitorial service, and it's one of the lowest-priced franchises on the market. For a $10,000 purchase price a franchisee is guaranteed $1,000 a month in janitorial contracts, and can get more on his own or from headquarters. Jani-King gets a royalty of 10 percent of the business billed. Franchisees are trained in cleaning and business practices and do their work in office buildings between six and nine o'clock at night. It's a system that allows people to keep their day jobs and make some income on the side, or, if they're ambitious, hire people and expand.

Cavanaugh pressed on until 1980, when he began hiring experienced managers, like Gene Nunn, to come on board. Like most entrepreneurs, Cavanaugh doesn't like handling the day-to-day operations of a company. He'd rather be opening up new cities, signing new contracts and motivating people. With Nunn's management ability and Cavanaugh's crusading, Jani-King went on a growth tear in the eighties that amounted to twenty-five new franchises per month by 1986, and a nationwide total of over 600.

It took a long time, longer than most people could hold out. But Cavanaugh's hunch had just too much logic to be denied. As he notes, "We know that dirt will always be here. Somebody has to be employed to clean it, and I would like to be the one to employ the people to do it."

In fact, in the burgeoning service industry, the janitorial

sector is ranked as the number one future job gainer by the U.S. Bureau of Labor Statistics. Between 1982 and 1995 more than 779,000 janitors will be needed by an unkempt nation, while only a quarter of that number will be required to work as computer programmers.

Jani-King is positioned to take full advantage of the forecast because Cavanaugh saw the future before the rest of the field. There are now more than a half-dozen janitorial franchise operations in the country, but when Jani-King started there were none. Getting there first is the essence of entrepreneurship. It requires doing what everybody else is not doing, and the social human animal doesn't always like it out there alone in the cold.

"If you're going to go out on your own," advises Cavanaugh, "there are going to be some very lonely, lean times, and if you're not prepared for those, then it's hard. It's so easy to just chuck it all and go back to living the easy life."

But as one who's conquered what he has, Cavanaugh rightly believes that if he can do it, anyone can—anyone who can bear the price of living with risk. He is an ardent believer in the possibilities of the least of us, who, if we would just believe in ourselves, would see the results.

Jani-King today employs fifty people at its corporate headquarters in Richardson, Texas, and another 3,000 janitorial hands in the field. It was ranked by *Venture* in 1985 as the second-fastest profit maker of all franchise operations in the U.S., an irony in which the long-suffering Cavanaugh takes great satisfaction.

After all those bus rides and bottomless cups of coffee at Denny's, Cavanaugh now owns a new Porsche 928 and two airplanes. He doesn't have to worry about his dad's old clunker breaking down anymore. In the old days he had endless battles with the station wagon's distributor misfiring and stalling out the car. "I got to where I could pull that distributor out and replace the pin on it in about ten minutes. Whenever I left for an appointment, I would leave with a ten- to fifteen-minute leeway, so I could stop and replace the distributor pin and get on to the next town.

"I knew where I wanted to go, and the car—or not having a car—wasn't going to stop me. I would get there one way or another."

THE EMOTIONAL ROLLER COASTER

Not every entrepreneur will suffer the same level of financial hardship as Jim Cavanaugh and have to take refuge in cheap motels. But the commitment to do so if necessary, to really go down to zero, is the fact that distinguishes all successful entrepreneurs. Yet there's something even harder to take than the loss of creature comforts. Possessions and bank accounts are tangible, physical problems that can be propped up with planning and juggling. Keeping the spirits up, though, is a much more difficult proposition. Riding out the emotional roller coaster of starting a business is the toughest of all.

On the scale of vulnerabilities of the species, the ego ranks a solid number one, well above Achilles' heels and weak knees. The ego is a fragile construct that most of us try to hold together with whatever half-way positive impressions about ourselves we can latch onto. Since much of ego is shaped by outside opinion, we try to insulate it as much as possible from exposure to what other people really think about our ideas, behavior, looks—us. The best way to do that is not to vary from a secure routine in which the risks of ego damage have long been smoothed over.

Anonymity may provide great protection for the ego, but, remember: once you begin a commercial enterprise, you are leaving anonymity far behind, making the very risky leap into conspicuousness. It's like raising your hand in class for the first time, or making a public speech. You lose the cover of the crowd. Starting a business is an outrageous act of individuality, a gesture that opens you up to the judgment of the pack. You are flagrantly bucking conformity, the tendency that Mark

Twain described as being "born of the human being's natural yearning to stand well with his fellows and have their inspiring approval and praise."

People don't like you to break rank and do something different. Your independence is seen as threatening, destabilizing. If successful, it reflects badly on those who've never tried. If struggling, it is an unratified shakeup of the accepted system. Permissible change, like Japanese tourists, only travels in the safety of numbers.

"My friends all thought I was crazy," says Soloflex's Jerry Wilson. "I was one of the boys, so to see somebody like yourself, another one of the boys, trying to step outside and become an inventor, they don't believe it. By doing something on my own I was rejecting everything the group stood for. I was violating the buddy system."

The conformist instinct makes people avoid boat-rocking—until everybody else is in the boat and you have widespread "inspiring approval." When you're eking by in the early days of your venture, your lack of public approval sticks out for a mile. So bystanders will shake their heads, avert their eyes, and smile contemptuously at your unsanctioned ruckus. Until the bandwagon forms, that is.

You have to get used to the paradox that although you may be pursuing the American Dream everyone extols, you won't be perceived as a frontiersman until your dream is a reality. Until then, you're a nut for having given up a steady job, and your fledgling operation is looked on as an amateur sideshow in a world of professionals. Americans may love underdogs, but only after they've established themselves as contenders.

Rejection. If you can't take it, you won't make it. Today Avi Ruimi and Avi Fattal are hailed as overnight sensations for the astounding success of the Auto-Shade. As Israeli immigrants, they are singled out as another example that the Dream still lives. It does, they found out, but no thanks to fellow so-called Dreamers. They took their cardboard windshield screens to swap meets. Nobody bought. They went to trade shows for years on end. Nobody bought. They contacted every auto-parts buyer in the country. No one wanted "a piece of cardboard with sunglasses on it."

They decided to take out some ads to sell their product direct to consumers. The designer they hired to do the ad asked Fattal, "Do you really believe you're going to sell this cardboard?" Fattal did the ad himself.

After two and a half years of trying everything, and spending every cent they could pool, over $50,000, all they had to show for it was constant derision and rejection. Finally, they decided to just give away a bunch of Auto-Shades. Maybe if they could get enough of them on the streets and get them seen, they could create a public demand that would force retail stores to carry them. They gave away thousands of Auto-Shades to employee associations at big corporations around Southern California, companies that had big parking lots with hundreds of cars baking in the midday sun.

Sure enough, Auto-Shades began popping up all over town. The eye-catching sunglasses captured motorists' attention and soon people were calling stores to try to find out where they could buy them. The buyer at Thrifty Drugs, who had rejected them on five separate occasions, called Fattal. "Sorry, I goofed," he admitted, and placed a huge order.

Within the year sales reached $3 million. The following year, 1986, sales had boomed to $12 million. Getting there took "three years of struggling and being frustrated and rejected, and wondering how am I going to feed myself," says Fattal. "There are moments of extreme aggravation. You wonder, 'are you having a failure'? Maybe we've fallen in love with a product that doesn't have any potential.

"You have to stick to it. If you really believe in it, you have to go for it. You know why we succeeded? Because we didn't have any choice. Either we were going to be successful or we were going to starve to death."

Richard Thalheimer got the usual flak from status quo society when he launched The Sharper Image. "I found out," he says, "that the world is definitely filled with nay-sayers, and everybody can find something wrong with an idea. Once you've done it, though, everybody's positive it's great."

Beating rejection can't be done when you're on the defensive. Just acknowledge to yourself up front that nine out of ten comments are going to be negative (and the other one a 'maybe'). Expect it, brush it off, and get on to the next case. Think of it, as any good salesperson does, as a game of mathematical probabilities. You have to spread your net wide enough to bring in the catch. Consider, too, that 90 percent of the disapproval is going to be uninformed, herd-driven "corn-pone opinions," as Mark Twain called them, born of the urge to deny what the majority has yet to validate.

Another way to stave off the debilitating effects of rejection is to harness it, and turn the negative into a positive. The most determined entrepreneurs use the rejection to fire themselves up to prove the skeptics wrong. One of Michael Crete's biggest incentives was "to prove to all those people who questioned, who doubted, that California Cooler could be something to shake the beverage industry."

You have to have a deep reservoir of self-belief to counter the drumbeat of gloomy assessments. Jazzercise's Judi Sheppard Missett says, "You have to be willing to lay down in the middle of the street for it. You have to be that convinced, because if you're not, you're not going to last, because people will tell you you're stupid, foolish, crazy. You've got to be really confident. You've got to know deep down inside that what I'm doing is one hundred percent right, and I'll stand behind it with my life."

Dave Bobert had to put up with more than the usual share of abuse. His product, a coin-operated vending machine that dispenses air for tires, was just the kind of left-field, oddball idea that the status quo seekers love to pounce on. "What? You're actually trying to sell *air?*" Corn-pone opinions engulfed Bobert in a sea of gibes and jokes.

Bobert was in good company. They had laughed at Henry Ford, too. King Gillette had to put up with years of jokes and harassment as he tried to find a way that everyone said was impossible to sharpen sheet steel for his new safety razor. "Well, Gillette," his friends would chuckle when they met him on the street, "how's the razor?"

Like Ford and Gillette, Bobert stuck it out and had the last laugh. He was able to build his company, Air-Vend, Inc., into a $5 million enterprise by, as his story illustrates, riding out the emotional rollercoaster with a constant supply of self-belief.

MAINTAINING AIR SUPERIORITY
Dave Bobert/Air-Vend, Inc.

At every trade show there are scores of new products presented by hopeful entrepreneurs testing the waters of commercial viability. They stand expectantly at the edges of their booths, psyched with enthusiasm, ready to convert any buyer they can flag down. The sales pitch is well rehearsed, voice modulated with enthusiasm. However, for the vast majority of first-time hawkers, the energetic smile will soon be replaced by the wan look of rejection as jaded buyers roundly dismiss the new-comer's wares.

Dave Bobert wishes someone had taken a picture of the expression on his face at his first trade show, the National Oil Jobbers Show. "I probably was the saddest-looking guy around," he says. Nobody wanted his tire inflator. "Virtually every guy that came by would look at the product and laugh derisively, or they'd say, 'You gotta be out of your goddamn mind. I'd never put one of those in my gas station.'"

If Bobert had been like most people, that would have been the end of it. The tire inflator would not have lived to rescue another flat tire. But Bobert wasn't going to be gotten rid of that easily. This son of an Illinois farmer was used to hard work, and he had a strong competitive streak. A track star in high school and college, he hated losing and wasn't about to this time.

Besides, he couldn't afford to. After the auto-parts manufacturer he worked for went bankrupt, starting his own company was the only job he could find. He had sunk all his savings, $11,000, into the tire inflator and there was no turning back.

No matter what anybody said, it couldn't alter the central fact in Bobert's mind: the need was there. He had done a survey of gas stations himself and found that hardly any Minneapolis stations had air on a regular basis. That service aspect of gas stations had disappeared with the oil crisis of the seventies, as dealers closed down, reduced extras, and self-service outlets proliferated with no air, oil, or windshield-washing facilities.

Bobert tried to get about a dozen people to invest in his idea, but everyone thought he was crazy, including his family. "Everybody had the same line," he recalls. "'Why are people going to pay for air when they can get it for free?' My point was that people couldn't get it for free that easily. They could if they were willing to spend a certain amount of time driving around looking for it. But my feeling was most people are either going someplace or coming back from there and they don't want to spend a half-hour looking for an air hose that works."

Since he couldn't get anyone he knew to invest in his idea, he took $11,000, all he had, and started himself. "It was do or die," says Bobert.

It was a scene unlike any he knew as a marketing manager for a big company. It required a substantial reduction in both lifestyle—and workstyle. Gone were the nice desk and office furnishings. When Bobert went down to zero, his "office" became a noisy, unused portion of a sheet-metal shop; the carpet "looked like somebody had drained the oil out of their car engine onto the rug and let it soak in a big, black pool."

The tire inflator is essentially a metal box with an air compressor inside. A coin meter activates the compressor and for twenty-five cents a motorist can fill up his tires with air. It was so simple, yet so hard to explain in a way that would translate into sales. Six weeks went by, Bobert calling on some forty gas stations around Minneapolis, but no one would take a chance. Things were looking pretty grim inside his oil-soaked nerve center. By this time, his credit terms were coming due with suppliers, and he didn't know where the $30,000 he owed would come from.

Then finally he got his first sale, though he didn't even make it himself. A friend in the vending machine business got him the customer. A second customer followed, buying five machines to take back to Detroit, where he was going to install them in gas stations and operate them on a vending route.

For the rest of his first year Bobert squeaked by on intermittent sales, on three separate occasions reaching the point where he was "nearly out of money and counting the days before I had to close the doors."

One of the most difficult things for him to take was the constant uncertainty and emotional swings. "When things were going good, I'd be really high. If I had a few downturns for any period of time, it was hard not to become discouraged. It was hard not to think: 'Boy, what's going to happen if this thing goes down the drain.' If you're an entrepreneur, you put your ass on the line and everything that goes with it. So the fear of failure is always there. It really keeps you motivated and keeps you going."

Two things helped turn things around for Bobert. A press release on Air-Serv (the brand name made by Air-Vend) was picked up by *Entrepreneur* magazine, which then ran a feature on the tire inflator. With the national exposure, calls started coming in from customers intrigued by the inflator's low cost ($1,400 retail, $700 wholesale, and no franchise fees).

For a minimal amount of capital people could buy up a few air machines, stick them in gas stations (with 25 percent of the revenue going to the stations, 75 percent to the Air-Serv owner) and make money on the side without scarcely having to lift a finger. There was no overhead, inventory, paperwork, or personnel required. It could be run as a family business or a tax shelter.

The other big boost came when Bobert was able to hire a sales expert, a former boss of his many years earlier. George Hean brought the kind of management expertise the entrepreneur so often needs to get beyond the fledgling state. He was able to help set up a sales network that raised sales from $500,000 the second year to $5 million by 1985.

By 1986 more than 20,000 of the machines that were laughed out of that first trade show were in operation across the U.S., and multiplying at the rate of some 700 new inflators per month. Instead of the one-room, greaseball office, Air-Vend was headquartered in a 6,000-square-foot complex in a suburb of Minneapolis. There were not only fourteen models of inflators, but also a coin-operated vacuum machine and a window-washing device. Bobert could be seen driving a Ferrari and jetting around Europe tending to the British Air-Serv dealers in France and Switzerland.

Though he had lived through hair-raising times, the risk had been worth it. Bobert's financially set, and, more important, is enjoying himself immensely. He looks forward "with great anticipation each Sunday evening for Monday morning to come around" so he can start a new week of work. How many of us can make that statement?

It was all made possible, he contends, by his not giving up on his product or himself. "I guess I always felt that I'd somehow save it or pull it out."

STATUS INTERRUPTUS

Strong self-belief is the sustaining element against rejection, and one of its nagging side effects, dwindling outward status. The loss of standing is another of the psychological risks you have to withstand in the early stages of starting a business. Going from a big company's letterhead to one whose clout is nil, from a nice office to a corner of your apartment, from an equivalent social level with friends to one too impoverished to mingle, these assaults on self-image can take a cumulative toll.

Faith Popcorn had held a prestigious creative director's post at a New York advertising agency. She had won many awards and had lots of connections in the business. She thought. When she started her own marketing consulting firm, BrainReserve, she discovered that "everybody I had done good advertising for over the years, I couldn't even get them on the phone." The numbers on her IRS return plunged from almost six figures to $8,000.

It can be tough when nobody calls you back, when officious secretaries stonewall your every move, when the receptionist you hand-deliver the package to asks you who the messenger service is, and it's you. It's disconcerting to be an adult in the prime of life with a good education and professional abilities to be spending your days packing boxes, licking stamps, and typing labels. The question may arise while you're standing in a two-hour line at the UPS office: "My God, what have I done?" Your lofty dream can seem absurdly removed from the trudge to the instant printer every time you need a single, lousy photocopy of something.

Isn't there an easier way? Sure, if you have an inheritance. If not, going down to zero is the name of the game, and that means you will have to have to dine on humble pie for a while. The entrepreneur has to accept a reduction of status and a serious plunge on the Keeping-Up-With-The-Joneses Index before the eventual triumph can happen.

You have to stoop to conquer. Whether it's Michael Crete scraping labels off beer bottles, or Mo Siegel stirring up tea with a grain shovel, successful entrepreneurs are the ones who get their hands dirty and their clothes wrinkled. They are the ones prepared to put out maximum effort toward the goal, regardless of how it may look to the outside world.

Being treated as a nonentity by the business world, and living a pauper's life, can gang up to create a feeling of illegitimacy that can undermine the confidence you need to sell your product. As hard as it may be to do, you can't let your personal straits interfere with the value offered by your product. You can be sleeping in your office and showering in a motel like Jim Cavanaugh, but the customer doesn't know that; if your product or service fills a customer need and you can persuade him it does, that's all that matters.

Entrepreneurs overcome status problems by constantly referring back to the need for their products, and their belief in themselves. According to psychologist Joan Harvey, what keeps them going is a "tendency to be internally validated and not having to look outside themselves for validation of their own ideas or feelings. It's a confidence that what you feel internally is correct, and you don't need someone else to tell you how to think."

SOLITARY CONFINEMENT

Man may come into the world and leave it all by himself, but he goes solo on these occasions only under the greatest duress. As social animals, we spend most of our lives in a pitched battle against solitude. There's an instinctual need for us to share with others of the species the thoughts, hopes, joys, and particularly the travails, of being human. When we can't share these feelings, can't connect with someone who understands our goals, our woes, we experience the psychological encirclement, the me-against-the-world alienation that is known as being alone.

Though most entrepreneurs start companies so they can be on their own, they usually only imagine the good side of independence, freedom of choice, doing what you want to do. But there's a downside to total autonomy, too. You can't delegate the pain of running a business.

Two entrepreneurial functions, researchers tell us, can't be delegated to anyone else: uncertainty-bearing, or, tolerating long-term inconclusiveness, and ultimate control and decision-making. Problems and crises can only be solved—and borne—by one person: you. Since the burden can't be shared, you have to figure a way out of every bind yourself. The resulting sense of isolation and loneliness has been found to be the number one cause of entrepreneurial stress.

It was a rude awakening for Dave Bobert. "The statement 'It's lonely at the top' used to mean to me that it's lonely up there because there aren't as many people up there as brilliant and successful as you are. What it really means is that when you're at the top of an organization, the buck stops there. When you get into a jam, you can't turn around to your boss and say, 'Help me out of this mess.' I had no one I could turn to. I couldn't turn to my banker—he didn't own his business. I couldn't turn to my accountant. It really brought home the true meaning of that loneliness at the top."

If you can't stand to be by yourself, don't even think about being an entrepreneur. If you can't go out in public except in the company of others; if you can't make decisions on your own; if you wouldn't be able to take being cut off from almost all social activity, you will not be able to handle the solitary confinement imposed by entrepreneurship. You have to work alone, think alone, get out of jams alone. There's no one to blame but yourself, and no one to commiserate with if things go wrong.

"You don't have a friend in the next office that you can complain to," says Faith Popcorn. "The loneliness comes from not being able to complain about your boss or the system. You are it. You have nobody to pass it off on."

In the end, independence is a cast of one. As John Godfrey Saxe wrote:

In battle or business, whatever the game,
In law or in love, it is ever the same;
In the struggle for power, or the scramble for pelf,
Let this be your motto—Rely on yourself!
For, whether the prize be a ribbon or throne,
The victor is he who can go it alone!

THE TWILIGHT ZONE

Uncertainty is the godfather of entrepreneurial risk. All other members of the risk family—from financial to emotional—derive their power from its unpredictable ways. The ability to confront it is what separates those who would like to start a business "someday" from those who actually do it. More than the potential loss of capital or reputation, it's the awesome specter of the unknown that prevents people from cashing in treadmill lives for other directions.

The thought of no steady paycheck and possible rejection and failure is enough to repel any urge of initiative in most people. For them stability and security dictate the course of inaction. The entrepreneur, on the other hand, while he or she may be anxious about the unknown, has enough self-confidence to believe that whatever fate throws up can ultimately be handled.

That self-belief is sorely tested by the chronic uncertainty of a new venture. You need to have what studies have isolated as one of the key traits of successful entrepreneurs—a tolerance for ambiguity, an ability to function in the midst of a netherworld of vague, incomplete, unstructured, or unclear situations. You have to make decisions in a twilight of shadowy information and sketchy resources, where the full outline of events remains maddeningly hard to make out.

As an entrepreneur, you don't know what's going to happen next. You don't always know how you're going to get out of this one. The uncertainties can range from how to meet your next payroll to how to deal with the threat of a price-slashing competitor when your costs are already out of line, to whether to increase your production based on intangible signs from the market, to wondering if the phone will ever ring with another order. Dilemmas pile up and vie for your attention. You take the most important ones first. Others must fester. For still others there may be no resolution in sight.

Surviving this state of siege without losing your mind or your shirt, or both, requires not only a tolerance for ambiguity, but also a tolerance for disorder and chaos. Drill instructors, train conductors and bureaucrats would never get out alive in this land where rule books, precise schedules, and order are thrown out the window. It takes a certain skeptical attitude about orderliness to put up with the litter of loose ends and unresolved problems strewn about. For neat freaks, entrepreneurship is a terrorizing spill-a-minute, an unending clutter of concerns that defy tidy arrangement.

How do you come out on top in this free-for-all? Being able to keep an eye on the forest through the trees is essential. Some of the less important problems just have to be ignored or transcended. You have to focus on the most critical issues without getting overwhelmed by the daily buildup of unresolved headaches. You have to get used to the fact that the desk is never going to be cleared.

THE POWER OF PASSION

In the dawn's early light of a struggling young company, there is a sense of stillness amid chaos, that for all the energy and effort and crises met and conquered, real progress is as distant as ever. The thought may occur in one of the few free moments off the battlefield, driving home late at night, or getting up in the morning, why bother anymore? Each day just brings more peril, not profit.

It's an endless split-decision. Sure, some people like your product. But not enough to get you anywhere. Is there a bigger market out there? There may be, but how will you ever get the capital for the expansion needed to reach it? Maybe your product's not going anywhere; on the other hand, maybe it's a question of just hanging in there longer. The conflicting signals line up opposite one another canceling out into infinity.

How do you keep going when logic, bankbook, family, and friends are telling you otherwise? Intense motivation, like financial desperation, or wanting to prove something to someone, is a key. Personality traits like pride, stubbornness and competitiveness are helpful. A significant factor, though, in the decision to press on is the level of faith in your product. Do you like what you're doing? Do you feel passionate about your product? When outside forces have eaten away at your gut instinct, you need something more to sustain you, what Celestial Seasonings' Mo Siegel calls "love of product," a personal tie and devotion to your creation that will not flag.

"If you ask me what got us through everything," says Lane Nemeth, who had more than her share of major stallouts launching Discovery Toys, "it was our product. It was something I understood deeply and had a huge personal attachment to. I had a mission. I was going to change the world with educational toys."

There's a bit of the crusader in all successful entrepreneurs; a sharpened sense of justice; a belief that their products are right, what's on the market—or isn't—is wrong; and that by providing a quality alternative the world becomes a better place. Only this sort of zeal can keep you going when progress is negligible, which it can be for years on end. That's why those who launch products just to make money, with no real interest in what they're marketing, usually don't make it. Once they run out of physical gas, there's no spiritual or emotional reserve tank to pull them through.

If Mel and Patricia Ziegler had been selling pallet nailing systems or vinyl extrusions, there would likely have been serious problems on the gusto front when it came to crunch time. But when the Zieglers were up against the wall several years into their travel and safari clothing venture, Banana Republic, it was a lot harder to give up on something that had wrapped up in it their two favorite things in life: travel and art.

Even though the debt piled high, and the thought of a less precarious life often crossed their minds, the psychic attachment to their product was a match for all obstacles. The Zieglers got through their years of living dangerously to build a $50 million company (as estimated by *Business Week;* the privately held firm doesn't release sales figures). They were able to outlast long-

term uncertainty by confronting it with something more enduring, the creative spirit. As their story shows, self-expression,
particularly for a journalist and an illustrator, is something
worth fighting for.

SURVIVING IN THE JUNGLE
Mel and Patricia Ziegler/Banana Republic

Anyone with an insistent creative streak who works for a newspaper finds out soon enough that imagination is not front-page
news. As a feature writer for the *San Francisco Chronicle,* Mel
Ziegler did his best to liven up the breakfast table reading of
Bay Area residents with articles that contained a human dimen-
sion, not just factual litanies. He tried to give readers an extra
twist, zeroing in on the emotion of a story about a regular guy
who rescues a woman from a burning house, or revealing the
manipulations behind the Werner Erhard "est" empire. Ziegler's
"gut-wrenching journalism" always got the phones ringing and
the letters written. But the response from his editors was more
unpredictable.

"Some of the best stories I wrote ended up on the spike,"
he recalls, "and some of the worst I wrote ended up on the
front page. I could never figure out the pattern, and there really
was no pattern. It was usually the editor trying to second-guess
the publisher. I got really tired of living in a world where people were second-guessing other people. I wanted to put my
own vision out there. And I didn't want anybody in the way."

His wife Patricia, an illustrator for the *Chronicle,* also saw
no outlet for her ideas. A fine artist with an interest in clothing
design, she found the life of courtroom illustration left a lot to
be desired. She was tired of sketching. She wanted to produce
full canvases, on subjects of her own choosing.

Instead of complaining about their jobs for the rest of their
lives like most people, the Zieglers came to the realization that
they had the faculty of free choice. They could do something
new. The usual stumbling block of indeterminate future funds

would not stop them. Getting away from the meddlers and the dictators was worth the risk. Mel decided to become a free-lance writer, while Patricia would open up some kind of clothing store.

Finally off the corporate reservation, Mel was now able to indulge his interest in travel. He angled for free-lance assignments that would take him abroad whenever possible. It was his custom on these trips to pick up representative army surplus gear from the host country. From Australia, for instance, he might bring back a British Burma jacket. Patricia would take whatever he brought back and customize it, adding some patches, a new collar, new buttons, updating the classic khaki look. The redesigned military castoffs began to attract some notice. People wanted to know where Mel got his distinctive duds.

That he could in any way be considered a fashion plate was a joke to him. "I've always felt great disrespect for fashion," he says. "It's ludicrous to the point of being funny that people will feel themselves inadequate this year in last year's clothes. I was very anti-fashion, so anti-fashion that my way of dressing I used to call 'First Available Chic,' whatever I pulled off the rack and put on my body was what I wore."

As a visual artist, Patricia had a keen eye for style. Her tastes leaned toward the independent classics so proudly displayed as nonfashion by her husband. She explained to him that his lack of style was, in fact, a style. And more than that, it was one that seemed to have some possible sales appeal.

"Patricia loves clothes," says Mel. "She wanted to get into the clothing business, but she had been an artist her whole life. For her to knock on the door and say, 'Could you hire me as a designer?' was impossible. So she had no way to do it but to do it on her own. Since she was anti-fashion as well, she was very interested in classic clothing, turning old surplus things into new outfits."

If entrepreneurship is a case of unearthing the unseen opportunity, this one was buried good. Nobody saw it in a truckload of used, unwashed, wrinkled-up Spanish paratrooper shirts. Nobody except the Zieglers, that is—and the Spaniard who unloaded the moldy merchandise. While on a trip to Spain, where Mel was working on a story, they stumbled upon this unclaimed prize, and decided to collar the market, investing the $1,500 they had in their savings.

When the shipment arrived in San Francisco six weeks later, so did the Real World of commerce. Inside the boxes were airplane parts (they had bought the shirts by the pound), an extra-grubby, reduced amount of shirts, and sleeve lengths four inches too short. They had neglected to try them on before they bought them.

Looking like you know what you're doing is a technique we all have to practice from time to time, but entrepreneurs have to be able to develop it to an art form. When things go awry or the knowledge isn't there, you have to bluff your way through. With the invention that comes from necessity, and a journalist's creative wiles, Mel dreamed up an elaborate explanation for the short-armed sleeves.

"I wrote a little sign—'Spanish Paratrooper Shirts'—for our booth at the Marin County Flea Market that explained that they were authentic Franco-era Spanish paratrooper shirts and the customers would please note the arms were too short. That didn't matter anyway, because it was not stylish to wear shirts with the sleeves rolled down, and, furthermore, the reason for the arms being short was, as everyone knew, Franco was a maniac and one of the most maniacal things he did was persecute long-armed Spaniards."

Customers bought the story and the shirts. Creativity had turned a dead loss of defective merchandise into a budding venture. Revenue from the Franco-wear sold at the flea market gave the Zieglers just enough money for a month's rent on a small storefront in Mill Valley. They couldn't afford to buy fixtures or even a cash register. With just the paratrooper shirts and a couple of other bargain-basement surplus items, the Banana Republic, true to its name, made a decidedly underdeveloped appearance in the league of fashion-states. With no capital, no business knowledge, and no precedents to follow in marketing these offbeat items, the Zieglers faced total uncertainty.

As for all entrepreneurs, that void was made bearable by the knowledge of another gaping chasm—their market niche. In 1978 when they began Banana Republic "the world had evolved to a point where fashion had replaced clothing," Mel points out. "Our concept was to sell natural fabric clothing in muted colors, primarily khaki, that was functional. Patricia was adding style, not fashion, to good, basic, classic clothing.

"We wanted to make the classics, but since we didn't have the capital, we had to find it from available resources, which was mainly the military surplus market. We'd buy items, tear the fabric out, and remake it into something else. We took whatever existed out there in the world of natural fabric and khaki and created our own look, sewed our own labels into it."

As befuddled customers wandered through their tiny store, though, it occurred to the Zieglers that the appeal of updated surplus, like that of paratrooper shirts, wasn't self-evident. Somebody had to explain what was going on, to turn the esoteric into a more marketable eccentric mix.

Mel came up with the Banana Republic catalog. His first issue, a hand-stapled, black-and-white booklet featuring Patricia's illustrations of their wares instead of photographs, outlined the marketing scheme that was to elevate humble supply-depot clothing to the heights of style. He made it romantic. Instead of bland product descriptions, he filled his catalog with colorful foreign correspondent-style dispatches. Drab army khaki came alive through images of game-filled savannahs and jungle adventure.

They printed up 5,000 copies of the first catalog at an instant printer and sent it out to everyone in their address books, which included a lot of journalist friends. Suddenly stories started to appear in the local newspapers and the shop began to attract customers. The fantasy grew. They turned army surplus into theatre. Giraffes and zebras roamed the aisles of the imaginary republic. Mel was known as Minister of Propaganda, while Patricia was Minister of Culture. They didn't miss a detail of the fantasy, down to the official seal of the Banana Republic, government-style, on the back of customers' checks.

But behind the fantasy there was a reality, the day-to-day torment of growing a business without capital and manpower. "We were tremendously over our heads," Mel relates. "Having to borrow money in order to buy the merchandise, in order to put the catalog out, we became further and further in debt on a short-term basis, and I began to work just to pay off the debt, even though we were profitable.

"It was an impossible set of circumstances because we never had enough money to hire the really good operational people who could make the damn thing work. We'd be working eighteen, nineteen, twenty hours a day and often we would disappoint people, and it broke our hearts every time we did. Somebody would call up and say, 'I ordered a shirt and you sent me a dress.' It wasn't us, of course, it was the poor guy we paid $4.50 an hour because that's all we could afford, and he probably couldn't read English."

The Zieglers were having their ambiguity-tolerating powers tested to the limit. In the classic entrepreneurial dilemma, sales were growing, people talking; things seemed to be onward and upward. On the other hand, every dime was going back into the company to pay for growth. So there was no cash to show for their efforts, only debt and the rapidly multiplying problems of a growing business. Like for all undercapitalized entrepreneurs, progress for the Zieglers was as slow and indiscernible as geologic history.

The trials mounted. Stores got robbed, employees quit with regularity, suppliers failed to ship. Going further and further into debt to pay for merchandise and production of an expensive catalog, the Zieglers soon found themselves slaving just to pay off the debt. This was not their idea of independence. They didn't own their business; it owned them. They couldn't even do the thing they set the company up to do. There was no time or money for travel.

It became obvious one day that the catalog was a money-loser. The stores were profitable, but to make money on catalog sales they had to mail out quantities they couldn't afford to produce. Mel weighed the death of his baby. "The logical thing was to kill the catalog," he says. "But I couldn't do it. The catalog was the fun part for me. And it explained the business. I was afraid if I took the catalog away people wouldn't understand what it was all about. When they understood the literary context in which it came about, the whimsy, the humor, the catalog created a whole atmosphere which made people want to go to the stores."

He made the classic entrepreneurial decision. Defy logic and go with gut feeling. His passion for his product would not allow it to be diluted in any way. He would stick with the catalog. "We knew in our heads," he says, "that we were going to make it. There was no turning back."

They coped with mounting uncertainty the only way entrepreneurs can and still maintain sanity. They transcended the larger anarchy and tackled the crises on a case-by-case basis. "It's an exercise in waking up and knocking down all the obstacles, ducking from all the people who are shooting at you, just saying 'You're not going to get rid of me until my idea catches.'"

By standing their ground, the Zieglers bought time for their product to become more established in the marketplace. After four years of persistence, the results were adding up to, if not big bucks, major influence, which, if played right, can eventually be felt financially too.

Their whimsical world of wanderlust was capturing the public imagination. Patricia's durable anti-fashion designs and natural-fabric concept were being praised—and copied—by tastemakers around the world. Bush jackets, Serengeti khaki skirts, Outback shorts, women's fatigue pants, and various safari-wear began to emerge as a vital sector of the apparel industry. Mel's catalog, featuring lively clothing reviews by top writers and celebrities, was capturing awards for design excellence from the direct-mail industry.

Influence can attract important people. Big companies, always on the lookout for growth areas they don't have to start themselves, wanted in on this safari thing. Several wanted to buy Banana Republic. The Zieglers held out. As much as they knew they needed a huge infusion of cash to be able to supply the demand they had created, they didn't want to give up their independence.

However, on one particularly bad day at the office, Mel got a call from a friend. He confided to him that if the right offer came along he wouldn't mind selling his company. Within five minutes the chairman of one of the biggest clothing retailers in the U.S., The Gap, was on the phone.

After months of negotiations to make sure their autonomy would be left intact, the Zieglers sold Banana Republic to The Gap in 1983. Mel remained president and Patricia executive vice-president. With the enormous resources of a major corporation behind it, the borders of the Banana Republic could be expanded to take in territory beyond the scope of its under-developed economy. By 1986 there were thirty stores nation-wide, with plans for upwards of one hundred by 1990.

Now the Zieglers spend up to six months a year trekking the globe and plotting new adventures, including books, maga-zines, and distributing folk art and crafts from around the world. It's everything they could have dreamed of achieving when they set out, and more.

"We wanted to travel, and we wanted to be independent," says Mel. "We didn't want to report to anybody. We never really thought about the accumulation of money. Money turned out to be the by-product. I believe we've made the money be-cause we didn't go after it directly."

Driven by the creative fruits of their labor, and pride in product, instead of by some big-buck end result, the Zieglers were able to persist long enough for their idea to take hold. "The thing we had going for us," declares Mel, "was that we had staying power."

JUST SAY YES

As any entrepreneur would tell you, persistence is the difference between success and failure. "Persistence," though, is one of those vague entrepreneurial clichés that doesn't really tell us much. There's more to it than just amorphous character traits like being stubborn or competitive. There's a very basic, practical technique that allows successful entrepreneurs to persist. They refuse to take "no" for an answer.

Negativity is drummed out of the vocabulary. "We banned the use of the word 'can't' at Banana Republic," states Mel Ziegler, "because if you use that word you create a reality where you possibly can't. But if you don't say that word, you put all your mind power, all your intelligence at the problem to find a way to 'can.'"

A "no" is never a "no" to an entrepreneur. It's an invitation to another approach, another avenue. Rejection doesn't repel; instead, like in an Italian playboy, it incites the sporting instinct. Repeated attempts will eventually meet with success.

State and federal authorities flatly rejected Michael Crete and Stuart Bewley's California Cooler countless times. The alcohol content was too high; the rules didn't permit wine to be sold in beer bottles, and on and on. Crete rejected the rejections and found ways around them.

An entrepreneur is told "no" so many times that it either breaks your spirit or makes you lose all respect for the word. The entrepreneurs who are able to stick it out are the ones for whom "no" loses all literal meaning, who strip the term of all finality. It's just another routine, uninformed opinion that you haven't rebutted successfully yet. Or a problem you just haven't thought of a solution for yet.

"When I'm in a tough situation," explains Netcom's Bill Tillson, "I only concentrate on what is wrong and how to correct it. I get absolute tunnel vision. I'm not the easiest person to talk to at that time because I'm only concentrating on a way out of that situation. The process of coming out of it does not include the possibility that you won't."

Persistence, then, is the power of positive thinking. You have to keep saying "yes" no matter how tough the going gets. Be stubborn. Plain old stubbornness can be a valuable entrepreneurial trait, keeping you at it when everyone and everything is telling you to do otherwise. A proud, intractable nature, along with "every book ever written on how not to worry," is what helped Faith Popcorn to stick it out. She was able to outlast five years of struggle to get her marketing consultancy business established. Today BrainReserve, Inc. is ranked among the top 40 women-owned businesses in the country (by *Savvy* magazine), and pulls in $23 million in annual sales. But, as her story shows, it would never have happened if she hadn't been able to persist long enough to find the key that opened the door to success.

Enduring Achievement
Faith Popcorn/BrainReserve, Inc.

As a creative director for a medium-sized New York ad agency, Faith Popcorn seemed to have it all; six-figure salary, the works in perks, and a prestigious title in a glamorous and highly competitive field. What she didn't have was creative satisfaction, personal fulfillment, or an ability to tolerate the arbitrary and cautious dictates of her superiors.

She grated at higher-ups whom she felt were doing half the work she was doing, with a fraction of the smarts. "I wanted people to think I was extraordinary, doing a great job," she says. "But I could never get that recognition in the company."

There was something else missing, too. Excellence. Everyone settled for the most expedient, most inoffensive advertising, instead of the most well thought-out, creative, long-term strategies. Advertisers should have been getting more than feel-good messages and incessant TV jingles that drummed home name identification. There needed to be more long-term strategic marketing advice and it wasn't happening.

"It really annoyed me," Popcorn recalls. "The ideas that were getting to the client were ones that were easy for them to buy, easy for them to run, but very little thought was ever given to the client's overall strategic problem. You need to figure out if you're going after the right market. Is it the right time? Is the age segment right? Is it meeting the trends? That's the kind of company I wanted to start, but, unfortunately, I was the first one to do it."

With an art director colleague and $20,000, Popcorn bolted from her high-paying agency job, and started Brain-Reserve, "a reserve of thinking for corporations to help them position and re-position products or develop new ones." Her company would conduct in-depth opinion surveys of customers and competitors, and do extensive market research so that corporate accounts could get a more vivid picture of where their products and markets were headed.

Corporate clients, though, didn't come running. Eight-figure campaigns did not materialize overnight in the hands of this twenty-eight-year-old woman working out of a Manhattan apartment. "I had never run a business before," she explains. "I had no financial backing. There was no real acceptance of this kind of category. We had to define the category."

She only got a couple of jobs the entire first year. "That year was mostly learning," says Popcorn. "I didn't even know there was such a thing as a correctable typewriter. I didn't know anything about office management, traffic control, or how to figure out if you're making money on something."

The second year was not much better. Because she was selling a new concept, a hybrid form of marketing consultancy that incorporated research elements, it was exasperatingly hard to break new ground in the established system. "We weren't wired into any network at all," Popcorn relates, "old boy or otherwise. We were creating our own network on a one-to-one basis with executives and it took forever to build it.

"There were times in the early years of the company when I got very, very tired and asked myself 'why am I doing this?' There were financial problems so extensive that I wondered if I would ever get through them."

Years three, four, and five dragged on with no real payoff in sight. But her fear of re-entering the job market again, and a proud, stubborn streak kept her soldiering on. "It was complete stubbornness," she agrees. "I just decided I would die or I would be successful, whichever came first. I was so burned out by the system that I just didn't want to re-enter at any cost."

She kept cold-calling new accounts, developing new leads, and trying to hone her concept into a more readily identifiable niche. Her perseverance led her to stumble upon an interesting discovery in her sixth year of operation. After years of doing opinion surveys, it occurred to Popcorn that consumers were giving her more than just "yes" or "no" answers about a new shampoo or camera. They would offer their opinions on values and attitudes that were important to them, such as the need for a product to have more integrity, or be more health-oriented.

Popcorn began to see this information as the basis of a trend-predictive capability that could be invaluable to corporate clients trying to forecast where the market is going. In interviews with business reporters, she began to predict where consumer trends were headed. She turned out to be right in 95 percent of the cases, and suddenly BrainReserve was a much sought-after product positioner.

Ironically, although she was in the business of positioning other people's products, it had taken her five years to clearly position her own. "The doctor self-administered," she laughs.

Polaroid, the Southland Corp., Anheuser-Busch, Pillsbury, Campbell's, Kobrand, and Quaker Oats were among the big accounts to come on board. BrainReserve's sales went over the million mark on an upward spiral that by 1986 was at $23 million.

Today, as she talks about expansion, adding a public relations wing and a promotion company to her holdings, the struggle of the early years is weighed against the rewards and to her, it's no contest. "It's unbelievably satisfying when you realize you've built something bigger than yourself, that will continue after you. You realize that you've contributed to a product's success and people's careers. I can't tell you how much I get back. Really, the price I ended up paying is a cheap price compared to what I've gotten back. When you're working for yourself, it gets to be ten o'clock at night before you even realize you're there."

Her advice to other entrepreneurs is, not surprisingly, persistence. "The more stubborn you are, the better your chances."

* * *

In the end, if the motivation and self-discipline are strong enough, and you maintain faith in your product, you will find a way to endure the hardships of living with risk. If being a bit player in someone else's game plan is distasteful enough; if being unable to get across your ideas is exasperating enough; if never making enough money to really get ahead of bill collectors is frustrating enough; if a lifetime of unfulfilling work is painful enough; your resolve will rise to the occasion to take on all comers.

9

The "F" Word

SPELLING OUT THE UNSPEAKABLE

Sometimes no matter how hard you try, how long you hold out, or how much you endure, you may have to face the fact that you've come up short. There aren't enough sales, profits, or positive trends to justify your efforts any longer.

It's the nightmare of every entrepreneur. Failure. All that effort, all that promise. Down the drain. The dream is dead and you might just as well be too. Devastating as the loss of a venture can be, it's not the end. It's just another step along the road to success—if you can rise above the setback and try again.

Failure is the last thing any of us expect in a culture bred for success. This is particularly true of our nation's most optimistic citizen, the entrepreneur. We expect to win at everything, from the Olympic stadium to the business arena. We don't give a moment's thought to anything other than the victory stand. We never hear about losers, only about winners. Triumph is trumpeted; failure mute. Victory has a hundred fathers; defeat is an orphan.

In an information age, there's only silence when it comes to the subject of failure. Unsuccessful people fade into the woodwork. They don't want to talk about it and expose shortcomings. (We wouldn't want to hear from them until they were successful anyway.) Everybody else is afraid to even mention the dreaded word.

"When that particular word arises in my head," says Discovery Toys' Lane Nemeth, "I just make it go away." For Society Expeditions' T. C. Swartz, it's "not in my vocabulary."

The silent treatment only makes matters worse, though,

should the unspeakable become undeniable. Because we don't know anything about failure, and can't even discuss it, we are at a complete loss to know how to deal with it. In the absence of discourse and knowledge, we exaggerate the consequences of non-success. We think we're the only person it's ever happened to, that we're a failure for life. We blow it all out of proportion.

The fact is, failure is not some curse of the gods or sign of eternal ineptness; it's just a normal part of the process of enterprise. It's how the market validates or invalidates ideas. It happens a lot. Five out of ten new businesses fail within their first five years, and eight out of ten fail before their tenth year, according to the U.S. Small Business Administration. The odds suggest that it will take an entrepreneur three tries to achieve a successful venture. Clearly, then, failure is an integral part of the system.

Whether it's a threat or an actuality, failure is a fact of life that must be reckoned with by every businessman or woman. You're never too far from a competitor muscling in and taking over your market, from a major blunder, from changing markets that may make your product obsolete.

Ignoring failure may work for the three out of ten entrepreneurs whose ventures are successful. But even among those, the fear of failing can cause such torment that the joys of success can never be appreciated. Gymboree's Joan Barnes believes that "making peace with the fear of failure" is one of the most critical elements in the entrepreneurial portfolio.

"I tried ignoring failure for a while, but that was a worse boogeyman, so I had to make peace with it by connecting with what it felt like to fail. Until I could really face it, I thought it would kill me. It would loom heavy over me. Now that I've pushed through and come out the other side, I feel I'm a more inspirational leader."

For the large numbers of entrepreneurs who do fail, though, the approach to failure can determine whether you throw in the towel and never make another peep, or whether you shake off the blues and come back fighting. Your odds of succeeding increase greatly the more you keep trying.

It's time to go beyond the superstitious avoidance and ostrich action, and confront the taboo head on. To start, we have to try to take failure out of its usual emotional context as a personal rejection, and view it objectively, as a natural consequence of risk-taking. Trying something new is a risky business; there's a chance it won't work. Attempting things, getting off your butt and taking action, and failing, go hand in hand. People who haven't had any setbacks, just haven't been trying.

Thomas Edison probably had more failures (including his bungled electric company and his ahead-of-its-time phonograph) than anyone who ever lived. But he also had more successes because he never stopped trying. Frank Carney, founder of Pizza Hut, has started sixty businesses and more than forty of them have failed. Take enough chances and you'll fail many times, but you'll also have successes that far outweigh the setbacks.

You have to accept failure as part of the package of a totally practical art like entrepreneurship. It just can't be proven ahead of time. Only by doing it can you know if a venture will work or not. Like anyone testing a theory, you have to expect that the results, subjected to the vagaries of unanticipated forces, will not always come out as predicted.

It's similar to the falsification process in science. We find out what works by discovering what doesn't. As in the scientific world, the failure of a business may disprove a theory, but at the same time reveal information that can be used to get closer to success the next time around.

USC's Richard Buskirk doesn't use the word "failure" at all to describe a business that doesn't pan out; it's too final. "I don't like that word," he says. "I call it 'process.' We get to success through this process, learning as we go along until we get all the pieces of the puzzle to fit right."

If you can see failure as part of a process of reaching your goal, instead of as a final result, then you can defuse one of the worst feelings of failure—that it was all for nothing. In the "process" of enterprise nothing is wasted. The knowledge and skills gained in one venture are applied to the next.

Henry Ford plowed the lessons of his first two auto failures into his legendary third venture, Ford Motor Company. Henry Heinz learned what not to do after his first company, which sold bottled sauerkraut and pickles, went bankrupt. He came back the next year with a more realistic approach to business and some new sauces, including a tomato blend that would become an American institution.

It took Rowland Macy seven tries to get his retail concept right. After a string of failed ventures from Boston to California, Macy turned his seventh stab, this one in lower Manhattan, into one of the biggest department stores in the nation. Aircraft entrepreneurs Juan Trippe and James McDonnell didn't give up when their first companies bombed out. They made the proper adjustments and followed up with Pan Am and McDonnell-Douglas, respectively. Even J. Paul Getty didn't make it his first time out. He had several oil ventures flop before he got on the winning track.

Failure has to be viewed in context particularly by first-time entrepreneurs. Whenever you do something for the first time, like riding a bike, you may fall off. Doing something new involves some acclimation, some flailing around for the right technique or knowledge. You just don't know everything that first time out. Your enthusiasm may run ahead of the realities. Your decisions may not be informed ones.

Look at some of the unsuccessful first ventures by entrepreneurs in this book. California Cooler's Michael Crete laughs today at his feeble attempt to sell macramé products. Celestial Seasonings' Mo Siegel began his entrepreneurial career with ideas that could never make him any money—an art store, followed by a health food store. Soloflex founder Jerry Wilson was never going to have enough customers for his rural air taxi service to take off. Jani-King's Jim Cavanaugh undersold his cleaning franchises, admitting he "just didn't know what things were worth."

How can we know how to do something perfectly if we've never done it before? Novelist Milan Kundera has observed, "Human life occurs only once, and the reason we cannot determine which of our decisions are good or bad is that in a given situation we can only make one decision; we are not granted a second, third or fourth life in which to compare the various decisions."

Businesses fail because we lack the necessary information to make the correct decision, or, as is the human wont, we just plain err. In short, we don't know what we're doing. We rush into the market without doing any homework. We don't plan. We don't keep proper books. We don't manage well. We lack the knowledge and experience needed to pull it off. According to Dun & Bradstreet, 54 percent of failures in 1983 were due to incompetence; 23 percent due to "unbalanced experience," the proprietor or partners being "not well-rounded" in all aspects of their business; and 9 percent was caused by lack of managerial experience. The vast majority of failures, then, could be corrected next time around with additional experience, the very instruction that might be gained from failure.

If we learn from it, failure primes us for success by pointing out pitfalls to avoid in the future. Failure is such a valuable teacher, in fact, that many venture capitalists regard it as a positive factor in an entrepreneur's bid for investment capital—if it can be reasonably explained. As venture capitalist George Crandall of Capital Venture Investors told the *Los Angeles Times,* "Failure tends to give people a more realistic view of the world than success."

COPING WITH THE NOT-SO-FINAL JUDGMENT

That failure is normal and teaches us valuable lessons may be all well and good, but when it happens, the philosophical view is eclipsed by other matters, like the knife twisting in your stom-

ach, the howitzers going off in your head, and the deep despair
and loneliness of feeling permanently exiled from the rest of the
happy and healthy human race. When the bottom drops out of
your life, and everything you've struggled for for years is gone,
it's hard not to take things personally.

When Hercules Computer's Kevin Jenkins' first venture, a
San Francisco magazine, failed after three years of 14-hour
days, "it was a devastating experience" for the gung-ho entrepreneur. "I had to admit it had been a business failure even
though I'd put my life and soul into it."

Massachusetts entrepreneur Jerry Goldstein has two successful ventures under his belt, including one, Clinical Assays,
that he sold for $20 million. But before success came failure.
He lost $50,000, and his way in life, when an earlier medical
venture came crashing down on him. "The financial setback was
severe," he recalls, "but the emotional setback was even more
severe. It took a long time to recover."

When your direction in life and self-image is that of independent entrepreneur, controlling your life, and suddenly you
have no control, and are relegated back to the dutiful corporate
role to pay bills, there's a sense of helplessness and futility that
you'll never be able to have any influence over your life. "You
think it's your last shot," says Goldstein.

This "final judgment" syndrome, the feeling that your misfortune is freeze-framed, like Pompeii, for eternity, is the biggest obstacle in dealing with failure. People think that it's an
indelible verdict on their abilities—proof for all time that they
just don't have what it takes. Or that another opportunity will
never come along. The feeling that the die is cast, that "I blew it
forever," robs the entrepreneur of his or her lifeblood—hope,
optimism, belief.

But it's not the end, the last idea you'll ever have. A good
entrepreneur never runs out of ideas. As soon as the anxiety and
stress subsides, and your mind can relax again, new ambitions
and dreams will come to the fore. There's life after failure.

"Failure is not final, and failing is not fatal," says Fran

Jabara of Wichita State University, "therefore the entrepreneur goes through it many times. It's one of the key points in entrepreneurship education. We say avoid failure, but if it happens, don't be destroyed by it."

Don't think in absolutes, that "it's over," "the end," "finished." Human beings, particularly entrepreneurs, are very resilient characters, constantly changing and adapting to new conditions. When a major setback occurs we can momentarily become prisoners of a particular time and place, limited by our imagination to see anything else. But as surely as time and place pass, so will the hurt and pain. Businesses may die but their founders live on to fight another day.

When you invest everything you've got—financial, physical, and emotional—in a venture, you and your project can become one and the same. If your business is rejected, you feel rejected. It's this intertwining of product and ego that must be avoided to get back on the road to recovery. You have to try to look at the situation realistically. What were the marketplace reasons your business didn't work out?

Once you start to assess the strategic and operational reasons why your business failed, you can see that the real cause of failure lies in the violation of business law, not in some diabolical fatal flaw. It all boils down to things like inadequate sales, heavy operating expenses, uncollectible receivables, poor location, and competitive weakness—hardly items significant enough to cause anyone to question their worth as a human being, or suffer loss of face for life.

"The main difference between those who are ultimately successful," says industrial psychologist Mark Held, "and those who give up, is how they deal with the failure experience. The successful ones can separate themselves out from the circumstances. They can say, 'Hey, I had a good idea, but, boy, I had the wrong timing, I was undercapitalized, and came at a bad time in the business cycle.' They don't take it quite so personally. The person who's going to fail says, 'I guess I'm just no good, I guess I'm not smart enough, I guess I don't have it.' And so they give up."

Author and psychologist Joan Harvey agrees. "People who succeed see a mistake as a mistake, something that can be repaired. You can go on from there. I've studied people who are so afraid of failure that they just never allow themselves to fail. They never learn the realities of failure. So they exaggerate in their minds what the consequences of failure might be. They feel like they would never work again, be bag ladies on the street."

Admitting failure is tough on entrepreneurs, who tend to be endowed with excessive amounts of pride and perseverance. But denial can only prolong the agony. Putting the blinders on to a rapidly deteriorating business can only succeed in digging a deeper hole. Worse still, the refusal to own up to an unsuccessful venture can paralyze you in a lingering state of anger and self-pity that block the only way out of the depression—a clean break, followed by new goals and new ventures.

There's a denial phase that entrepreneurs go through that can be much more destructive than admitting the end of a venture. Jenkins used to say that "I'm going to do this magazine if it kills me. I just won't give up. Finally, I began to physically suffer, and my wife said you've got to get out of this thing. With her help she managed to persuade me that it was better to get out of it, to admit failure and go on."

One of the hallmarks of successful entrepreneurs is that they're willing to admit when something's not going well. They cut their losses and get out of a bad situation before the damage is too catastrophic. This way they still have emotional and financial resources to start over, the quickest route to success.

"Coming to grips with failure and understanding it is very important," says New York entrepreneur Linda Enke, herself a victim of the flip side of success. "You have to understand that a failure isn't a total failure of you as a person. It isn't that everything in your life failed. But you did fail at something and you have to face it."

Enke had to confront a failed first business, plus a second one that almost fell apart. But she fought her way through the hurt, rage, and depression to establish a thriving business. The founder of Anne Rothschild & Co., a $10 million marketer of promotional apparel and retail giftware, Enke offers some battle-sharpened lessons on how to make it through the fire.

STARTING OVER
Linda Enke/Anne Rothschild & Co.

It never crossed Linda Enke's mind that she would not be successful. She had been on a fast track since she walked into a Mankato, Minnesota, department store looking for a cashier's job and was made the buyer for women's wear. By the age of twenty-two she was ensconced at Montgomery Ward headquarters in New York and in no time was the buyer for the chain's women's sportswear department.

There was talk that she might be Ward's first woman vice president. But she made a sudden about-face and chucked it all to follow her new husband and his job to Buffalo. "I'm not the type of woman who makes career changes because her husband has a job in another city," says Enke. "But I did it. Why, I don't know."

In Buffalo Enke wasn't able to find a job that challenged her like her big-time New York post, so she created her own. With $10,000 of her own money and a $10,000 SBA loan she started a sophisticated art/gift/plant store.

Within a year her store was very successful, and she was a respected lecturer around town on plant care. "It was another example of how I really couldn't do anything wrong," she says.

But just as suddenly, someone pulled the plug. The competition attacked with better facilities and prices and siphoned off all her business. Her first reaction was denial. "Entrepreneurs are all overly optimistic," she points out. "I ignored warning signs like a drop in sales, and escalating inventory. I wouldn't lay off my part-time person because that would be a sign of pulling back and the possibility of failure, which I refused to admit. There were steps I could have taken that I didn't because I kept hoping it would get better."

In the end, though, there was no getting around it. Enke had failed. Like a boxer sent to the canvas, she was stunned. She now had to try to figure out what hit her, to go through the replay and re-evaluation process that determines whether the entrepreneur fights another bout. And that's not easy when you're in a weakened state, broke, dejected, embarrassed, stripped of purpose. On top of all that, Enke's marriage, which had gotten her into the mess in the first place, had also failed.

The entrepreneur at this point, reeling from feelings of inadequacy, loss of face, and self-doubt, has to focus through the disorienting maze of bad news on the best path to restore shattered confidence and spirit. In Enke's case, she returned to a scene of past successes, her old job at Montgomery Ward, where she knew she wasn't a failure, but a capable, talented, respected person.

"I came back with the feeling of having really failed for the first time in my life," she recalls. "There was an element of 'I've had it with being an entrepreneur. I'll go back to where I was this kid on the fast track.' I was in a sense going back to the womb after having ventured out into the hard, cold world of owning your own business."

In time, after she'd regained her strength, she was able to look on her failure more objectively. "I was able to take credit for the fact that I failed. That doesn't mean I was no longer good to people, and I was no longer smart. But I did fail at a business, and those things happen. Initial businesses fail often because entrepreneurs don't want to take full responsibility for their failures. You tell yourself it's all going to work out. Well, it doesn't. If you can't take responsibility for that failure; if you really extend yourself on your payables; if you don't pay your taxes on time, you're kidding yourself and life isn't like that."

One surprising side effect of failure is that, if you don't let it destroy you, and once the wounds have healed, the experience only intensifies the appetite to go out on your own. You've learned that you can put your ideas into practice, that you can go into action, if only temporarily. The mysteries of business are do-able—with a few less mistakes and a few more breaks. After running her own show, Enke found it hard to tolerate corporate regimentation.

"I felt like a totally ineffectual person," she relates. "I had a lot of people putting restraints on me and there was this sense that I couldn't move any faster than the Montgomery Ward system. I found myself approaching thirty saying, 'I'll be lucky if I make merchandise manager by the time I'm forty-five.'"

She took a job in the sales promotion business, where she saw an opening for her next venture. She was selling corporate premiums, such as caps and jackets, that companies give out to sales forces or customers at reduced prices to stimulate sales, when she noticed that the area was completely devoid of style, fashion, and originality. All the giveaways were stock items, polo shirts or baseball caps to which people were just attaching corporate logos.

"I saw the possibility of doing much more sophisticated apparel promotions for consumer product companies," says Enke. "The idea of taking a cosmetic bottle and designing an original print around it, and then turning that into nightgowns and robes; nobody did that. The field was wide open."

Though she had no money to get her idea off the ground herself, she figured a good-sized order from a top manufacturer might be able to bankroll her. An order in the corporate promotion business can routinely average $500,000, and that kind of money can attract backers in a hurry, suppliers and vendors anxious to be cut in on the action.

When she had an opportunity to bid on a job for 50,000 jogging suits for Fabergé, she quickly lined up an established factory as a partner, and made her pitch. Her new company, Winslow and Rothschild, though it had yet to conduct a single day of business, won the job over four established companies. "I'm a very convincing salesperson," adds Enke.

The order turned into 100,000 jogging suits, a $1 million job, and Enke was definitely in business. She and her partner each put up $5,000 and the factory's credit took care of the rest of the financing. Operating as a one-woman company with a desk and a phone at her partner's office, Enke brought in an astounding $7 million worth of business her first year in 1982.

With the large premium companies not straying from stock sizes and styles, Enke filled the void with a range of colors, sizes, and original designs tailored to the given product. She was amazed that larger companies, out of sheer laziness to customize, would leave such ripe pickings all to her. "When Avon places a $1.5 million order for 80,000 nightgowns and 30,000 robes," she notes, "they're entitled to get anything they want."

All looked rosy. She made the front page of the *New York Times* business section. More and more blue-chip clients were coming her way. But then a partnership fight broke out that put all her work in jeopardy. Her partner sued her for $4.5 million, and all the money in her company, about $500,000, was handed over to a court-appointed trustee.

"All of a sudden I didn't have a company anymore," she says, recalling the dread of yet another failure looming in the distance, "and not because I did anything wrong either. They called me everything but a whore. My partner assumed he would break me, that the financial pressure of defending myself in a lawsuit would be too much. But I am a very strong-willed person. I felt very motivated by the fact that I was right and that I knew I was right."

She won a settlement, but it cost her $500,000 in legal fees to do it. She was in that awful place again, of having to start all over. But she'd done it before, and there was no way she was going to be defeated again. "The way I came out of my first failure was that it's inconceivable that I will fail. In my mind it's impossible and whatever I have to do to keep it from happening I'll do it."

She scrapped back and by 1986 had rebuilt her company to $10 million in sales, producing custom raincoats, leotards, lingerie, sweaters, and shirts for companies like Cheeseborough-Ponds, Revlon, and Johnson & Johnson. She had also expanded into retail giftware, opening up Anne Rothschild Collection stores in New York and Washington, selling high-end European gift items.

Today Enke has no doubt that the struggles and setbacks were worth it. "It's enormously satisfying to be building something. It's not power; it's a more subtle form of power. I have a sense that owning my own company allows me to be the very best that I can be, and I can't imagine a corporate situation that would give me that flexibility or creativity."

Her scrapes with failure have made success all the more sweet. They've also taught her that the best way to avoid failure is not to avoid it. "Temper your zealous enthusiasm with some cold, realistic looks," she advises. "Evaluate your worst-case scenario. You never allow that the worst can happen, but the worst can happen just as easily as the best."

THE ROAD TO RECOVERY

Getting over failure isn't something that happens overnight. Like any serious injury, the damaged psyche takes time to heal. It's going to require a patient, one-day-at-a-time approach to regain lost spirit and confidence. The road to revival is a gradual process of disengagement from the one-tracked obsession that has ruled your life for so long. You have to discard old dreams, old habits, perhaps even your old image of yourself. And you have to develop new interests, new directions, a new attitude.

Here are a few guidelines that can help develop the new perspective:

1. ADMIT IT. Look in the mirror and face the fact. You're not invincible; you're mortal. Welcome yourself to the human race. If it was a bad idea, admit it. If you bit off more than you could chew, own up to it. We all make mistakes. That's why we have erasers and correctable typewriters.

2. ACCEPT RESPONSIBILITY. Don't assign blame. Take re-

sponsibility. This way the anger and bitterness doesn't continue to hold you hostage to the past. Recognize your own mistakes and forget everybody else's. They don't matter anymore.

3. GIVE YOURSELF CREDIT. Don't wallow in your mistakes. Take some credit for all the obstacles you did overcome along the way, and for the daring challenge you mounted. You would think someone else who went through as much as you did, and took such a valiant risk had a lot of guts. Give yourself the same respect. You had a great idea, but maybe it just wasn't achievable given your resources and timing.

4. IGNORE BYSTANDERS. Don't make yourself a victim of loss of face. You didn't worry about the nay-sayers when you started your business. What they think of you now is just as meaningless, and irrelevant to the self-determined life of an entrepreneur.

5. AVOID PROPHECY. Don't crystal-ball yourself into a life of failure. Failure doesn't make you a fortune-teller. You have no idea what's going to happen down the road, so can the pronouncements of doom.

6. GET OUT OF YOUR HEAD. Don't withdraw into an interior isolation cell, ceaselessly replaying what's over and done with. Get connected to the world again. New faces, experiences, and interests can begin to put distance on the past.

7. TAKE IT EASY. Don't rush into another project before you've had time to recuperate. Take a little time off from the wars with an easy workaday job, weekend trips to the mountains, or a longer vacation, if you can afford it. The psychic toxins have to be cleansed from the system before you can start again at full strength.

8. GET PHYSICAL. The best way to improve mental health is by improving physical health. The stress of failure can leave

you physically drained and weakened. Poor physical health only adds to the feelings of fragility and helplessness. Start a vigorous, and daily, exercise regimen, and with newfound physical vigor will come new emotional strength.

9. TALK POSITIVE. To develop a positive frame of mind again, start using positive language. Drop conditional phrases like "if everything goes right, I'll do such-and-such," to "I'm going to do it"; from "if I have another idea" to "when I get my next idea"; from "hopefully" and "maybe" to "I will," "I'm going to." Speaking positively again helps psyche you up to act that way.

10. REPHRASE THE LOSS. You have to find another way of looking at it. No failed project is for nothing in the "process" of enterprise. If you think hard enough you can find valuable knowledge, contacts, methods, and personal insights about yourself or others that are worthwhile and reusable. You are a lot more prepared for the next battle.

The best way to get over failure is to learn what you can from the experience, and move on. Failure, because it doesn't encourage the repetition of routine behavior as success does, can be a valuable teacher. As Wichita State's Fran Jabara notes, "If you fail, you get smarter."

The experience makes you wiser, toughens your resolve, and makes you better able to handle challenges in the future. It can reveal who your true friends are, and make you reassess destructive habits. Jerry Goldstein, for instance, learned from his failure to correct his workaholic sixteen-hour workday and enjoy life. He learned how to take a vacation.

"The sooner you can convert it to a learning process, the better off you are," notes Berkeley psychologist Ellen Siegelman. "What can I extrapolate from this mess that I could use somewhere else? Change the emphasis from how you missed out or lost out to how it could be used to build something else."

One of the things you learn from failure is how to deal with it, which can be a significant asset in taking future risks. The knowledge that you can recover from failure allows you to look at risk more objectively. Getting the monkey of "the final judgment" off your back frees you to be more open toward risk and make crisis decisions based on the facts and not on emotional, exaggerated fears.

Most entrepreneurs think that if they contemplate the smallest hint of failure, they doom themselves to it. Yet being prepared for it doesn't invite disaster; instead, like a seat belt, preparation is only there if you need it. And if you do, having it around can prevent serious injury.

If you can anticipate the very worst that might happen with your venture and have a plan to meet it—getting another job, having another idea in reserve—you will have gone a long way toward defanging the most destructive effects of a failed business, which are psychological, not financial. Recognizing that life goes on, that your struggle is a series of skirmishes, a process, instead of one final conflict, gives you the upper hand over the failure whammy.

COMEBACK COUNTRY

It may come as a shock, but the most winning-obsessed culture in the world, home of the world's worst losers, is also the most tolerant of failure. We hate losing so much we refuse to dwell on it for very long. We're an optimistic society whose attention is focused straight ahead on eventual triumph. A dynamic culture full of dramatic turnarounds doesn't linger long on bad news.

Failure in the U.S. isn't nearly as devastating as it is in other places around the world. "The U.S. is probably the only place in the world," says Baylor University's Don Sexton, "where you can experience a failure and not suffer all kinds of social indignation, and get chastised for it for the rest of your life. You fail; you pick yourself up; and start all over again."

A bankruptcy in Japan can disgrace an entrepreneur and his entire family for life, giving him a lifelong black mark, and shaming him into never trying again. The Europeans, too, take a dim view of those who step out of line. In an insular, tightly structured society, there's nowhere to hide for those who make a spectacle of themselves pursuing nontraditional paths.

"The social impact can be disastrous," says Dieter von Graffenried, a Swiss entrepreneur who publishes an art magazine, *Parkett*. "A society with a clear code of social standing judges failure very harshly. In fact, very often you find people who have a failure in Europe leave for America because it's the only way to start over."

From the beginning America has been comeback country, home to failures from around the world. Failure has never been considered a permanent position in the U.S. You can be down one minute, up the next. People who try hard but miss aren't written off and ostracized as they might be elsewhere around the world. You can still get another good, responsible job. You can still get another loan. (Studies have shown debtors find it no harder to get credit after a bankruptcy.) And, importantly, there's always another chance in the opportunity society.

The anonymity of rugged individualism is such that we can work through our more unfortunate moments on our own without the paralyzing social stigma of hierarchical societies. Mobile, rootless Americans are used to fending on their own without support systems like extended families, "home" localities or tradition. In a classless society we make our own expectations, so we're free to fail on our own as well as succeed.

Tolerance of failure plays a major role on the financial, as well as social, side of American enterprise. Very effective bankruptcy law shields entrepreneurs from irrecoverable ruin. If you form a corporation and your business fails, the corporation has the liability, not you. The aim is to help get reeling people and companies back on their feet and productive again. If you can't pay your debts, you'll never get back into the credit stream and become a contributor to the economy. By keeping risk-takers from being destroyed bankruptcy helps perpetuate risk-taking. It recycles the enterprising to try again.

It wasn't always so easy. Failure used to be a very incapacitating affair. Debtors became slaves and could be killed or sold in Roman times. After the American Revolution there were more people in prison for being in debt than for any other reason. In one such debtor's prison, an abandoned copper mine in Granly, Connecticut, bankrupted individuals spent their days chained by the neck to roof beams, and had their feet fastened to iron bars. Robert Morris, founder of one of America's first banks, and one of the richest men of the Revolutionary era, wound up behind bars when some of his land and financial deals collapsed. Even visits from his good friend George Washington were not enough to spring him. He served three years.

Today bankruptcy has become a routine part of business life, further eroding the stigma of failure. High-profile bankruptcies like Continental Airlines, Wickes, Toys 'R' Us, Osborne Computer, Gavilan, and all the Silicon Valley busts are bringing failure out of the closet for a more objective appraisal.

"Bankruptcy is part of the business philosophy today," says Ron Michaelman, a Los Angeles bankruptcy attorney. "When you start a business today, you anticipate eventual problems. It's that analytical chess play that when you go into a situation, you string it all the way out to the end. The end in business is bankruptcy."

Once again, we're back to thinking the unthinkable, to planning for contingencies. Setting yourself up to avoid failure doesn't invite it; it's just good business sense. Insulate your liability by forming a corporation. That way, if something should go wrong, you can get out of it alive.

Dusting yourself off, shaking off the bruises and bouncing back has always been the approach to failure in a land where fortunes are never fixed. No matter how desperate, even ridiculous, your straits may be, even the most hopeless situations can be turned around with the right idea, execution, or effort.

Tom Monaghan, a bankrupt pizza retailer staring down the

barrel of 150 lawsuits, had no apparent prayer of pulling out of his nose dive. Yet by living a pauper's existence, working eighteen-hour days, and applying a lot of resourcefulness he was able to come back and make Domino's Pizza the largest privately held pizza chain in the world, a near-$1 *billion* company.

Even by Lazarus-style American standards, though, Dal La Magna seemed to be a hopeless case. He had a string of failures spanning seven different businesses and a dozen years. Yet demonstrating a talent for reincarnation that could surpass some Hindu deities, La Magna outlasted it all to strike paydirt with, of all things, eyebrow tweezers. La Magna's epic journey through nonstop rejection and misfortune to boss of Tweezerman provides ample lessons in how to avoid failure, learn from it, live with it, and overcome it.

Into Each Life Some Rain Must Fall
Dal La Magna/Tweezerman

It started off promisingly enough. Dal La Magna had been accepted at that gateway to fame and fortune—the Harvard Business School. But before the energetic New Yorker had even gotten to his first class things began to turn sour. He blew his first student-loan check, $3,500, playing the stock market. As he tried to recoup that loss, he began to pile one disaster on top of the next until by the time he graduated from school he was $100,000 in the red.

There was the ill-fated drive-in disco. La Magna thought he could convert drive-in movie theatres into drive-in dance joints. He forgot two things, though. One, it was 1969 and the Woodstock generation wasn't big on dancing, and what frugging it did do was confined to live rock concerts. Two, the weather.

"The kids were supposed to get out of their cars and dance under the screen," La Magna explains. "The first 11 times it rained. I booked the show north in New Hampshire and down in Rhode Island, thinking that if I spread it out far enough it couldn't rain in both places at the same time. Well, it did."

He lost $30,000. He decided next time he would do something indoors. So he opened a psychedelic light store on Harvard Square. He started manufacturing a light box that plugged into stereos and flashed lights to the beat of the music. But his invention "broke when I shipped it, so the stores sent them all back."

La Magna's next maneuver was to turn his light store into a waterbed store. It just barely kept him afloat.

So by graduation day he was $100,000 in the hole. It was an amount no corporate job was going to make much of a dent in. "Gillette wanted to hire me, Columbia Records," he notes. "But on $25,000 or $30,000 the most I'd be able to save a year would be $5,000. I felt I had no choice but to continue on as an entrepreneur and go for the score."

For the next 11 years La Magna searched in vain for the idea that could put an end to his jinxed existence. Since his goal in life (besides getting out of debt) was to be in the movie business, his efforts included several film projects. He decided to leave the scene of his setbacks on the East Coast, and go to Hollywood to become a movie producer. But stardom was nowhere in sight. He wound up living on $7 a week, and at no fixed address. "I would go from friend to friend and when my welcome wore thin I moved on."

You would think that someone so battered by defeat and devoid of resources couldn't even think about another project, let alone be taken seriously if he did. Yet there was one thing La Magna wasn't low on, and that was ideas. As bad off as he was, he still had the entrepreneur's imaginative faculty of quantum leap. He could still envision the right idea getting him out of his mess.

The La Magna Lasagna Pan had to be it. For Italian food lovers, a baking pan perfectly sized for lasagna would, he figured, be a ticket to the pasta firmament. He had learned from his light box fiasco not to make a product he couldn't sell, so he decided to sell a product first, then produce it. "I convinced manufacturers of lasagna noodles to put my coupon on the side of their box. I tied up six million boxes of lasagna that would carry my coupon every year, and I was all set to go with it. When I went out to get the pan, which I assumed was just a stock item, I couldn't find that pan anywhere in the world. The best I could do was $25,000 for tooling for a company to make a minimum run of 5,000 pans. I needed $50,000 to start the project."

Needless to say, La Magna's Lasagna Pan Inc. didn't have a spare $50,000. Once more La Magna took one on the chin, and this time he was really sent reeling. "It had gotten to the point," he admits, "where I really thought there was something wrong with me. You start to hate yourself, and you think you're a failure, and you think whatever you're going to do will fail. I was pretty frustrated and callous towards getting ideas and making them happen."

He went back to Boston, where he got a job as an accountant at an electronics firm. He lived at his mother's house and rode his sister's bicycle to work. He was thirty-two years old. At his ten-year reunion at Harvard he lowered his class's average income by $80 a person. His average earnings for the first ten years out of school were $1,400 a year.

Yet a compulsive entrepreneur like La Magna has a hard time turning off the spigot once it's been turned on. At the electronics company he noticed something that gave life to an inspiration he had dismissed for lack of spirit or means in his bummed-out, post-lasagna-pan days. While sunning in the buff on a Venice, California, rooftop he'd gotten a backside full of slivers. As he tried to extract them with a standard blunt-end tweezer in one hand and a needle in the other, he found the available tools left a lot to be desired. What the world needed was "a tweezer that was a needle to take splinters out."

La Magna spied that very tool on the assembly line at his job. Workers were handling capacitors and diodes with a tweezer device that had opportunity written all over it. The

Splinter Remover was born. With $500 and two credit cards, he was off and selling.

Lumber yards and hardware stores weren't as excited about the Splinter Remover, though, as La Magna. The general verdict was "nobody comes in here looking for those things." While La Magna looked for a wall to bang his head against, a woman friend suggested that if he could get her an eyebrow tweezer that was as precise, but not so pointy, as the splinter remover, that she might be able to sell some in her beauty salon.

From the same supplier who sold him the splinter remover, he got a model perfect for eyebrow tweezing, and started in 1979 for the umpteenth time to promote an idea from scratch. Despite the fact that the splinter remover had just gone down the tubes, despite all his past setbacks, despite his chronic lack of means and clout, he was still able to muster the confidence and enthusiasm to sell a new product. He knew that it didn't matter to accounts or customers where he'd been, or how destitute he was. All that mattered was the product. The right opportunity gives the entrepreneur all the optimism and the credentials needed to push ahead.

Slowly but surely the hi-tech tweezer began to raise eyebrows at the beauty shops he called on. Its fine-point precision was clearly preferable to the cheap, clumsy, blunt-end variety that dominated the market. La Magna couldn't believe his eyes. His company, Tweezerman, was actually going somewhere. For two years he steadily built his eyebrow tweezer into a steady sales producer. Then he started adding other products, a line of nail clippers, hair scissors, callus removers, and a direct-mail catalog that sold his products.

By 1986 La Magna had sales of $2 million and new ventures around every corner. He had become a partner in the Italian factory that makes his tweezers. He was trading hundreds of thousands of dollars in foreign currency, and cooking up movie projects. He was well underway on his lifelong ambition, to produce a movie.

"The thing that makes me laugh," says the budding movie mogul, "is that people aren't investing in the movie because they think it's a great project. They're investing in it because I'm telling them to and they think I'm a successful guy and everything I do works."

"I can't tell you how powerful I've become in the sense that I'm able to carry out my ideas now that I have a base. I sit here and watch my ideas happen instantly. When you're trying to make something go, you've got to do it all yourself; it takes forever to do everything; and you get bad luck. If you just get a toehold somewhere and you don't give up, you're in. And once you're in, it just progresses geometrically."

La Magna's advice on overcoming failure is to learn from it. "The only thing that got me through it was just my compulsion to move on, to keep trying and not make the same mistakes twice. I'm now selling an eyebrow tweezer that I can fit five hundred of into the space of one light box. The disco drive-in was such an outrageous idea it was impossible to make it happen."

His biggest mistake, and one he thinks many entrepreneurs could learn from, was that he would always blast off into a project without doing any homework. "I wouldn't make sure the idea was totally sound before I'd run off and do it. It's gotten to the point where unless I can sell my friends, I won't do something. With my tweezer I was able to sell anybody."

Surviving the hazards of an entrepreneurial career, La Magna has learned the hard way, requires "focus, persistence, and frugality." It also takes an ability to "live with debt. To be an entrepreneur you have to be able to go into debt. You get some people who just won't do that. They'll never get very far."

10

What's Luck Got to Do with It?

THERE BUT FOR FORTUNE

If it wasn't for a last-minute bail-out from an angel, Michael Crete and Stewart Bewley wouldn't have survived their first few months in business, or become millionaires marketing California Cooler. Except for a phone call out of the blue, Discovery Toys' Lane Nemeth wouldn't have made it, either. She was out of cash and about to go out of business when a venture capitalist she'd never met called to offer her the funds she needed.

Norm Pattiz was a small-time radio syndicator, struggling to make ends meet, when the FCC decided to deregulate the nation's airwaves. With airtime freed up for new programming, Pattiz was deluged by stations suddenly in need of his product. In the right place at the right time, Pattiz was able to parlay the bonanza into a $50-million business.

As these fortuitous events illustrate, there's another element to the success equation. You need a little luck, too. You need some breaks. You can have the best idea in the world, but unless you get some people to take a chance on it; unless your timing is right; and unless you can avoid or minimize bad luck (big accounts that go bankrupt, product liability suits, natural disasters, etc.), you may not get your product out of the starting gate.

When you're playing long odds, as the entrepreneur does daily, it helps to be lucky. Because entrepreneurship involves the taking of continual risks and chances, it exposes you to more brushes with fortune—both good and bad—than the average person. Luck also plays a more conspicuous role when you're starting with nothing. The need for a first break—an order, an investment, a mentor who can provide key knowledge to get you rolling—is greater for those lacking connections, money, and other resources.

USC's Richard Buskirk believes luck plays a distinct role in the success of a venture. "Some entrepreneurs do nothing wrong, really. They're smart people; they've got good products, but they just don't get any breaks."

There's no denying the influence of luck in a field that begins as a hunch, and lives at the whim of so many outside forces. There's certainly no other word but "lucky" to describe the first person on the market with a new product. Getting out there first is an almost miraculous accomplishment in a nation where umpteen millions probe the market daily for opportunity.

And who can deny the imprint of fate on the wild card of entrepreneurship—the unforeseen, the unexpected, the uninvited? You have to be lucky to survive the onslaught of Mr. Murphy and his Law. You must be fortunate enough to not be buried by some of the more creative consequences of risk, like the unheard of bad weather that wiped out Mo Siegel's peppermint crop (and Celestial Seasonings almost along with it) or wars, such as the one that cost T. C. Swartz hundreds of thousands of dollars in bookings to Afghanistan when the Russians invaded and created too much adventure for Society Expeditions.

There are so many close calls and down-to-the-wire incidents in getting a start-from-scratch company off the ground and threading it through the obstacle course that no successful entrepreneur can deny the importance of having the fates on your side from time to time. The feeling that "there but for fortune go I" is one entrepreneurs can readily relate to.

Artesia Waters' Rick Scoville believes "there's somebody out there with an invisible fishing rod and reel, with a hook on it, reeling me in. Because I don't think I'm any better than you or anybody else. I was in the right place at the right time and seized the opportunity."

Lane Nemeth, saved by the bell countless times, says, "I've looked at luck a lot. I think people are surrounded by an aura of magic of sorts that anyone can grab onto. We're all surrounded by little cushions of something nice. If you take it, and say, 'I'm going to put every bit of energy and drive and excitement into it,' then I believe good things happen to you."

MAKING LUCK LUCKY

It's an age-old debate. Is talent or luck the better part of good fortune? In a broad sense, we're all products of circumstance, of who we happen to be born to, where we happen to grow up, the people we happen to bump into along the way. We're steered toward careers by a friend, a teacher, an item in a newspaper. Do successful people just stumble on a better mix of happenstance? Or do they just select more skillfully from the random events that drift their way?

Philosophers and poets have tried to pin that one down since the beginning of time. "Character is destiny," proclaimed the Greek sage Heraclitus. The Roman, Appius, postulated that "every man is architect of his own fate." Other more contemplative types through the years have found Fate a tougher customer. The Japanese writer Saikaku, for instance, noted that "to make a fortune some assistance from fate is essential. Ability alone is insufficient."

While we don't expect to resolve the issue in these pages, there is evidence that in at least one small corner of human existence self-determinists have the upper hand. Much of what passes for luck in the entrepreneurial arena is the result of actions and attitudes that create the conditions for good fortune to strike. You can make your own luck.

As T. C. Swartz says, "People make their own opportunities. Luck is nothing more than making good choices, and following your intuition."

Air-Vend's Dave Bobert recognizes that he got some breaks, but he also knows the effort it took to get them. "With a little bad luck, we wouldn't be having this conversation," he admits. "There were some crucial crossroad points where if money hadn't come in a couple of weeks, the company might not have survived. But I'm also a firm believer that you make your luck. We've had a lot of people tell us that our timing was just perfect. They don't know all the rejection that took place in the beginning, that the market really wasn't ready for tire inflators. We forced the market to accept an idea it wasn't really ready to accept."

It was a masterstroke for Rod Canion, Jim Harris, and Bill Murto to hook up with venture capitalist Ben Rosen. He not only provided a capital windfall, but it was his connections that opened doors in the press, and with strategic accounts, like Sears, that enabled Compaq Computer to break out into the open.

At the same time it took proper follow-through for this lucky encounter to produce any luck. "It wasn't really luck," explains Jim Harris, "that we engineered a product as good as we did. It wasn't luck that we put together a manufacturing facility that could ramp as fast as it did. It wasn't luck that we put good control measures in our accounting systems, so we could grow. It wasn't luck that we decided to hire the best possible managers. Those were all conscious decisions we made."

If we look closely at the critical junctures, breaks, and turning points of the entrepreneurs in this book, we can see definite patterns that suggest that lucky accidents become that way more as a result of initiative than rabbits' feet or good karma. When Michael Crete and Stuart Bewley talked a wealthy commodities trader into funding California Cooler just as their money ran out in the first month of the venture; it may have been a wondrous eleventh-hour stroke, but it came after they had tried some 200 other potential investors. They forced the laws of probability to work for them.

Some might say Philip Hwang was just in the right place at the right time when Atari handed him the $150,000 order that got Televideo going. He was—but only after three trips to

Korea and thousands of dollars had put him there. It was his extraordinary commitment to make a quality TV monitor, his personal zeal, not the luck of the draw, that led Atari to reverse several decisions against him and take a chance on a jet-lagged Korean immigrant with a dream of running his own business.

To get luck you have to put yourself in a position to receive it. Positioning yourself for potential opportunity and advantageous situations is the whole basis of the entrepreneurial approach. It's the key to our search for the link between talent, luck, destiny, self-determination, and the stunning transformation of ordinary wage earners into epic success stories.

Let's take a look now, then, at how our entrepreneurs positioned themselves to take control of the seemingly uncontrollable forces of fate. We'll explore the two main categories of entrepreneurial "luck," the corralling of the lucky concept, and the first break (or two) that got the entrepreneur out of the starting blocks and on the way.

SPREADING THE NET

You have to be, as James Michener says, "eligible for luck" to get it. It doesn't just happen. You need the knowledge to know where to look, the alertness to recognize it, and the willingness to act on it. We touched on some of this in Chapter 3 when we discussed the idea process. We're now going to probe a bit deeper into the constituent parts of what most people consider the "luckiest" aspect of entrepreneurship, hitting on the right idea.

Ben Rosen, whose firm Sevin-Rosen Partners helped start Lotus and Compaq Computer, calls coming across winning ideas the art of "studied serendipity. If you build the web wide enough you will eventually trap a good idea," he told *Fortune*. He constantly monitors some 2,700 contacts and thousands of proposals looking for lucky formulas.

To increase your luck potential you need to expose yourself to as many people and areas as possible. Talk to everyone. Be gregarious. It was the urgings of friends that caused Mo Siegel to start selling his tea, Michael Crete his wine cooler, and John Todd his hotel amenities. It was his insatiable conversational habit that caused Jani-King's Jim Cavanaugh to uncover a cleaning business while small-talking with the night janitor.

An archeologist T. C. Swartz met on a trip to Easter Island tipped Swartz off to the notion that started Society Expeditions. "Why don't you put together some trips for people to come to Easter Island to study the monuments, and I'll lecture to them about the history and archeology," suggested the Chilean tipster.

In his fascinating book, *The Luck Factor,* Max Gunther calls this networking process "the spiderweb structure." He believes that "the bigger your web of friendly contacts, the better the odds in your favor" of acquiring luck. Even though you don't know in advance which people are going to bring a break your way, a web with many lines increases the statistical chances that something good may happen.

A key aspect in spreading the web is breaking from routine and exposing yourself to new environments. When Bill Murto, Rod Canion, and Jim Harris journeyed from Texas Instruments to California to check out suppliers for TI products, they had placed themselves in the vicinity of new ideas and potential luck. Mingling with scores of entrepreneurs marketing fresh new concepts and having fun was the beginning of the end of the corporate road, sparking a search for an independent route that would lead to the Compaq portable computer.

Pursuing interests or hobbies is another way to increase your chances. Getting deeply involved in an activity allows you to explore an area thoroughly, leading to interactions with like-minded enthusiasts and an exposure to the intricacies of a subject that might toss up an opportunity. Plus, if you like your pastime enough, you have the motivation to try to find a way to do it full-time.

Lifeguard Ron Rice's desire to incorporate the beach life-style into his work triggered in his subconscious the possibilities of coconut tanning oil, observed on the beaches of Hawaii. Likewise, Jim Jenks's love of surfing positioned him with the inside knowledge—the instinct—that something was missing from surf culture: namely, authentic surf clothes.

Whenever you feel passionate enough about something to spend a lot of your time at it, you acquire an intuitive feel for it that can be instrumental in the unearthing of opportunity. Intense familiarity with a subject, whether friend, lover, or a hobby, develops intuitions and hunches that tip us off to things before other people know it.

Intuitions are the stuff that entrepreneurial "luck"—often called "timing"—is made of. You are in the right place at the right time because you've spotted a convergence of factors that hasn't yet become apparent to the rest of the world.

The enthusiast/hobbyist's tip to opportunity often comes from an urge to enhance the appreciation of a pursuit, to do it the way they know to be "right." Whether it's two computer nuts who feel everyone should have their own personal computer (the genesis of Apple Computer), or, like Jenks, the surfer who knows his tribe isn't being dressed right, the moment of destiny stems from a nagging urge to perfect a private passion.

When a favorite interest is misrepresented or limited, it could be the start of something big. Because there are no doubt lots of other people who feel the same way you do. Your intuition may start as nothing more than a desire to improve the avocational experience for yourself or a small circle of acquaintances. But if the commitment to make things better is strong enough and the improvement needed enough, it can develop into a bona fide entrepreneurial opportunity.

It was this "crusader" instinct, the need to get the true gospel out there, that placed Judi Sheppard Missett at the vortex of opportunity. A hunch that her consuming interest—dance—wasn't being presented right turned her into a best-selling author, a gold record-selling artist, and chairman of a $42 million health and fitness company, Jazzercise. Hers is a classic study in how good fortune presents itself, of the signals, suggestions, and suspicions that combine to create opportunity, and of the instincts and initiative that seize it.

MOVING TO THE CUES
Judi Sheppard Missett/Jazzercise

Judi Sheppard Missett always thought she'd make a living in the dance world. From the age of three, when she took her first dance class, she had her sights set on only one objective: to keep on dancing. She was working in theatrical productions by fourteen, and in college studied dance at Northwestern University.

Dance for this one-tracked woman was more than just artistic expression, or the applause of an audience. It was her life source, where she got her vitality, her energy, her good health. She lived for physical movement. Her philosophy: "When you move, your whole life moves."

Like all aspiring dancers, she dreamed of performing on the world's top stages. She could have been "a Broadway gypsy" her whole life, she says, traveling from one audition to the next, except for a trait that was to radically alter this seeming destiny. She had an independent streak as feisty as Patrick Henry's.

"I don't like being condescended to very much," admits Missett, a lithe, buoyant woman with close-cropped blonde hair. "That's what the theatre world is like. I did well in it, but I just don't like going into that audition. 'Yes, my dear, and what can you give us today.' I just hated that."

Disenchantment with cattle calls led her to take a more active interest in her "day" job as a dance instructor, which she sandwiched between theatrical assignments. She was teaching at the Gus Giordano Jazz Dance Center in Evanston, Illinois, when she began to notice something curious about her classes. Not all her students were staying. It was an observation that could have easily been dismissed. After all, not everyone's cut out to be a dancer, or can keep up the discipline. But Missett didn't file the thought, she did something about it.

"They'd come and take a few classes and then were gone," she recalls. "I thought, 'Judi, you have to reach out to these people because you want them to get that wonderful feeling you get through self-expression, through dance.' I thought that the reasons they were not staying were (1) dance is too disciplined, too structured, too rigid and (2) it's too negative. People are coming in the door, I thought, and they're being told 'Your toe isn't pointed right, your head is inclined wrong, your arm's in the wrong position.'

"I asked the owner of the studio if I could try something different. He said, 'You bet.' I turned people away from the mirrors. I based what I did on dance technique, but I made it real simple and easy to follow and lots of fun. I put in lots of positive motivation, like when they looked good, I'd tell them they were fantastic. It was successful right away."

Fate had sent a small signal of potential luck. Unlike other dance teachers across the country who no doubt saw the same thing in their classes, Missett took the cue. Her passion for dance wouldn't allow her to let other people miss out on its wonders. She had no profit motive behind her response. Simply, the crusader's instinct had been stirred.

"It was not even in my mind that it would become a business," says Missett. "In fact, my mother was an accountant and she used to say, 'Judi, you're never going to be any good if you go into the field of business, because you don't have a head for figures.'"

As often happens, a change of scenery provided the next link in the chain of opportunity. Two years later, she and her husband, a reporter for a Chicago TV station, moved with their four-year-old daughter to San Diego. Missett did some TV work in L.A. ("The Tom Jones Show," among others) but finally decided she'd had it with show business and casting directors. She'd run her own life, go at teaching full time. She loved watching her students grow. Plus, she could still get her performance kicks dancing for her classes.

Missett started up her hybrid dance/fitness sessions again,

running them out of local YMCAs and schools around San Diego. It didn't cost her anything to get started. All she needed was a few pairs of leotards and a stereo. Student fees easily covered the nominal rental fee on rec rooms and school gyms.

Jazzercise, as she began calling it in 1974, had no trouble finding students. The move to southern California had placed her in the health and fitness capital of the world. Word traveled quickly about Missett's fun mixture of calisthenics and jazz dance movements. There was nothing like it around. The options until then had been joining a health club and staying motivated on your own, trying to keep up in a difficult dance class, or bouncing between one-shot weight-loss clinics that never kept the weight off for long.

Her twist of adding easy workouts, dance-style moves, lots of positive encouragement, and a musical beat to it all created a whole new niche in the market, one that didn't exclude anyone. The women ranged from socialites to housewives to career women, even the occasional hoofer. They were undergoing major conversions at the hands of their charismatic leader.

"They start to feel more confident," says Missett. "They come up and say, 'Since I've been a part of this class I'm feeling better; I'm looking better. I feel so much more motivated. I'm going to finish my college degree.' Husbands write and say, 'My wife is totally different. It saved our marriage. Now she's an exciting woman again.'"

Within a few years by 1977 the crusading dancer was teaching twenty classes a week around San Diego. Customers wanted her to start classes in other parts of town, but the boundlessly energetic Missett had reached her limit. By Fridays she was talking in a whisper. She had developed nodules on her vocal cords. A friend suggested she train other instructors and expand.

It was another signal, offering possibilities but also pitfalls. Should she stay small or grow? Like many entrepreneurs before her, she faced the dilemma of giving up some control of her baby for the first time. At first she resisted, thinking it was "my own special personality and the way I was that made it work. I didn't think it would be successful at all if I trained someone else." In the end, though, she listened to the crusading voice that told her dance-fitness must be available to more people.

She trained five other instructors in the Jazzercise technique. It worked as well for them as it had for Missett. "Pretty soon we needed more instructors and people came to me and said, 'Can I train? Do you think I'd be a good teacher?' That's the way it developed."

One of her students provided the next fortuitous suggestion. Ever the good listener, Missett picked up on it. The student asked her if she'd like to do a book on her program. Missett's wide net of contacts through her classes had snared a big one. *Jazzercise—A Fun Way to Fitness,* co-authored by Missett and Dona Meilach, went on to sell over 500,000 copies.

It was how Missett worked that break, though, that made it one. She didn't leave it to chance that her story would get out there. She promoted it hard. When a San Diego TV feature neglected to point out Jazzercise was a San Diego company, she complained to the producer. She got a bigger segment the next week "because I had the guts to call her up and tell her how to produce her own show." Making breaks, she believes, "is not being afraid to do that kind of thing."

"Don't believe that everyone knows more than you. Everybody's insecure. Johnny Carson's insecure. Don't worry that you feel insecure, because so do they. Just go in there and say to yourself, 'I know more about my subject than anybody else does, so I want to make sure that whoever I'm talking to understands this."

Missett understood that success, and breaks, come from visibility. So like many entrepreneurs with limited budgets she worked the promotion circuit hard. "I would do almost anything for free," she laughs. "Anyone who asked me to do any kind of demonstration, who asked me to speak in front of a women's club, I always said 'Yes.' It was another project that promoted what I was doing."

When Jazzercise outlets opened around the country, press releases were sent out to the local newspapers. "Instead of doing expensive ads, I wanted an article. Because there's much more credibility in that." The coverage brought in customers, and then after the class was built up, Missett would go back to the same media and hit them up for follow-up stories—"These are your readers and they'd like to see a story about themselves."

With all the media exposure, more good things came her way. There was a gold-selling record album, *Jazzercise,* which she promoted herself. "The record company didn't do anything," she says proudly. "We did it and that's why it went gold." A best-selling videotape followed. There was a regular spot on "PM Magazine."

As a result, requests for franchises came in from around the country. The lowest franchise fee in the business ($500) and almost nonexistent overhead spread the Jazzercise concept quickly. It's the ultimate service business. No inventory, no buildings. All you need is a hall to rent, a tape player, and a little promotion. Missett supplies training, new choreography every eight weeks via videotape, and national advertising.

By the early eighties fitness had become the rage. A whole new industry, a sport, even, had grown up around Missett's concept. "Aerobics" it was called, and Missett had center stage. She was definitely in the right place at the right time, but it took ten years for the timing to catch up to her.

"Which came first," she muses, "Jazzercise or the fitness craze? I'd been doing this for a long time and I think our exposure and growth helped increase the interest out there in fitness. At the same time, because that was apparent other people entered the market, like Jane Fonda. So it just continued to elevate the awareness of the public. We helped inspire that awareness."

By 1986 Jazzercise was a $25 million business with 3,000 franchises in the U.S. and fifteen foreign countries. There was a Jazzercise mail-order catalog selling dance-fitness apparel, and a

Jazzercise shoe on the market. Missett had a syndicated newspaper column and was continuing to promote the gospel of fitness tirelessly every chance she got.

On the set of a cable TV show she had just taped, she reflected on her success. "To some it means power, some it means money. To me it means accomplishing things, being productive. The more I accomplish, the more productive I feel, the more excited I feel.

"I never got into this to make money. My motivation was that I enjoyed what I was doing. I just wanted to pass on the excitement and joy of dancing. I truly believe that's why it has been good financially."

What does luck have to do with it? "It's being in the right place at the right time, that's true. But how did you get there in the first place? Because you worked and figured out that I better be here on a certain day, because if I am, I'm going to be in the right place at the right time.

"It's just tuning in, listening to those messages and cues that are out there, saying, 'Hey, I better do this.' Trust your instincts, that's all."

FORTUNE FAVORS THE OPEN-MINDED

The thing that causes more opportunity to be squandered than anything else is not being ready for it. We get so preoccupied by routine that we can't see the openings around us. A force field of habitual behavior keeps unfamiliar, potentially lucky data from entering our consciousness. You may have gone to school to become a teacher, so you have to stay one your whole life. You doggedly pursue your fixed course, oblivious to non-teaching career signals.

Routine can lull you into a sleepwalking state, oblivious to all outside the humdrum, and confine you to a reactive, exclusionary mode, keeping out all unfamiliar information. The same goes for a rigid, doctrinaire personality. If you always know best, and can't accept any hints or suggestions you haven't thought of, you wall off the people and ideas that can lead to new choices.

It's called a rut. If you're in one, and don't want to be, you have to start taking steps to increase your acceptance of change. You have to be open to new information, to allow for the possibility of doing other things with your life, before any new leads can even register in your brain. You have to have the welcome mat out for new ideas before any will call for a visit.

A major factor in your readiness for good fortune is your level of contentment, specifically, how satisfied you are with your job and the accoutrements it brings. If you've got a good salary, and nice perks, even if you hate your job, the comfort zone may be too cushy for you to risk a change. Even the most obvious signals of opportunity will be ignored for fear of jeopardizing your lifestyle.

However, if the benefits don't include fulfillment or a requisite amount of meaning, the urge to grow personally may be enough to overcome the safety needs. The search for growth is a clear sign you are open to new possibilities. Follow the urge and a more complete path may turn up.

If you're unhappy with your work, and have made either a conscious or subconscious admission that you have to find something new, you automatically become much more receptive to the prospects of change. The more open you are to finding a new route, the more likely you are to follow up stray notions that may have merely glanced off a closed mind. The most open-minded anyone can get, of course, is to be out of a job. Then you're ready for anything. It's not so surprising, then, that unemployment is a frequent bearer of entrepreneurial luck.

When you're forced to investigate new avenues for your own survival, everything gets a fair hearing. Desperation allows you to entertain ideas you never would have otherwise. If he hadn't gotten fired from his TV sales job, Norm Pattiz would have probably collected a handsome, but corporate, salary his whole life. Instead, being out of work caused Pattiz to be receptive to the signals of a radio broadcast, which tipped him off to a totally different career, his own radio dynasty, Westwood One.

When the company Dave Bobert worked for eliminated his position in a cost-cutting move, he says he had to be open to any career suggestions. "I had to get out and get going. I looked at it as an opportunity. I was presented with a choice. Either I could keep looking for a job or I could do something on my own." An idea he had dismissed when he was comfortably employed—a coin-operated tire inflator—now took on new-found viability.

This is not to say you should hit your boss up for a pink slip to find suitable inspiration. But it's that kind of flexibility and urgency that are needed to grab the chance when it pops up. You have to act fast. Because the window of opportunity is only open for an instant. As Bill Poduska, an entrepreneur who has started two hugely successful companies, Prime Computer and Apollo Computer, explains: "Opportunity may knock at your door several times in life. But each particular opportunity will only knock once. That means you better react to it pretty quickly or it's going to disappear."

JUMP TO IT

Stalling or postponing a decision can leave you open to second thoughts or a competitor beating you to the market. Remember, that for any idea you may come up with, there are plenty of people in a country of 240 million people who've thought of the same thing. If you don't move on it immediately, you're going to be scooped.

When the idea presents itself as a commercial possibility, you have to act decisively to turn luck potential into the real thing. Successful entrepreneurs make their luck by going into action as soon as an idea assumes a business profile. The idea may have been around in a different form for a while. Michael Crete, for instance, mixed his wine cooler for several years without ever sensing commercial prospects. He did it for fun. But the night his cooler tasted so good he felt he had to bottle it, he immediately went into action. He got right on the phone to a lawyer to see if he could patent the idea.

Over and over the story of seizing opportunity is one of lightning-quick reflexes. The day after Norm Pattiz got his tip over the radio, he was down at the station that broadcast it, investigating the possibilities. The same morning John Todd dreamed up an amenity shampoo business while showering at a Hyatt Hotel, he was downstairs asking the Hyatt's manager if he'd be interested in his potential product.

Passing thoughts of potential opportunity have to be followed up by at least some tangible move or they will drift off into the ether. If the idea has merit, the first investigative steps serve to not only get the ball rolling but also to validate the concept and inspire further activity.

Unlike most people, who procrastinate and put off action until the time is right—until they have enough money, or expertise, or energy, or until they can find an easy way to do it—thereby losing the initiative, entrepreneurs are propelled by the after-burners of their own instincts. They reach a state of maximum psychological readiness, where they've mentally made the break from their past course. Chronic job frustration and personal aspiration hits a kind of critical mass, that instinctively erupts when triggered by the fateful stimulus.

The Sharper Image's Richard Thalheimer calls the lucky encounter "preparation meeting opportunity. If you're prepared to take advantage of opportunity when it comes along, then you will see the door and be able to walk through it."

Alan Rypinski saw the door, in fact, millions of them on the day he came prepared for opportunity. He had gone to the Briggs Cunningham Museum, a classic car gallery in Costa Mesa, California, looking for advice on how to restore the leather on an old Jaguar he was fixing up. The upholstery was as brittle as a leaf; the rubber had turned white. Rypinski asked the curator if he had anything that could bring the car back to life.

"He didn't say," Rypinski remembers. "But he went into the back room and pulled out a gallon of this milky-white substance. He said, 'This is the greatest stuff we've ever found. We've been using it for ten years.' We splashed it around the car on all these surfaces and I went absolutely out of my mind."

Rypinski didn't hesitate. He had just quit his job with Subaru and was ready for something new; not just any old job, either, but one of his own. He was "looking for a product to market. I didn't have any limitation as to what business it would be in."

After working in real estate, the gift business with Hickory Farms of Ohio, and Subaru America, Rypinski had had his fill of selling other people's products. Now it was his turn. He had a sense of readiness so complete it felt like destiny.

He pounced forthwith on the museum curator, who told him he got the magic formula from a chemist. Rypinski called the chemist, who had just made a deal with another company to market it. Even if someone else had spotted the opportunity, the fact that another company was already selling it would have put an end to the matter. But the supercharged Rypinski was not to be denied from fulfilling his destiny.

He made a deal with the company to distribute the product. They hadn't done much with it in two months. After a year of hard selling, he bought the product from them. From there he built Armor All protectant into one of the most popular household products in the land, with sales of more than $200 million a year.

A chance trip to the museum had created a Sunday morning institution, "Armor Alling" the car, rated up there with mowing the lawn and watching football in the pantheon of Americana. The ways of fate can indeed yield bonanzas. Yet Rypinski was not the first to see the white gold in action. It had been used at the museum for ten years. He was just the first to come looking for it, and the most ready to do something with it.

What does he think about the role of luck? "There's no

such thing as a lucky person," he says. "He or she is aware and looking for opportunity. I don't think there are breaks; there are opportunities that you find. I found this product. I knew I could put it together, knew I had the horsepower and vitality to do it. I made my own breaks. My goddamn phone didn't ring. No customer ordered Armor All for over a year."

THE BREAKS

One of the biggest misconceptions about entrepreneurs is that they do it all themselves. To a great extent they do, dreaming the whole thing up from scratch, producing it and marketing it. Everything stems from the initiative of a single enterprising individual or partnership. Yet whether that initiative goes anywhere in the venture's earliest, unproven state is often in the hands of someone else. In short, no matter how great your concept, or how hard you work, you need someone or something to open the door a crack so you can get your foot in.

"Any entrepreneur who says he's a self-made man is fooling himself," says Artesia Waters' Rick Scoville. "I had so much help it's hard to even list it."

No man is an island, not even an entrepreneur. Entrepreneurship is a daily exercise in getting others to reciprocate to your overtures. It's a two-way street of coaxing, convincing, cajoling, badgering, trying to get people to buy your product, distribute it, print it cheaper, extend your credit terms, bail you out with a one-time-only loan, promote it, write it up in the media.

Once you've established yourself and your product cooperation is easier to come by. However, in the early days of a shoestring venture, certain key assistance—a break or two—can be the difference between getting off the mark or not.

A few entrepreneurs maintain they got no breaks at all, that no one ever extended a hand. Most, though, who've been through the early crisis days of a start-up can testify to the saving grace of a well-timed break. Bill Tillson, for instance, remembers all too clearly how his firm, Netcom, teetered on the edge. After a year in business, he was steadily increasing his billings, but his uncollected receivables had him in a big hole. He was on his last try for a $50,000 loan to tide him over. The loan officer at his bank refused to part with the cash, insisting that Tillson's company had to be in business three years to qualify for a loan.

Then, just a few days before Tillson would have run out of money, the obstinate loan manager was transferred to another bank. His replacement thought Tillson had been treated shabbily and took a special interest in his case. She pushed through the $50,000 and saved a desperate entrepreneur. "If that loan didn't come through, I was through," recalls Tillson.

Breaks can come in this inexplicable style, seemingly from the hand of fate, and on both the plus and minus side. Norm Pattiz was lucky to be in perfect position when deregulation came down out of nowhere and catapulted his radio syndication business into the big time. But he had been unlucky, verging on collapse, when his top client canceled his business. If Pattiz hadn't overcome that piece of misfortune, and gotten the client back on board, he wouldn't have been around to accept the windfall later.

In the high-stakes entrepreneurial game, there are many points that a venture's fortunes can turn on. Some cataclysmic events are beyond control, but many other critical junctures are determined by something entrepreneurs can have some influence over, the human element. As we look over the moments considered the key breaks by the entrepreneurs in this book, we find that most involved some kind of personal assist.

It's the same at the start of any career. Someone has to go out on a limb and take a chance on you. Some brave soul has to see something beyond your lack of credentials and come through with that first funding, an order, or some critical instruction. Who are these rare individuals and how do entrepreneurs locate them? That's what we're about to find out.

But let's first define what we mean by the word "break."

We're not talking about sheer dumb luck, like being discovered by a Hollywood producer while you're walking down the street. Entrepreneurial breaks are the result of a course of action you set in motion. As entrepreneurs like to say, you make your breaks—through the quality of your product, your persuasive powers and persistence.

For our discussion, a break is any boost from fortune, whether person or event, without which a venture may not have gotten out of the starting blocks; or, once off the ground, any major turning point that allowed a company to move from a perpetual start-up state to the big leagues.

Making breaks involves a confrontation with several entrenched aspects of human nature—habit, the herd instinct, and the tendency of society to treat beginners like pimply freshmen in high school. Breaking this resistance down and getting people to accept something different, as yet unapproved by the masses, and from a new face, requires that you switch energy, enthusiasm, confidence, and people skills into overdrive.

So successful entrepreneurs go at it with a frenzy, substituting passion for track records and wherewithal. That's how Philip Hwang got the break from Atari that enabled him to get his company going. Without that $150,000 order, he says, "Then that's it. I'm looking for a job and I may never be thinking again about my own business, I'd be so discouraged."

It was Hwang-the-human-air-cargo, the trans-Pacific shuttling entrepreneur, who could not be ignored, that forced Atari to buy product from him. Once Hwang's product was established as competent, the decision to buy would be based, as it often is in business, on personal intangibles. And the irrepressible Hwang stuck out a mile among the competition. Hwang's efforts were so Herculean it didn't matter that he spoke poor, broken English. His determination got through and Atari had no qualms about going with him.

Creating a personal link, connecting on human as well as business terms with a wide variety of people is what helps to win breaks. You have to distinguish yourself as well as your product from the pack. Because, essentially, you are your product. Standing out from the pack as an individual is important to making yourself known to people who could direct you to a break, as well as making yourself someone others would want to lend a hand to.

The best approach is to be genuine. Forget the fake sales pitches, and put your soul into it. Level with people. If you're just starting out and need help, don't pretend you've got it all figured out. Don't masquerade and project total control. No one will think you need help and thus you won't get any. Obviously, there are times when it's better to let a client think you know more than you do and that your company is bigger than it is. But not all the time. The more you let people know where you stand, and what you need, the better will be your chances of getting it.

To get people on board in the early days of a venture, you need to demonstrate something of your vision, your integrity, your individuality, and, importantly, your commitment. The more of an honest and singular impression you create, the better the odds of influencing someone to cough up a good turn.

Making an impression is something that comes naturally to Kevin Jenkins. Co-founder of Hercules Computer, a Berkeley, California, firm that manufactures add-on graphics cards for computers, Jenkins is not your typical computer nerd. He dresses flamboyantly in electric-pink shirts and skinny ties and is considered "a wild guy" by colleagues. But what's really unorthodox about him is his candor. He speaks his mind.

It's this trait, along with a huge stockpile of ambition, that enabled him to string together a remarkable series of coincidental contacts and events that netted a $35 million business within three years. Jenkins's story shows that good things can come to one who speaks forthrightly. Candid, garrulous behavior leaves no doubt as to who you are, or what you want, giving someone in the network a chance to provide it.

HE HEARD IT THROUGH THE GRAPEVINE
Kevin Jenkins/Hercules Computer

Kevin Jenkins has never been one to mince words, a trait that hasn't always served him well. In his younger, blunter days it was more of a contentious device than a conversational one. He was fired from at least forty of the fifty restaurant and factory-type jobs he worked at through his high school and college years because he was never shy about expressing what was on his mind.

Jenkins was something of a rebel, a feeling engendered by the maverick times in which he grew up, the late sixties, and by the fighting instincts that can develop when you're a "Yank" at a British boarding school. When his adman father got transferred to a post in London, Jenkins had to spend his high school years amid the bizarre authoritarian rituals which clone English conformists.

The experience no doubt contributed to a common entrepreneurial characteristic: hatred of arbitrary authority. The thing he couldn't take about working for other people was "putting myself in a position where I can be subject to the whims of somebody's opinion of me and what I can do." He wanted control over his life. So much so that he turned down a job offer from a Big Eight accounting firm after he graduated from UC Berkeley and started his own business instead.

His reflexes were still running ahead of his talents, however. Though he had no background in writing or publishing, and made no effort to research it first, he decided he'd put out a magazine. After three years of publishing *Boulevards,* a new wave lifestyle book for the Bay Area, he had to admit that his spontaneity had gotten the best of him. Like many impulsive entrepreneurs before him, he had rushed into the marketplace for no other reason than he wanted to do it. *Boulevards* was a flop.

"It was a devastating lesson," he remembers. "I had to admit that it was a failure even though I'd put my life and soul into it. I worked sixteen-, eighteen-, twenty-hour days at times."

So far the fates seemed to have had it in for Jenkins. Yet he hadn't done much to help them along. He had completely ignored the cardinal feature of a good opportunity—timing—not to mention the most rudimentary analysis of his project to see if it was worth doing.

Now a much wiser entrepreneur, Jenkins decided that his next venture would be done right. He would research it first. As he started investigating potential growth industries, like solar energy, jojoba oil, and computers, he began to place himself in areas where opportune occurrences tend to congregate— around emerging, breaking developments.

He was fortunate to be searching for a new business right at the most explosive moment in the growth of the new personal computer business. But it was no accident that he narrowed his choice of a new venture to the computer field. That was pure entrepreneurial timing. Jenkins, like a host of other opportunists, could see niches being opened up every day by the hi-tech boom. It was 1982 and Apple was leading the manufacturing charge. Computerlands were opening up all over the country. And the industry was abuzz waiting for the IBM PC to come on line.

Into this fluid situation came Jenkins, knowing nothing about computers but learning fast that this was where fortunes were being made. He bought a kit and assembled his own computer, read every computer magazine under the sun, and started rooting around for a niche. He toyed with opening up a computer retail company with a friend from the magazine business, but "decided I didn't want to be a retailer. I'd seen many retailers in the course of selling ad space. I didn't think you could make enough profit as a retailer."

"I wanted to be a manufacturer," says Jenkins. "I specifically wanted to manufacture add-on products for the IBM PC. I knew that people would make a lot of money on products like that because people had made a lot of money making products for the Apple. I thought, 'Boy, wouldn't it be great to sell boards for the IBM PC. They'll probably sell a ton of these machines.'"

Personal computers, like cars, don't come fully loaded. You get a basic model and add on extra capabilities later. Jenkins knew that the history of Apple's add-on success would repeat itself with the IBM, and then some. He also knew everybody and his brother would be trying to exploit the same observation.

(That's the trouble with high-growth, opportunistic areas, as opposed to not-so-obvious niches like safari clothing or environmental music. Everyone's onto it and it's a race to the finish.)

Timing would be even more critical than for most startups. Jenkins's tiny window of opportunity was already closing by the time he spotted it, due to intense competition and rapidly changing events in the computer world. When timing is such a marginal affair, it sets the stage for critical moments, and breaks are the order of the day.

Since Jenkins was no computer expert he needed a partner on the technical side to help him design his product. Where in the world could he find the right person? By tapping all his contacts and acquaintances. He had built up a lot of connections through the magazine, and due to his own gregarious personality. He started putting the word out to anyone and everyone. He took ads out.

"I met a bunch of weird people," laughs Jenkins, "including a sixteen-year-old kid with a three hundred-pound mother. Finally through a friend of mine I had met at Berkeley I got a couple of names. The first guy wasn't right and I knew it within five minutes on the phone. The second guy was from Thailand.

"I was looking for somebody to build a board for the IBM PC, and here was this guy who had an idea for a board for the IBM PC. He had bought one of the first IBM PCs to write his Ph.D. thesis, and he was looking for a marketing guy and somebody to run the business. It was strange that he was looking and I was looking. If he'd been two months further along it probably would have been too late."

Vann Suwannukul was in the process of designing a high-resolution graphics board that could be added onto the IBM PC hardware. It would allow him to write software so he could program in the Thai language. Jenkins told him to forget about the Thai market. "They'll probably never sell more than a hundred PCs there, and you'll be lucky to sell fifty software packages. Let's just develop the hardware for the U.S. and let the international market grow."

They each chipped in a couple of thousand dollars, Jenkins hit up friends and family for additional funding, and with a grand total of $23,000, the odd couple opened up Hercules Computer. The shy, studious Suwannukul juggled school and a day job as a digital designer with late nights designing the graphics board. The brash promoter Jenkins fanned out to parts suppliers for PC boards and components, and to advertisers, plotting his marketing strategy.

The Hercules product was a 13-by-4-inch wafer, wired with video data, that plugged into the innards of a PC. It gave IBM users a much higher-resolution graphics capability than the board that came with the machine. Developing the board took only about two weeks, but it seemed like two years to Jenkins, afraid with each passing day that someone was going to beat him to it.

"I was always pushing Vann," he says. "I poured over every ad. I was almost afraid to look at them. I was real nervous."

Once the production board was done, it was time for the next link in the opportunity chain. Through a friend Jenkins used to swim with at Cal, he had met a woman who was starting up a computer magazine. Aware of Jenkins's publishing background, she asked if he'd be interested in doing some consulting work on the new venture.

"I told her about my plans with the graphics board," he recalls, "and I said that I'd be interested in trading some ad space for my consulting fees. I probably talked with her for about four hours and wound up getting six full pages of ad space, which was worth several thousand dollars. I don't know if what I told her was helpful, but the magazine was *PC Magazine*, which turned out to be the most successful magazine launch ever."

The ads ran, and Hercules was flooded with calls from buyers. They were selling a hundred boards a month at $500 each, of which $350 was profit. Jenkins was ecstatic. But he quickly discovered that although he had a market, his product wasn't marketable.

"The advertising was slick enough that people were convinced this was a great product. We could sell it, but they couldn't use it. It didn't have the software. I didn't know enough about computers and never even really used them to know what a serious drawback that was to the product. Van said, 'If we just put it out, someone will write the software for it.' I said, 'But we can't put it out without any software.' It was a Catch-22."

It was time for a break. Jenkins mounted an assault on the software companies of the land, trying to talk one of them into writing the software that would allow the Hercules board to do its thing. But in the standard response to upstarts, the reaction was, "Who are you?"

One day while fielding phones at Van's house, Jenkins got into a long conversation with a customer, as was his talkative wont. The caller wanted to know what software ran the Hercules board. Jenkins didn't hide anything. With his usual candor he told the customer the whole story. By airing out his problem Jenkins had made it possible for someone to offer a solution. If he had pretended he had everything under control, Jenkins may not have gotten the tip that was to alter his life.

The customer told him there was a new software firm coming out with a product that might be what he was looking for. The company was called Lotus; the product was 1-2-3.

"As soon as we hung up," says Jenkins, "I called up information in Cambridge, Massachusetts, and asked for the number for Lotus. I called up and asked for Mitch Kapor. He came on the line, and I said, 'Hi, I'm Kevin Jenkins, president of Hercules. We have the new Hercules graphics card and I'd like to see if you'd be interested in supporting it.' He said, 'Sounds real interesting.'"

Jenkins sent Kapor his first board, and kept calling him

every week for a couple of months until they met at the Comdex trade fair in November 1982. Finally, Lotus agreed to let Hercules design a "driver" that would connect the graphics card with Lotus 1-2-3. However, he couldn't get Kapor to incorporate the new design into the first release of Lotus a few months away in January 1983.

"I was pushing, pushing, pushing," says Jenkins. "Come on, we can get it in. He said, 'Look, we closed the software two months ago, and I won't make any changes.' I said, 'Please, please.' He said, 'No, I can't do it.' We had to wait for the next release seven months away."

While Jenkins sweated it out, his company's future on hold, his customers wondering how they could make his product work, Lotus 1-2-3 shot to the top of the software charts. Would the hot-shot guys at Lotus stick to an agreement made in distant pre-launch days? Jenkins hoped, but wouldn't believe until he saw it.

In July, the new Lotus 1-2-3 came out. It had the Hercules support. Sales of the graphics card shot up from 152 in May to 1,140 in July to 3,300 in August. Hercules was suddenly doing $1 million in sales a month.

"It was unbelievable!" gushes Jenkins. "I thought, 'Christ, finally.' I was driving this car that had the rear window shot out. I had the trunk chained down. We had no side panels. My wife wasn't too wild about all this."

The Lotus break propelled Hercules to sales of $35 million by 1985. Jenkins and Suwannukul owned 95 percent of the company. It was a success beyond their wildest fantasies.

"There's no doubt about it," says Jenkins. "Lotus was essential to the success of our company. Ninety percent of our sales were to people who were buying the board to use with 1-2-3. It made the company. It's as simple as that."

That break and some of the other quirky events in the saga of Hercules have caused Jenkins to muse often on the role of luck. "There's a temptation to think that there's some sort of guiding hand principle, because luck seems too arbitrary and things seem to work together so well in sequence that you think chance could not have put it together as smoothly."

The hand, however, was Jenkins's, aided by that of his partner. Hercules was the end result of a long process of independent investigation, countless decisions, and producing leads through an active networking channel.

For good things to happen, agrees Jenkins, "you have to be looking. And when you're looking, you have to be able to discard the junk."

THE SIX FACES OF FICKLE FATE

Breaks come in many different forms. Some are dramatic—such as Hercules Computer's rescue—and bring instantaneous results. Other breaks might not be fully appreciated until long after the fact. While financial breaks are the most common among bootstrap entrepreneurs, the turning point also may be provided by a key advisor or by a story in the media.

People who provide breaks may be total strangers or long-time acquaintances or friends. Running the gamut of backgrounds and means, from wealthy angels to salaried middle managers at important accounts, all seem to possess one characteristic—the capacity to be intrigued. Something in the vision, the character, or the presentation of the entrepreneur captures their fancy and prevents them from writing off the upstart. Enthusiasm or logic busts through, causing them to go out of the way in some fashion for the entrepreneur.

At one end of the spectrum, there are mentors, usually fellow small businessmen who take entrepreneurs under their wings, more out of compassion and solidarity than out of any financial gain. At the other end are calculating businessmen who may take a chance and place an order with your small company over larger competitors because they are impressed with your commitment to service their account.

Breaks break down into five main sources the entrepreneur has some capability to effect, plus one sheer-luck category.

*   *   *

Mentors. When it comes to critical junctures, it's hard to top the first few weeks of a venture. Everything's foreign; nothing works right; there's no money coming in yet. You can be tempted to give up before you hardly get started. That's why several entrepreneurs acknowledge the role played by people who stepped in with a helping hand right at the most confusing, impoverished part of the adventure, the beginning.

These Samaritans tend to be fellow small businessmen who've "been there," who offer advice or facilities or both to an entrepreneur lost in the maze of enterprise. They don't expect anything in return for their services. They take satisfaction in showing someone with promise the ropes.

Air-Vend's Dave Bobert remembers the help of Gene O'Brian, a sheet metal shop owner. "He said, 'I like you Dave, and I think it's a good idea." He helped Bobert design the tire inflator and produced the first fifty on extended credit terms. He also gave Bobert a corner of his shop for an office.

"The guy really gave me a break. It probably provided me with the incentive to say, the hell with it, I'm going ahead, because I don't have to lay out a lot of money, sign leases."

Jerry Wilson's "patron" was a steel distributor, Arthur Curtis. He showed Wilson how to weld, provided him with scrap metal to build his prototypes, and gave him encouragement to build his Soloflex home gym.

T. C. Swartz had a travel agent friend who let him use his office and phones at no charge. "If I hadn't had a guardian angel like that I don't know how I would have financed myself in the beginning," says Swartz.

Buyers. A turning point for many entrepreneurs is getting that first big order. You can survive on subsistence accounts for a while, but to really get things rolling, it's often necessary to land a top, influential customer, who can then bring other big boys on board. The providers in this case are corporate executives who, unlike mentors, don't give a flying fish about the entrepreneurial struggle. Their only concern is how your product will make them look to the boss.

It would seem like a lost cause for most entrepreneurs. But, surprisingly, there are those who will take a chance on the newcomer. What motivates the break? It can be a buyer's hunch that your product is an up-and-comer. Or the decision may turn on value or service. No matter how small your company is, if you can offer a better value, in product or price, and demonstrate a willingness to service the account to death, you can swing powerful purchase orders.

As you will recall, John Todd got his first break from an executive at Marriott Hotels. Though he didn't even have a company at the time, Todd convinced the exec that he could give Marriott a better sample shampoo deal than Procter & Gamble or Helene Curtis. "We gave them something the giants couldn't give," Todd explains. Custom bottle, packaging, and service won the $1 million deal that launched Guest Supply, Inc.

It was the same pitch of more attentive, custom service that loosened up the $500,000 order that got Linda Enke and Anne Rothschild & Co. going. Same, of course, for Philip Hwang's Atari deal.

The breakthrough for Mo Siegel came when he got a distributor to carry his tea. As a barn operation, Celestial Seasonings couldn't get near the big distributors. But Siegel was able to find an up-and-coming entrepreneurial distributor to take on his product. This technique of finding compatible fellow travelers is an effective way to create breaks.

Angels. Without the seed capital to get started, some entrepreneurs wouldn't have made it. Jim Jenks gives the nod to Bob Driver, a friend whose $50,000 credit line got Ocean Pacific Sunwear off the ground. "If it wasn't for that initial credit line, I'd probably still be sanding surfboards today," says Jenks.

Stuart Bewley's eleventh-hour sales pitch to a wealthy

commodities trader got the bulk of California Cooler's $150,000 start-up capital to come on line just as the product was hitting the stores. Bewley's pitch that investment opportunities in Cooler were going fast, plus the investor's own sixth sense, closed the deal. As with Jenks and many other entrepreneurs, Bewley was an acquaintance of his investor.

Bankers. Financial aid is the major source of breaks for shoe-string entrepreneurs, both in getting companies going and bailing them out as they operate on the edge through the early years. Since new businesses don't yet qualify for needed loans, most financial breaks tend to come through a back channel, usually through a personal connection of some sort.

As you'll remember, Rick Scoville got his first break from his banker of many years. Carl Clemons authorized the initial signature loan of $10,000 that got Artesia Waters started, and then came through with another loan of $15,000 because Scoville was a personal friend.

It was a neighbor of Boyd and Felice Willat who prevailed on a banker friend to grant Harper House its first big loan. Once John Todd got his $1 million order from Marriott, he wouldn't have been able to manufacture it if his partner hadn't called in a favor from a banker buddy that resulted in an SBA loan.

Media. Getting a start-up out of the fledgling state is a matter of reaching a larger audience. Doing that without dough isn't easy. It may be that the thing that can give your sales the critical boost is a shot of publicity. Judi Sheppard Missett's press releases, and particularly her Jazzercise book, helped break her company wide open.

Mo Siegel credits an appearance of his tea on "The Tonight Show" with being a key break for Celestial Seasonings. After receiving a fan letter from actress Susan St. James, Siegel persuaded her to become a stockholder in the company. When St. James did a guest spot on "The Tonight Show," she plugged the tea. "After Susan served tea on Johnny Carson that night," says Siegel, "it was really easy for us to go to our customers and say, 'Maybe you need two bags of Red Zinger instead of one.'"

It was an ad in *Entrepreneur* magazine that turned the tide for Dave Bobert's tire inflators, which languished unsold until his small ads started bringing in customers.

Cosmic Breaks. Just as bad breaks like war, pestilence, and accounts that go bankrupt can wreak havoc, good breaks may appear out of nowhere to spruce up the fortunes of struggling entrepreneurs. There's no rhyme or reason to these windfalls. It's classic Lady Luck, and becoming a beneficiary is as random as winning the lottery.

The only common denominators are that (1) the entrepreneurs were in need, (2) they were in a position to do something with the gift, and (3) they did something with it. They capitalized.

Lane Nemeth and Discovery Toys were rescued by such a cosmic stroke. She remembers that she "was desperate. I didn't know what to do. I couldn't meet payroll. I couldn't buy any toys." Out of the blue came a call from a telepathic venture capitalist, who offered the needed capital. The man's wife had seen Nemeth's product, liked it, and got him to call.

Deregulation was the lightning bolt for Norm Pattiz and Westwood One. For T. C. Swartz a major turning point in the fortunes of Society Expeditions was sparked by a competitor's cruise ship running aground. As the only tour operator left offering cruises to Antarctica, Swartz swooped in to make the most of the void. He charged one-quarter the rate of the grounded competitor, and filled his chartered ships to capacity.

THE BOLD ONES

If there's one conclusion that can be drawn from entrepreneurial good fortune, it's that it derives from visibility. You have to be out there. You have to be constantly pressing your case to anyone who will listen; and double your efforts with anyone who won't.

You don't find breaks by keeping things to yourself, by being subtle, secretive, or self-absorbed as an all-conquering one-man band. Overweaning pride, paranoia, or propriety cuts you off from the network that transmits favorable incidents. It's exposure, the aggressive, persistent display of your project that sets the chain reaction of luck in motion.

Luck specialist Max Gunther has noted that "as a group, lucky people tend to be bold people. The most timid men and women I've met in my travels have been the least lucky." It's his contention that "little bits of potential luck drift past nearly everybody from time to time. But they are only of value to those bold enough to reach out and grasp them."

Andy Lewis, an entrepreneur who invented the LED moving message signs we see in banks and shops, sold his first programmable signs with just such a combination of luck and boldness. It was 1977 and Lewis had just produced the world's first LED moving message "Scanvertiser." His first sales calls for the new product were turning up nothing at the large hotels on the Las Vegas Strip. After a rejection at the Flamingo Hotel, Lewis was headed outside when he overheard a ruckus in the office he had just left. That night's headliner, Helen Reddy, was ill and the hotel had to get the word out to ticket holders. They had to hire a sign company to rush "canceled" notices into the lobby and casino.

Luck had presented itself. Though he had already been turned down, Lewis saw his moment. He quickly programmed his sign and barged back into the office. He plugged in his sign for the startled executives. It read: DUE TO ILLNESS, HELEN REDDY WILL NOT BE PERFORMING TONIGHT. IF YOU BOUGHT TICKETS, SEE CASHIER NUMBER 6 FOR A REFUND. They wrote out a check for six $1,800 LED boxes on the spot. Boldness had cashed in on opportunity, and started the life of Lewis Lektronix, Lewis's new start-up.

If you want to make your luck, instead of always having it pass you by, you have to make a move. The words of that great entrepreneurship expert, Virgil, ring clear some 2,000 years later: "Fortune favors the brave."

Starting Smart

YOU'RE NOT SUPPOSED to be able to pull a John Styth Pemberton anymore. The days when the corner druggist could whip together a concoction that changes the drinking habits of the world are long since over, it's said. Those quaint scenes of Coca-Cola founder Pemberton stirring up potions in his house in a thirty-gallon brass kettle or bottling his drink by hand in recycled beer bottles are the products of that golden age of entrepreneurship, the late nineteenth century.

The Cokes, the Pepsis, and the Anheuser-Busches are entrenched now. The big corporations are all set. The only areas for major conquest open to the entrepreneur are hi-technology, telecommunications, and genetic engineering.

Someone forgot to tell Michael Crete, though. He didn't know the Pemberton days were done for. There was Crete, almost a hundred years later, stirring up his concoction in a five-gallon Coleman jug, soaking labels off beer bottles, so, like Pemberton, he could refill them by hand. People explained to him—four out of five, in fact—that beer salesmen making $25,000 a year just don't take on the biggest beverage corporations in America. But Crete kept stirring and mixing and blending and bottling.

His friend and partner Stuart Bewley was just as stubborn. Together they descended further into their folly of marketing a wine cooler that Crete promised would "shake the industry." They had $10,000 when they started down this obviously lunatic path to the poorhouse. Five years later their company was doing $150 million in sales, had created a $700 million industry, and had spawned over 100 imitators, including those all-powerful, omniscient goliaths, like Gallo, Heublein, Seagram, Coors, and Anheuser-Busch, who had faithfully copied their invention to the letter.

So much for corporate America having things all locked up. The story of California Cooler shows that, far from shutting out the small entrepreneur, today's economy of hulking, Brobdingnagian mega-corporations has actually increased the chances of finding an exploitable opportunity. As the giants get bigger and bigger, and the variety-seeking market gets more and more segmented into smaller and smaller subdivisions, the big boys cede many profitable niches to small companies because they aren't cost-efficient for the big machine or they're flat overlooked by ponderous, inflexible bureaucracies.

"Size is not necessarily the key to success and survival on the corporate battlefield," say Paul Solman and Thomas Friedman, authors of *Life and Death on the Corporate Battlefield*, "difference is. A tiny twenty-four-hour convenience store can't compete with Safeway, but then Safeway can't compete with the convenience store, either."

Entrepreneurs are finding that, like a fast-breaking six-foot ball handler, they can compensate for size on the court with quickness. Guest Supply's John Todd, marketer of hotel amenities, notes: "There are a lot of niches out there that the big companies can't effectively service. Today they're very big and lethargic. I look at Procter & Gamble, and Colgate-Palmolive. By the time they go in and make a presentation to a hotel, it takes them a year to turn around and do it. It takes me just a month. It's a great opportunity for companies to fill that flexible, service-oriented niche that they're leaving open for us."

Dal La Magna of Tweezerman agrees. "These companies are so big that they're creating enormous opportunities. There's not one major company that's been able to knock me off. I feared that. I used to hide my product. Revlon can't work on the margins I do. They're too big."

Because the market is always changing, there are an infinite number of these niches left unfilled by the major corporations. Capitalizing on them, though, requires careful execution and extraordinary resourcefulness by the fledgling entrepreneur. The low-budget venture doesn't leave much margin for error.

To see how rank amateurs get it done right, and implement product niches they've snatched right from under the noses of the establishment, there's no more instructive lesson than the story of California Cooler. Michael Crete and Stuart Bewley made far less of the usual beginning blunders, and played it far smarter all the way down the line—from educating themselves sufficiently ahead of time on their product and market, to corralling reluctant investors, to positioning their product, to outfoxing government regulations, to overcoming production handicaps, to enticing distributors, to stretching cash flow—in short, everything a new company has to do to make it big. Their tale is a shining example of upstart success.

Two Guys From Lodi
Michael Crete, Stuart Bewley/California Cooler

California Cooler has its roots, as might be expected, in a wine-growing town. Lodi, California, midway between Sacramento and Stockton, sits at the epicenter of the great San Joaquin Valley, the fruit and produce capital of America. Orchards, vineyards, and agribusiness have paid the bills in these parts since the first settlers started farming the area back in the mid-nineteenth-century. There are over 14 wineries located in Lodi, and the town's class-A baseball team, a San Diego Padre farm club, is called the "Crushers," as in grapes.

Michael Crete's family there goes back five generations. His great-grandparents on his mother's side had their own vineyards, and as a kid he trimmed grapevines, irrigated, and worked as a sugar tester. Today people tell him it was destiny that he should make his mark in the wine business. But it never looked that way to Crete. He would stare into the future, but all he could come up with was a blank. He didn't know what he wanted to do with his life.

Whatever it was, it wasn't going to happen in Lodi, a small town of 41,000. Young people with ambitions can be inclined to side with the refrain of a 1969 Credence Clearwater hit, "Stuck in Lodi again."

He attended UC Santa Barbara, where he took up studies in history, because it was "interesting." During summer vacations back home in the baking heat of the central valley, he and his friends often made use of an escape route to ocean-cooled Santa Cruz, ninety miles away, where they recouped at an old beach house. Anywhere from four to twelve of his chums would spend weekends majoring in partying. In the college tradition, the troops were wild and restless. And thirsty.

There were cases of beer and jugs of wine on hand, as well as a wide array of juices, liquors, and mixes to create custom grog. Crete was something of a hobbyist when it came to mixing drinks, and cooking, too. His creative talents in the area led him to be the designated Mix Master at these events. He took requests—margaritas, daiquiris, etc. But he also made some compositions of his own. This Saturday in the summer of '74 he seemed to be particularly inspired. He peered into the two-and-a-half-gallon Coleman jug where he was working on a wine cooler, and decided to go all-out. More pineapple here, maybe a dash of grapefruit. Suddenly, cherry syrup, coconut, and citrus juices splashed down like brushstrokes from a possessed painter. He gave it a taste. *Damn, he really topped himself this time.* The gang expressed their agreement by polishing off the Coleman forthwith.

Some people have a talent for remembering numbers. Others never forget a face. Michael Crete was born with an unfailing memory for cocktail ingredients. If he mixes it once, it sticks—even spur-of-the-moment concoctions—down to the last ounce of grenadine. So he remembered his mad improvisational recipe, and decided it would make a nice item to reprise on social occasions. Over the years it became known to fellow revelers as the Island Wine Cooler for its tropical, tangy taste.

Crete went on to graduate from college, but found that his degree in comparative communist theory had resulted in no discernible career. He did some work toward a Masters degree at

San Jose State, and tried going for a teaching certification, but he "didn't like cutting things out and putting them up on bulletin boards."

He came back home, where he worked with his father, a professional photographer and inventor. The experience with his dad taught Crete some valuable lessons on how not to be an entrepreneur. His father accepted little advice or ideas from the outside, including his son, and held onto projects long after they had proven unfeasible. Though he had a half a dozen patents to his name, none had amounted to much. One, once a promising idea for a portable television studio, had been passed up by technology, but he wouldn't let go of it.

Entrepreneurs have to be able to recognize and admit to unworkable ideas, junk them, and move on. This, plus the need to listen and not be a "know-it-all," were key lessons Crete picked up from working with his father.

Studies have shown that having a self-employed father makes the children much more inclined to starting businesses themselves. But it wasn't just Crete's father who was independent. There was hardly a relative on either side of the family who was not running his or her own business. Surprisingly, he admits to "no compulsion from birth to be an entrepreneur." But the family influence and his own desire to get pent-up ideas into action were slowly nudging him in the entrepreneurial direction.

He found himself taking a $400 weekend course in entrepreneurship in San Francisco. He learned about setting goals, surrounding himself with talented people, and recalls that it was the first time he heard the marketing truism "KISS"—Keep It Simple, Stupid. Though the generalities were on target, and the power of positive thinking got him all revved up, the specific advice of the instructor left a little to be desired. Crete was told that macramé was where it was at. "I thought, gee, that doesn't sound worth a shit," he says with a laugh, "but I bought about $300 worth of assorted garbage."

Thus began his first venture, like many first-time efforts an awkward attempt to try to get a feel for the commercial realities. His company was called Buyer's Desires and he sold gift and craft items to a few shops in Stockton. It didn't take long, though, to realize that the hot tip from the entrepreneurship course was a bum steer.

He landed a job as a salesman for a Coors distributor. "I can't tell you what a pleasure it was selling Coors beer instead of Illusions and Macramé," he says. "I got a feel for what the beer guys were doing out there, what a battle it really was between Anheuser, Miller, Coors, keeping your shelf space, people pushing your product off to the side, merchandising."

Calling on bars and liquor stores in the Lodi and Stockton areas, he was getting a brew's-eye-view of the most important part of the beverage business—sales. He was picking up shelf-level insights and valuable account friendships that would be instrumental in the marketing of his own product down the road.

One night in October 1979, after a hard day schlepping Coors, Crete decided to unwind with friends over a batch of his favorite wine cooler. He mixed up his fruity concoction, took a swig, and the cooler stopped him cold. It had done more than hit the spot. It had hit an entrepreneurial nerve. Standing in the kitchen smacking his lips, he was seized by a tantalizing thought: "Why doesn't somebody put this in a convenient package?"

He immediately said to one of his friends, "What do you think of this wine cooler in a bottle or a can? I want to patent it. I want to patent premixed wine coolers." The same night he was on the phone to a patent attorney trying to protect his discovery.

Unlike thousands of backyard bartenders and even professionals who may have thought they hit on the ultimate blend, Crete was brazen enough, and ready enough, to act on his impulse. Since he left college he had been in search of a direction. He had been shuffling from job to job, unable to settle down to the white-collar corporate life. The restlessness he felt was the symptom of an urge for independence that had been gathering steam for some time. Like the temblors that precede a volcanic eruption, his dabblings in entrepreneurship courses, his gift company, his experience selling alcoholic beverages, and the years of making a product everyone seemed to love, had built up to an explosive realization that the time was right for action.

LEGWORK OF SUCCESS

After finding out that his cooler couldn't be patented (it wasn't any new breakthrough; just a "logical progression" in something people had been making for years), the next thing he did was to sit down and write out a prioritized list of what he had to do to find out if his idea was feasible. "One of the first questions I asked," he recalls, "and, damn, I was smarter than I thought I was back then, was, 'Will this stuff last in a can or a bottle?' My experience in the beer business really brought that out in me. There is a 120-day rotation policy for beer. After that you're supposed to rotate the old out and put the new in. I learned that old product will kill you. There's nothing worse than someone opening a bottle of your product that's rancid or turned."

Other questions would lead him to Stockton's main library where he holed up with books and trade journals on the beverage industry. He examined the size of various markets, including the juice segment. If he could pull in the beer audience and the juice market with his natural fruit juice cooler, the prospects could be staggering. From another book, "a dusty, old softdrink manufacturer's handbook," he learned about the carbocooler and the complicated process of carbonation.

By spring of 1980 he began the process of trying to gauge customer support for his product. Thus began the amazing bathtub bottling works. Crete was living, appropriately enough, in the middle of a vineyard at the time, in his grandfather's house. With the spirit of grapes past and present egging him on, he set up a cottage winery in his house. As he'd make the rounds of his bar accounts, he'd buy up long-necked, returnable beer bottles (cigarette butts in them and all) for $1 a case (24 bottles), instead of the going rate of seventy cents.

"You put them in the bathtub," he explains, "with hot, soapy water and soak the labels off. It's basically an overnight process. You get a knife or a razor blade out and you scrape the darn things off. Then you put them through the dishwasher twice for sterilizing."

The concocting took place in a five-gallon Coleman jug. He'd mix all the ingredients and then pour it from the spigot into one of his squeaky-clean bottles. He had rounded up a bunch of soft drink crowns and with an old manual crowner he then capped his creation, one bottle at a time.

As he'd make his rounds for Coors, and for a later job selling wines and brandies for Eastside Winery, Crete would present his home brew, chilled in an ice chest, for sampling by bar and liquor store owners. It was a relaxed, casual survey typical of Crete himself. He was never the high-pressure, glad-handing salesman. He had the gift of being natural, in an outgoing way. He made friends easily, and in the tightly knit central valley where everyone knew everyone else he got a lot of helpful feedback from his customer/buddies.

At the Shamrock Bar in Stockton, which he'd hit every Thursday, he had the proprietor, a former softball star named Bill Simone, make him a wine cooler. "That's pretty good," said Crete. He pulled out a bottle of his own cooler. "What do you think of this?" he asked the bartender. "It's great, better than mine," Simone replied. "That's my wine cooler," beamed Crete. He continued to talk it up every Thursday at the Shamrock and wherever he called on customers. He thought he wanted to put his cooler in cans. Simone told him he was crazy. It had to go in bottles. A year later the bar owner would become one of a handful of insightful investors in California Cooler.

MOTIVATION TIMES TWO

In June Crete got a call from an old high school friend, Stuart Bewley, who had been working in Portland as a commodities trader selling beans and lentils. He was tired of the corporate grind, though, and was back in Stockton to do something on his own. When they got together they swapped aspirations and decided that both essentially wanted the same thing: a company of their own. Two days later Bewley called his friend. "Mike, do you need a partner?" he asked. They were off and running.

As uncertain as Crete had been about what he was going to do in life, Bewley seemed to have things plotted out from his teenage years. The son of a dentist, and the third of four children, he had shown initiative early on, doing 4-H projects, raising popcorn and selling it door to door; raising chickens and selling eggs. When he started working he decided he wouldn't stay at a job for more than two years, so he could get the broadest possible exposure to the working world. He clerked at a pawnshop and a hardware store, worked for a chemical company, was a construction worker and a guitar teacher.

Very methodical, he knew in his college days that he wanted to run a business of his own one day. So he sought out successful businessmen for advice and opinions that he felt would give him a foundation on which to build a successful organization later on. After graduating with a degree in Business from the University of Oregon, he went on to take a graduate degree in International Business from the Institute for Business Studies at the University of Rotterdam in Holland.

Out of school he was thrown into the frenzied, wheeler-dealer world of international commodities trading, first at a firm in New York, and then at North Pacific International in Portland. The corporate life only made him more determined to extract the knowledge he needed, and then take off on his own. He recalls some of the frustrations. "When you work for somebody else, your boss will say you're not paid to think, or some guy at an upper level can't see the wisdom of an idea, so you never get to try it. Or the politics of the situation won't allow anything new. Creative people end up being very frustrated and there are many ideas that die. Running your own business allows you the opportunity to try a new idea or a different way of doing something.

It would be hard to imagine a twenty-seven-year-old first-time entrepreneur more prepared for the job than Bewley. Unlike most rookies in the venture game, he knew exactly what he was getting into. When he returned to Stockton to start hatching a business of his own, he immediately started cutting back on his living standard, and started hunkering down for the sacrifices ahead. His family owned a couple of abandoned farmhouses, part of an old condemned farm-labor camp, and he renovated one of them to live in, doing all the construction work himself, installing a wood stove to cut back on fuel costs.

Bewley was so intent on starting a business that he went through the elaborate process of quitting his job, of outfitting the farmhouse and preparing himself mentally and physically without knowing what venture he was was going to start. He just knew he would come up with something. He had ideas, one had to do with the surplus and salvage of electrical equipment. But nothing that met his rigorous requirements for profitability and potential (see Chapter 4 for Bewley's "Five Truisms"). Until Crete's special blend.

"It tasted great," he remembers. "It was a quality product. It was the right time. And it fit in with the direction that people were going."

THE NICHE

Changes in lifestyle and social attitudes had left a gaping hole in the beverage market. There was a national trend toward healthier food and drink. Natural products were becoming the rage. A wine cooler made with natural fruit juices could tap the growing health-consciousness market. Another element that Crete and Bewley pinpointed about their market niche was the immense potential it held for women. From his years as Mix Master, Crete knew that most women weren't big beer drinkers, and they got tired of the only other option being plain wine. A huge population of more independent-minded women were looking for an alternative.

As for the men, they were just as bored with their chronic

six-packs. Besides, the cooler was a better thirst-quencher than beer. On a hot day or after a game of tennis or racquetball, "a cool one," as Crete likes to call it, was the best refresher. The other major plus for the product was their idea to sell it in single 12-ounce servings, right out of the liquor cold box, to capitalize on its sating powers.

The major beverage companies had never thought of any of this, nor one final important ingredient, unknown even to Crete and Bewley. Their drink was the logical heir to the Pepsi Generation. Lou Gomberg, a wine industry consultant with fifty-one years in the business—who admits he overlooked all these factors himself—explains that the upstart cooler was tailor-made for a generation of palates weaned on soft drinks. "The average person grows up drinking soft drinks after leaving mother's milk or cow's milk. All the soft drinks are sweet; all are carbonated and all the soft drinks are served ice cold. The cooler fits right in." Beer wasn't sweet enough and wine not carbonated or ice-cold enough to fill the bill that the cooler did.

In retrospect, of course, it all seems perfectly obvious. But for two upstarts with $10,000 between them, the treasure was a long way off, buried at the bottom of a murky sea. They had to do a lot of exploring in treacherous waters to produce the prize. One of them alone might not have made it. But as a partnership they measured up well.

Crete made a good creator/promoter, developing the product, package design, and promoting it with his gregarious people skills in the sales and distribution areas. Bewley brought the business tools that were essential to the organizing of production and capitalization. Crete notes that it was "a shot of adrenalin" when Bewley joined him. "We made a nice mix. I wasn't anywhere near as aggressive or assertive in trying to get things done as Stuart was. The strengths that he had were my weaknesses and my strengths were his weaknesses."

The system they came up with was that Crete would keep his job and his sales channels going at Eastside Winery (where he was set up in his own small distributorship of wines and brandies), while Bewley would go at it full-time from his farm-house once he got it renovated. By fall 1980 the two set up their first office in an adjacent building of the condemned farm complex. They borrowed two desks, hung up a couple of bare light bulbs, and their funky war room, dubbed "Hog Hollow," was born.

OVERCOMING AMATEURISM

Then it was head-first into the question quagmire. Where do you buy bulk wine? Where can you get green beer bottles? Where do you get the caps? The foil? Who are the people who do the graphic artwork on the labels? You would think that suppliers would be happy to oblige future customers, but the fact is that the establishment is one big club, and it doesn't like to let in new members. The novice has to put up with all kinds of static from grizzled grumps guarding the specifications of widgets like sacred tablets.

At the first sign that you don't know the arcane field as well as the supplier, one of two things will happen. He'll get irritated with your questions and not take your business seriously; or, he'll jack the price way up, sensing a pushover.

One principle they developed to counteract this was Always Call the Guy You Don't Want to Work with First. This way they could pick up the all-important lingo or key buzz words from the supplier they didn't want to do business with, and then contact the quality firm and speak knowledgeably on the subject. Bewley used this trick to master the jargon of printers. The first one he called to ask about cardboard four-packs spewed out the choices: litho, flexo, or rotogravure; on 18- or 21-point board. Bewley didn't know rotogravure from Roto-Rooter. But he felt free to ask all the questions he wanted without worrying about looking dumb. He'd be smart by the time he called the next printer.

Another tactic they used to fight the neophyte image was to present themselves to suppliers never as the principals of the company but only as salesmen. It gave the impression they had a substantial firm behind them. It also bought them some time if they didn't know something. They could say they had to check with the "home" office.

OVERTHROWING THE GOVERNMENT

They confronted their biggest obstacles in Sacramento and Washington, D.C. The government bureaucracy was at a loss to know what to do with a product that wasn't covered in the rulebooks. They were told flat out many times that there was no way they could get a license to sell their wine cooler. The attitude, says Bewley, was if "it doesn't fall under the regulations, it's against the law. We said, 'We don't care if it's against the law, we're gonna do it. Move the law, change the law, reinterpret it, whatever it takes.' We just kept looking through the regulations until we found a loophole or a spot that allowed it to happen. You might talk to eight people who say you can't do it before the ninth says, 'I know how you can do it.'"

The government said they couldn't put their drink in beer bottles. Why not? Wine could only go in wine bottles, of course. The size closest to a 12-ounce beer bottle, 375 ml., called a "split," cost $5, while a case of beer bottles was only $2.50. Their cooler had to go in beer bottles. It was half the price, plus they'd built their design and distribution around it. Finally, Bewley found a loophole. If they lowered their alcohol content from seven percent to six they wouldn't be classified as a "wine" anymore and could switch to beer bottles.

Meanwhile, the most grueling battle, getting a license to sell their product in California, was reaching new heights of absurdity. The state Alcohol Bureau of Control first decided that Crete and Bewley were a "bonded winery" and needed a bonded winery license. After filling out the papers and satisfying the requirements of that category, they were then told that they weren't a bonded winery at all, but, in fact, a "wholesale warehouse seller." Time dragged on, more paperwork, and then it was concluded they might be a wine grower. Now they needed a wine grower's license. To be an official "wine grower" you had to have a grape-crushing machine. Bewley pointed out that his company didn't crush grapes. It didn't matter. In the book it specifically said that a "grape-crushing machine" was mandatory and until they had one they couldn't get the wine grower's license.

At times like this the only course open is to suspend all rational thought and outdo the law in illogical compliance. Two can play this game. They didn't have enough money for a grape crusher, so they borrowed a run-down, dilapidated one and stuck it in a corner of their warehouse. When the inspector came by to check it out, it was immediately rejected because the broken-down device wasn't installed and was obviously inoperable. "We said, 'Look, in the regulations it doesn't say that it has to be installed,'" Bewley remembers with satisfaction. "'It doesn't say it has to run. It just says we gotta have one. There it is.' He had to sign the papers."

Another roadblock was being thrown up by the federal government. The Bureau of Alcohol, Tobacco, and Firearms, which authorized approval on a national basis, sent back their bottles of cooler stamped REJECTED. The drink had bacteria in it, according to the BATF. The entrepreneurs were incredulous. They took the bottles to UC Davis and had them thoroughly tested. The researchers realized, though, that someone in Washington had looked at the fruit particles at the bottom of the bottle and had decided they were bacteria. After a long delay, a second sample was finally approved.

As part of their continuing education in the process of beverage making, they did a lot of their best research on local college campuses. A professor of Food Technology at UC Davis analyzed the properties of their cooler and determined that it had biological staying power on the shelves.

Students were asked to give their opinions on the drink in cardtable taste tests at Cal State Chico. At the University of Pacific a marketing class took up discussion of the project. The students decided that the name of the product, "Island Wine Cooler," needed some work. Grapes, vines, and islands didn't add up. Driving home from a skull session at UOP, Crete was thinking "grapes, wines, vineyards" and looking for inspiration when he caught sight of a vineyard out his window. It was staring him right in the face: "California" Cooler.

Production graduated from Crete's bathtub works to a 15-gallon beer keg. The ingredients were poured in, and then each of them would stand on one side of the keg and shake it to mix it up. A garden hose ran out of the bung. One would fill a bottle with the hose, the other would cap it. In March 1981 they moved out of Hog Hollow into a run-down warehouse on a Stockton back alley. They converted a 1,500-gallon water tank into a wine mixer and set about mastering the process of carbonating the concoction. Crete credits Bewley's mechanical expertise for riding herd on all the technical hurdles to get the secondhand gear up and running.

Though they were still a long way from producing California Cooler for store shelves, they had to keep a steady stream of it flowing through the long months of demonstrations to future customers, suppliers, and investors. They estimate they filled upwards of 4,800 bottles by hand-held garden hose. The taste testings usually gave them positive feedback, but that didn't mean anyone liked it enough to sink cash into it. "People said maybe the idea's good, maybe the name's good, maybe it tastes good," notes Crete, "but the two of you?"

CORRALLING THE ELUSIVE INVESTOR

They were looking to raise $150,000. They approached over 200 potential investors with a business plan that laid out the trends toward low-alcohol, natural products, how their product had no additives or preservatives and fit right in with the changing tastes. The plan also described how they would market it and distribute it. Crete already had some accounts lined up to take the product.

He didn't lack contacts in the close-knit central valley, home to some very wealthy agribusiness figures. He and Bewley blanketed the community in search of cash—Elks clubs, local businesses, service organizations, friends of their parents, friends of friends—the usual entrepreneurial hunt for anyone with a wallet. After eight months on the trail they had accumulated over forty prospects.

By the middle of July 1981, though, none who had expressed an interest in investing had yet written a check, and California Cooler was supposed to hit the stores in August. They were $27,000 in debt and the bills were mounting. Something had to be done to get the fence-sitters to commit. Crete and Bewley went around together in a last-ditch attempt to get cash confirmations. They explained that, no hard feelings, but they had to know now. Were they in or out? Every last investor begged off.

When the sun went down that night in Lodi two shattered entrepreneurs began to think that maybe it wouldn't come up on another day of California Cooler.

Bewley decided to play one last card. He dropped by the office of his former boss, a multimillionaire bean trader, who had first set him up in the commodities business out of college. Though he had his whole life on the line, Bewley tried to silence his pounding heart and play it cool, as if he was just in the neighborhood and came by to chat. He swung the conversation around to his wine cooler. He just happened to have a case and prospectus in the car, if anyone was interested.

An impromptu tasting was held. One of the vice-presidents said that this tropical-type drink would go over big in Puerto Rico, where the company had business interests. Maybe they could get an exclusive for that market. Bewley nonchalantly mentioned that with an investment that could probably be arranged. There was a huddle and the big boss was called in to discuss it. How much of California Cooler was still available? In fact, the only checks Bewley had were from his dad, and a telephone company worker who had invested.

But he didn't want to give an impression of his company not happening so he said there was 25 percent left. He got a commitment on an option for 25 percent that would be confirmed within forty-eight hours. The commodities king also wanted an option on anything else that wasn't sold by that time. The critical first break had come through at the wire.

There's nothing more important to raising capital than getting a lead investor, someone who can validate the project and start the bandwagon rolling for all those nervous investors who don't want to be first on board. This particular fellow was one of the most prominent business figures in the central valley, and his seal of approval immediately made it possible for Bewley and Crete to lean on the handful of investors who had told them to come back when they had gotten some money.

"Everybody in town knew this guy," says Bewley. "All of a sudden because he thought it was a good idea, then it was a good idea."

When Bewley's father heard about the millionaire's involvement, he doubled the amount of his investment. Other investors quickly wrote checks, including an accountant, Crete's bartender friend Bill Simone, a telephone company worker he had met at Simone's bar on one of his sampling sprees, and Bewley's brother.

D-DAY

The cash came none too soon because California Cooler was already on the market. On August 15, 1981, the long-awaited state license finally came through. Bewley got on the phone to Crete and excitedly announced: "We got it!" They immediately loaded up a 1953 GMC pickup and tore off to deliver their first cases to retailers. Almost *two years* had passed since that night in October 1979 when Crete first got his idea.

Crete's retailer friends provided the next break, by giving him space in their stores. "They figured they had to buy it," he says. I'd been talking it up for a year and a half. I think they saw the potential, but they were giving us a break because they knew we started from scratch."

His buddies at Flame Liquor, Sell Rite Market, Top Value Food Store, and Lodi Avenue Liquors weren't taking that much of a risk, five cases at $13.50 each—a total of $67.50. But they probably wouldn't have bothered if it wasn't someone they all liked and respected. "It wasn't really the taste of the item," says Top Value's Mark Nishizaki. "We did it because we knew Mike. He's always been real good to us, so we figured we'd help him out a little bit."

The partners held their breaths as they waited for the sales results. After five days the verdict was in from the dozen stores who took their product: those Coolers were moving. Most had sold out of their initial five cases. Crete and Bewley were ecstatic. People do want it. The idea was valid.

It was beginning to look like the concept of selling wine in new bottles did, indeed, have the broad appeal they projected. Although major wineries had made stabs at marketing wine coolers in the past, they had neglected three important parts of the California Cooler equation: carbonation, convenience, and temperature.

The amazing thing is that none of the big companies figured out the obvious point about a cooler—it had to be served cold. Other attempts were packaged in tall wine jugs far from the cold box of the liquor store. Once again, the entrepreneur was able to see something that insiders were blinded to by lock-step rituals.

So California Cooler, looking as frosty and upscale as an imported beer in its green bottle and gold foil wrapping, sat in the cold box alongside the fast-moving beer and soft-drink items, and traded on the traffic for ice-cold, instantly quenching beverages.

BUILDING A DISTRIBUTION NETWORK

The beer strategy was just as important on the distribution end as it was to consumers. Using beer distributors to sell Cooler opened up the broadest possible market, from corner liquor stores to Safeway. Plus, it fit with the image Cooler wanted to project, an Everyperson drink, not to be sipped daintily by the highfalutin'. The approach would be hailed later as a brilliant stroke of marketing. For Crete it was an obvious conclusion drawn from his own days wheeling in cases of Coors. He knew that the hard-working beer distributor clearly had the edge in rapport with store and bar clerks over the more snooty wine and spirits reps.

"The beer guys," he explains, "could relate one-on-one with the clerk at the Seven-Eleven or the Safeway. They're hard-working sons-of-guns. They get down on their knees and work cold boxes. A lot of these wine and spirits people would never dream of working a cold box in a liquor store. They would often show the clerk how classy they were and how much more they knew than the clerk did. In California they don't appreciate three-piece suits in a Seven-Eleven."

They knew who they wanted to sell California Cooler. But how could they get crusty beer distributors to take on a start-up product? Setting up a sales network is where many promising ventures bog down. But Crete and Bewley had a plan. They wouldn't try to do it all at once. They would build their sales apparatus one distributor at a time. They got quite a few rejections, but eventually they were able to persuade a Coors wholesaler to see the logic of simply taking over the accounts that they built up for him. "It was a no-brainer," says Bewley. "If it was one thousand cases a month at three dollars a case we effectively said to him, here's a check for three thousand dollars.

They then helped continue that distributor's success by working with his salesmen and training them and building the sales further. Once that distributor was happy, they went to the next one. He would be reluctant, citing the usual drawback, no advertising support. They would agree, but then mention that California Cooler seemed to be doing fine without TV in Lodi, and give him the name of the distributor who was making a tidy profit. The money sounded good. After that distributor was making a comfortable cut from Cooler, then it was on to the next regional wholesaler, in Sacramento, then the Bay Area.

SOLVING PRODUCTION HANDICAPS

Increasing sales means increasing production and credit problems. They were getting more orders but didn't have the money to buy the equipment to get production volume up. They were still using a hand filler for the first eight months of operations.

One method they used in the early short-handed days to get product packaged was to stage bottling parties. They'd get together family and friends for 50-case bottling sessions, after which there would be barbecued hamburgers and chicken. "Mike would make sure the barbecue kept flickering out," says Bewley. "We didn't want the grill to get ready too early so everybody would quit bottling and start eating."

MAKING SURE THE CASH FLOWS

If starting a company is a series of nonstop Odyssean sagas, then the growth phase represents the battle with the Sirens. As orders mount, so does the temptation to fling oneself onto the rocks of excess spending. The sights and sounds of a rapidly growing company can overwhelm the reality of minimal cash reserves. California Cooler experienced phenomenal growth, but it wasn't seduced into spending money it didn't have to meet increasing demand. Bewley and Crete had this one figured out, too.

Between 1982 and 1983, California Cooler registered a mind-boggling 2,700 percent growth rate, with sales rocketing from $1.5 million to $39 million. Naturally, as a start-up, they weren't going to get any help from banks to help finance that growth. Their solution was a Just-in-Time approach to inventory, combined with a swarming attack on the collection front.

They couldn't afford to wait the standard 30 days for payment from accounts. They needed the money to keep production rolling. With wily persuasive skill, they talked new accounts into paying cash up front on the first order, and then paying on net fifteen days after that. In addition to that, they were able to get many of their suppliers to extend them thirty days' credit, an amazing feat for a brand-new company. This allowed them to generate cash faster than they spent it.

The Just-in-Time inventory system made sure they turned inventory quickly. "We didn't carry much finished inventory or raw materials," explains Bewley, "especially the expensive materials like glass. I had my glass supplier keep high inventories in his warehouse so I didn't have to."

After four years of word-of-mouth promotion only, California Cooler finally began to advertise in 1985, as the major beverage companies reversed their myopia and jumped into wine coolers with a vengeance. The biggest competition came from the biggest wine company in the world, Gallo. In what Crete calls "deceiving to the public," and Bewley a "galling" irony, the Gallo ads for Bartles and Jaymes portrayed the product of a monstrous corporation as if it were the handiwork of a couple of entrepreneurs.

As the competition heated up, with over one hundred coolers in the race by 1985, California Cooler decided it needed some help to fight off the titans. Bewley and Crete sold their company to Kentucky distillery Brown-Forman, makers of Jack Daniels, Southern Comfort, and Old Forester. "As a five-year-old company," says Crete, "our pockets were only so deep to play the game that has to be played."

The deal was for $63 million down, with incentives based on sales that could go to $146 million by 1988. Crete and Bewley, who held 51 percent of the company, were very rich men at the age of 33.

By 1986 California Cooler was a $150 million company and owned one-third of the $700-million wine cooler market. California Cooler was also becoming one of the most popular drinks in Japan. There was an orange-flavored Cooler, a tropical punch blend, and a peach model.

With careful preparation and planning, and hard-nosed persistence, two people who weren't given a prayer of succeeding proved that it can be done. "You have to be willing to hang in there and buck the system until the system changes," advises Bewley.

"If you have an idea for a product, you have to follow through," Crete believes. "And more than that, you have to be able to recognize your strengths and weaknesses and surround yourself with the people who are good in the areas you're not."

In 1986 Michael Crete resigned from the company that he had built from his bathtub into an industry power. Later in the year, Bewley left, too, to pursue other interests. Yet it didn't mean the end, but only another natural phase in the entrepreneurial cycle. When entrepreneurs are too successful they can wind up tangled in the very corporate structure they set out to avoid. When the creative forward movement that's the lifeblood of the entrepreneur slows to a crawl, the restless pioneer goes after new conquests.

Crete has since formed his own investment company, Fountainhead, to invest in other promising ideas. "Starting things is the fun part," he says. "That's where I get my creative charge."

Revolt of the Wage Slaves

YOU ARE NOT ALONE.

A battle for independence has been declared. More and more employees are answering the call and turning themselves into independent business owners and employers.

In the 1980s it has become clear that the best company to keep is your own business. More than 600,000 new business incorporations were recorded in 1986, a quantum leap from the 90,000 started in 1950, or the 180,000 in 1960.

After decades of decline, the number of self-employed proprietors hit a record level of over 500,000 in the mid-eighties. Altogether, it amounted to a pace of one million new ventures annually. According to one study, more than one-third of American men now want to run their own companies, while an astounding 47 percent of American women aspire to head up their own firms.

A good wage at a big company is no longer the end-all and be-all of life that it was a generation ago.

In 1980, at the age of thirty-four, Rick Scoville didn't dismiss his aspirations and merge his identity with a corporation as his father felt compelled to do. He was part of a generation whose expectations wouldn't be traded in for customary security and seniority. He couldn't settle. The fulfillment factor—things like quality of life and job value, making a contribution, feeling a sense of accomplishment, creating something—were more important to him than job titles, company cars, and bonus clauses.

Scoville had been making his living selling glue, lots of it, the kind that comes in huge steel drums. As a salesman for one of the nation's largest industrial-strength glue manufacturers, Scoville spent his days like most salesmen, traveling the highways and byways of his district, cold-calling any firm he thought he could convert to the superior adhesive properties of his product.

We tend to be defined by the work we do and for Scoville that meant only one thing: he was stuck. For six years his energy, his ideas, his hopes, his car, his house, his life seemed inextricably joined to the ebb and flow of glue. But deep inside he knew that there was more to him than glue. As he would say later, there are only "so many days you can get excited by selling a fifty-five-gallon drum of glue."

His path up the corporate ladder was blocked and he couldn't see wasting another six years of his life beating the pavement making sales. Like most of us, his destiny was being ruled by a chance job opening. As a child, he hadn't dreamed of growing up and making a name for himself in glue. Simply, he got out of college, needed a job, and there it was.

Instead of surrendering his whole life to that one fluke event though, he reached the conclusion that he was a free man in a free country and he ought to be able to exercise some of that fabled free choice. His impulse to act put him in the right frame of mind to seize on an item he saw in a *Wall Street Journal,* as he waited in the lobby of a bottling account.

It was another story about Perrier water that caught his eye. This was in 1979 and Perrier's sales of bottled water were going through the roof, as high as $120 million in U.S. sales. Reading the piece on Perrier in the *Journal,* Scoville asked himself why no American company had challenged the French in what was obviously a lucrative market.

He couldn't find an answer. So he decided to do it himself. He quit the glue business, and started his own bottled-water company, Artesia Sparkling Mineral Waters, in San Antonio. What did he know about bottled water? Nothing.

How much money did he have to get his company off the ground? None. "I was the typical American single adult," he says. "I was in deficit spending like the government. I had more liabilities than assets."

But he was determined to get out of a job he hated, one

that offered no chance of progress or promotion. He was at a point "where getting up in the morning and going to that job was almost like going to a hospital to visit cancer patients."

With a $10,000 signature loan from his long-time banker, Scoville was on his way to a world as remote from the monotony of nine-to-five as New York City is from Pitcairn Island. It was a place where his wits, his instincts, his decisive powers, his stamina would be tested every day. There would be no more coasting, no more boredom, no more of the endless blending of one routine day with the next.

People told him it was impossible. "When I told them what I wanted to do they all laughed," he recalls. "They said, 'Scoville, you're making forty grand a year and working twenty hours a week. Sit back and enjoy life. Perrier's got that market wrapped up.'

"I thought I would just give it a try until I hit a big enough obstacle that would turn me away. But I never hit that obstacle, and finally I got to the point where it became a challenge."

He got a small mom-and-pop bottler to pack his product, and drove the length and breadth of Texas selling Artesia Water out of his van, since he couldn't get any distributors to take his product on. It was back-breaking work loading two hundred cases (about 4,000 pounds' worth) into his van and then unloading them case by agonizing case at convenience stores, markets, and nightclubs.

It was a bitter, hard-fought struggle. Like all entrepreneurial battles, it wasn't won overnight. He was terrorized by bouts of near bankruptcy; his nerves frayed to the breaking point. But he stuck it out and slowly Texans began picking up on his brash crusade. His press releases started getting picked up, and he was seen in the papers and on TV pushing his home-grown water with the motto: "Kick Perrier in the Derrière."

Five years later his break with the corporate world had made him rich and independent. He could come to work and "do what I want and wear what I want. I could have meetings in my baseball shirt."

Scoville's Artesia Waters isn't up with Perrier yet, but at $2.5 million in sales in 1985 Scoville was on his way. His water had moved from Texas throughout the southwest to California. When the 1985 rankings of the fastest-growing small businesses in America came out in *Inc.* magazine, Artesia Waters weighed in at a healthy 95.

Being your own boss is no longer a Walter Mitty fantasy, "someday" talk with co-workers in the canteen. An increasing number of ordinary citizens are now looking to themselves for career direction instead of some corporate personnel office. Instead of living to work, people are working to live, putting the unanalyzed work ethic under the scrutiny of a new worth ethic.

Scoville, and the fellow individualists of our generation, have the notion that you should get something more out of a job than a paycheck.

Everywhere you go, you run across them now, people in their late twenties to early forties, reassessing careers that have stalled out in the middle rungs of the corporate ladder. They may even have worked their way up to just shy of a top executive post. And now they're asking themselves, "What difference would it make if I got the top job?" A few more bucks that disappear as fast as the old wage, and round-the-clock responsibilities for something they had no real interest in anyway.

We are witnessing the emergence of a powerful force in working America—the fulfillment factor—as more and more people plot their escape from corporate life, toward a career that offers them more meaning and achievement—entrepreneurship.

The days of universally compliant wage earners, grateful just to have a job are over. Today's generation demands job value, psychological as well as financial. Satisfaction now outranks salary as the chief job reward, 56 percent to 27 percent, according to a *New York Times* survey. Because only 25 percent of us profess to be "extremely satisfied" with our jobs, that has left a lot of us in search of alternatives, with entrepreneurship an increasingly preferred option.

As psychologist Douglas LaBier explained to the *Los An-*

geles Times, "People have always been dissatisfied with work. That's human. No one has the ideal job or an ideal environment. But in the fifties, careerists wanted to quell those feelings. Having come through the sixties, the younger careerists come into careers expecting, wanting more opportunities for fulfillment and development. There's a lot of latent idealism. Unlike their older counterparts who were able to put up with it, younger people don't want to put up with it."

This generation, our generation, wants and expects a say in where their lives are going. A growing majority of Americans, 54 percent, believe they should have the right to take part in decisions affecting their jobs. They want a sense of movement, of progress, of input, accomplishment, feelings antithetical to the anonymous corporate machine which dominates most of our working lives. They want the fulfillment factor.

Enthusiasm and ambition are quickly muzzled by corporate policy. Stuart Bewley, of California Cooler, was constantly headed off at the pass in his days as an underling in a large corporation. "The boss won't allow you to do anything new. He'll do it the same old way. He's so worried about failure that he'll never let you try something different."

Another disgruntled employee, Discovery Toys' Lane Nemeth, held a variety of civil service jobs as a social worker. "I was never happy," she says, "because I'm a very creative, energetic person and I always had some boss who was going 'slow down; no, we don't want to do it.' I would come in with all these great ideas and rock the boat. But nobody wanted the boat rocked. I didn't understand why I wasn't appointed director of the organization in six months. I always thought I knew more than they did."

Mark Held, an Englewood, Colorado, industrial psychologist who specializes in treating the anxieties of corporate life, thinks that "people find corporate life controlled, mechanistic. It doesn't allow much creativity and is very regimented. People see entrepreneurship as a way to break away from the controls and limits the corporation has."

High achievers get lost in the shuffle of faceless management hierarchies. "If you're a high performer," recalls TGI Friday's Dan Scoggin about his Boise Cascade days, "you are being averaged in with the low performers, and they're benefiting from some of your success. I wanted to go out and if I was good, when I turned the crank six times I wanted to have six pieces of corn come out. And if I wasn't any good, then I'd starve to death. I didn't want to be averaged into an organization."

It was the same squelching of individual accomplishment that drove Hercules Computer's Kevin Jenkins out of a potentially lucrative career with a Big Eight accounting firm. "The thing that worried me was being put in a position where I really wanted someone to like me, and I would not be able to prove to them by virtue of performance that I had done a good job. The cards would always be stacked against me and by any objective standard I would not be able to prove to them that I had done a good job and deserved to be promoted.

"I like to be able to do it and say, 'If I screwed up, I lose a lot of money and I fail. If I do it well, I succeed and I'll get the rewards for it.'"

THE CORPORATE DROPOUTS

Guided by an internal quality-control mechanism much more exacting than that of any employer, the future entrepreneur weighs his chances for movement within the traditional corporate context, and after butting heads one too many times with "company policy"; enduring one too many idea-less, sycophantic staff meetings; feeling that the moss is starting to grow on his north face; he reaches a stage where his distaste is so great that he has only two options. He quits or gets fired.

These corporate mutineers represent a radical new force in American entrepreneurship. The traditional entrepreneur was the compulsive self-made man who began starting ventures as soon as he left the homestead, a rigidly anti-authoritarian type who would never work for anyone else. In the late nineteenth century, the scene of the last great wave of entrepreneuring, the breed was defined by the Armours, Kelloggs, Fords, people not long off the farms, who were weaned on the principles of self-reliance and controlling their own destinies. They had their sights set on only one career objective—running their own lives.

What has fueled the entrepreneurial boom of the last 15 years, though, has been the emergence of the latent entrepreneur, the corporate dropout, that person who undergoes a conversion to self-employment after getting his or her fill of company policy.

The country has never seen anything quite like this group of people, who turn their backs on steady paychecks, pensions, company climbing and gold watches.

Actually, the nation saw these same people reject similar tried and true paths before, in the late 1960s. Most commentators are baffled by the supposed "turnabout" of the baby-boom generation, from demonstrators against the establishment to drivers of hi-tech companies and BMW I's. No less eminent an analyst than economist Peter Drucker has stated: "Something, surely, has happened to young Americans and to fairly large numbers of them—to their attitudes, their values, their ambitions, in the last 20 to 25 years."

What's happened is nothing. This generation is doing precisely what it espoused in the sixties, rejecting impersonal, authoritarian, inflexible institutions and seeking self-expression and individual fulfillment by shifting from social to financial rebellion.

Once again the motivator is growth, for advancement on one's own terms. No period in U.S. history has seen an explosion in the pursuit of self-improvement as took place in the sixties. The spirit of questioning authority, being open to experimentation and new ideas, the revulsion to bigness and anonymity, the emphasis on individual rights and freedoms, and the quest for quality and meaning in life—all of it led directly to the era of entrepreneurship in full flight in the eighties.

Boyd and Felice Willat, living in the Haight-Ashbury district of San Francisco in the late sixties, were vigorous participants in the quest for alternatives, a search for identity that would lead them 15 years later to produce the symbol of their generation's new establishment identity. The Day Runner time-management system, has become the definitive appointment book/life organizer for upwardly mobile baby-boomers. The Willats' company, Harper House, sold $15 million worth of them in 1985. Boyd Willat believes that his generation was forced into being more self-reliant because the stances it took cut it off from traditional options.

"We were cleaved from the side of the giant institutions," he says. "We made a statement that separated us. Even though we did it in a naive way, we found that we were left out. So it was either sink or swim."

Our generation explored the globe in search of new alternatives, perspectives, information—elements of curiosity and receptivity key to the entrepreneurial process. The baby-boom generation's most fabled entrepreneur, Apple's Steve Jobs, wandered through India. Andy Lewis of Lewis Lektronix studied yoga in India.

Mo Siegel, a college dropout from Boulder, Colorado, explored South America. Siegel went into the tea business because he had a missionary belief in the correctness of his healthy teas. But even in his most Bohemian hour he never denied his capitalistic goals. "I always wanted to be a millionaire by 25," he says. He was. But on his terms.

Bill Tillson, a native of Vermont, spent a couple of years roaming through Europe on $3 a day as a street musician. He would return to the Continent a decade later as founder and president of the world's largest satellite transmission company, Netcom. He is no more ambitious today than he was in his guitar-playing days. Back then, he confirms, "I thought I was the next Bob Dylan." The fact that he's now seen as the next Bill Paley, the CBS founder, isn't the result of any conversion to capitalism. Tillson, like his peers, was never averse to money, just to the conventional ways of acquiring it.

Siegel, Tillson, and their cohorts of the baby-boom generation underwent the ideal psychological training for entrepreneurship. They had ideas on how life could, or should be different, which, as you'll recall from Chapter 3, is the essence of innovation. The pursuit of better socio-political mousetraps was a staging ground for financial/business mousetraps down the road.

Baby-boomers, those born between 1946 and 1964, represent the biggest surge in population this country has ever seen. There are 76 million of them, almost one-third of the U.S. population. Because there have been so many of them flooding the job market, and because they are now, on average, well into their third decade, the traditional mid-life growth phase, you would expect them to have a major impact on the economic fortunes of the country. But it's not just numbers that are responsible for the distinctive way they have influenced the course of capitalism.

Their values are different from any other generation. John Naisbitt, author of *Megatrends,* explains, "During the fifties, we turned our souls over to the corporations, our kids over to the schools, our health care over to the medical establishment and our welfare over to the government. It was the boomers who started to reclaim these things for themselves."

According to Daniel Yankelovich, founder of the research firm Yankelovich, Skelly and White, "Previous generations saw work as something that had to be done, but their real lives were lived with their families. They didn't look to their jobs for self-fulfillment. The baby-boom generation makes work the arena for success, for winning."

Yankelovich concludes that there are three main differences between this generation and others. One is an idea of personal success, as distinct from material, worldly success. "Personal success," he says, "is the perception and development of some inner potential—athletic, artistic, or whatever—and living your life in a way that fulfills that potential." Number two is an emphasis on fun now, not later. The third thing has to do with autonomy, "being your own boss, having something to say about your job, your relationship, everything in your life."

Baby-boomers have chosen to combine those qualities, he says, by starting a business. "Entrepreneurship has everything, autonomy, pleasure, winning, and personal success."

"It was just dogma that people came to college to become slaves of the corporation," says USC's Richard Buskirk, a pioneer in the entrepreneurship movement on campus, "but the students in the late sixties became disillusioned with the large corporations. Then during the seventies the corporations breached their implicit contract of lifetime jobs and started putting guys out on the street."

As that generation went out into the work force, their maverick ways waited in the wings for an opening, provided inevitably by the strictures, stagnation, or cutbacks in the corporate job market. When it came time to make the break, these people had an entire alternative ethos to fall back on. Its most symbolic element, rock music, with its mythologizing of rebellion, nonconformism, independence, and self-expression, had suggested to a generation that it was possible to challenge the knee-jerk procession of life and make some good bucks at the same time.

It would be stretching things to say that we have moved, as Drucker says, from "a managerial economy to an entrepreneurial one" because of pop culture. Quite a bit, in fact. But as the central symbol of a generational shift in attitudes, away from the days of The Organization Man to the era of the maverick Start-up Man, or Woman, pop culture has had a major role in making nonconformism a mainstream virtue. Rock icons proved that you didn't have to wait until retirement for the goodies in life. They made flouting convention conventional. A generation weaned on individualist anthems found career rebellion a natural next step.

THE SELF-MADE AGE

The story of today's wave of entrepreneurship began in 1972, a year in which an astonishing thing happened. The nation's self-employment rate went up for the first time in over 100 years. It's been on the rise ever since.

Since the 1850s, when a majority of Americans were entrepreneurs, the self-employment rate had plunged steadily downward every year to 7 percent of the population in 1972. But since then a historic turnabout has taken place. Between 1974 and 1984 the number of nonfarm, nonincorporated, self-employed persons rose 38 percent, according to the Bureau of Labor Statistics. The number of self-employed women shot up to 31 percent of all self-employed proprietors. Women in the mid-1980s were starting businesses at a rate three times faster than men.

The fever to go independent had reached such a level by the mid-1980s that it had given rise to a new labor phenomenon, the two-job person, not the kind who needs a night job to make ends meet, but one who develops an entirely alternate career on the side. Moonlighters may be mild-mannered administrative assistants and market researchers by day, but by night they are designers and consultants.

One moonlighter, who by day works as a television network personnel manager, in her off hours runs a small personnel training company with a friend. A management reorganization reduced her responsibilities—and achievement horizons—and boredom drove her to start doing something on her own. She told the *Wall Street Journal:* "'I started moonlighting because nobody here cares.'"

Rill Goldstein, editor of a magazine for moonlighters, *Sideline,* says what's behind the do-it-yourself phenomenon "is a need for independence, control, being your own boss. It's both a creative outlet and something they see turning into a full-time business down the road."

What's causing so many people to leave the safe corporate womb all at one time? Partly, the surge is due to the baby-boom demographic. The group is now well into its thirties and forties, the career-building phase of life. Many, particularly women, are peaking out within corporate structures. "They're topping out at the middle-management level," says Lisa Amos, a business professor at Tulane University, "and having a hard time making that leap into top management. So they start looking for alternatives, like entrepreneurship."

Economists cite financial reasons for the wave of entrepreneurship. They point to changes that liberalized the capital gains provisions in 1978 and 1982, that increased the return on investment in start-up companies. When new ventures like Apple Computer and Federal Express began to strike it rich on Wall Street in initial public offerings, that further sparked investment, triggering a flow of venture capital into new ventures. However, less than one percent of start-up companies attract venture capital, and only an infinitesimal number of new companies will ever be big enough to have stock traded publicly.

The shift from an industrial age to the information age, and the rise of new technology, is also given as the reason why so many of our friends and neighbors are going out on their own. This despite the fact that hi-tech still only employs about one percent of Americans, and that even among the fastest-growing, most dazzling new companies, as listed in the *Inc.* 100, only 25 percent are hi-tech. The fastest growing employment sector of the economy is temporary help services, a far cry from semiconductors.

Hi-tech's biggest contribution to the self-made age has been its role in recasting the image of the entrepreneur from an uneducated, small-time operator, to an imaginative, resourceful David, who doesn't just outsell the corporate Goliath, he out-creates him. The idea of creating something new, not just selling things, struck a chord with the best-educated generation in American history. People began to see business as the truly creative process it is.

The catalyst for the surge to independence, though, was the mass layoffs at America's biggest corporations through the seventies and eighties. More than 500,000 managerial and professional jobs were axed between 1979 and 1985 in corporate mergers and cutbacks designed to make operations more efficient and get costs in line with foreign competition. In 1982 and 1983 alone, 56 percent of the country's major corporations had tossed middle managers out on the street.

Between 1985 and 1986 300 major corporations drastically pared their staffs. Apple Computer lopped off 20 percent of their work force; Arco, 18 percent; Greyhound, 21 percent; CBS, 14 percent; even AT&T, 10 percent.

A traumatized work force reached the conclusion that one of the unwritten bulwarks of the corporate system, job security, was gone. As a *Wall Street Journal* article reported in 1985, "The womb-to-womb concept is dead. People used to be able to count on the organization and its stability. But the myth that institutions will take care of us has been shattered."

Gone, too, was corporate loyalty. A *Business Week/*Harris Poll of middle managers found that 65 percent are less loyal to their companies than they were ten years ago.

TAKING CONTROL

"We're being forced back on our own devices," says industrial psychologist Roger Hawkins. "It used to be that someone could start out as errand boy for a company and maybe be president some day. That's not true anymore. Most of us have to be confronted with the reality that we are not only going to make changes from one company to another—and maybe two or three—but also that we're going to have to make career changes."

Working for somebody else is almost as risky as going out on your own. More and more people are concluding that the only way to get the upper hand on runaway destinies is to simply seize the means of financial and psychological power. Be the boss.

Owning your own business allows you to finally break the salary deadlock that keeps us constantly living up to our means—or beyond it—but never getting past break-even. A piece of the action—equity—in a successful company is really the only way, aside from winning the lottery, to ever get ahead of the money game.

"I'm never going to be a millionaire with a salary," points out Mack Davis, an entrepreneur with two companies under his belt, and an instructor in USC's entrepreneurship program. "If I make $100,000, I'm broke; if I make $40,000, I'm broke. You just have better toys. If I have equity, I can't do anything with that equity, but it's building all the time and when it's time to cash it in, you're wealthy. On equity I'll pay capital gains tax; on salary I'd pay 50 percent."

A check of the *Forbes* 400 list of the richest Americans shows that, other than inheriting it, entrepreneurship, not high corporate office, is the surest way to make a million. A lifetime of corporate promotions can't come anywhere near the take-home pay of a successful entrepreneur.

As an investment, there's no stock on Wall Street that can produce a return like that of the start-up stake. Philip Hwang's $13,000 investment in Televideo Systems is now valued at $150 million. The $10,000 sunk into Westwood One by Norm Pattiz is now worth over $20 million. Those are publicly held companies. But the payoff is equally astounding for private firms.

Ron Rice, who began Hawaiian Tropic Suntan Oil on $500, now runs a company doing $120 million annually. His salary as a high school football coach was $4,300. The $500,000 a year he now makes fits comfortably with his net worth of over $15 million.

While these stories represent successes that are well above average, it doesn't take much to outdo your old company wage. After working for a semiconductor company in the Silicon Valley, Andy Lewis started his own electronic sign company. Though eight years later his firm is still doing just $2 million in sales, it's plenty enough to have made him a wealthy man. "I started with nothing," he declares, "and now I have net assets of $4 million and net worth of just under $3 million. If I was going to sell my company I could sell it for ten times its assets.

I've become a multimillionaire. I could not have done that as an employee of a corporation."

ALL THE FRINGES

Besides financial independence, there are freedoms even more valuable that being your own boss can provide. There's the fulfillment factor—the freedom to achieve, to create, to express yourself, to get your own ideas out unfiltered by committees and bosses.

"It's a creative license to do what you want," says California Cooler's Stuart Bewley. "I think a lot of people feel down deep that they can do something. But when you work for somebody else, you aren't given the chance to do it. Creative, capable people end up being very frustrated and there's a lot of ideas that die. Running your own business allows you the opportunity to do new things, try different approaches. There's a tremendous sense of freedom."

One of the key benefits of entrepreneurship for every self-starter is the freedom to live his or her own lifestyle. For the new generation of entrepreneurs success isn't just the accumulation of dollars. Quality of life, working where you want, at something worthwhile, in a style that lets you be yourself, is what it's all about. The fulfillment factor—the entrepreneurial lifestyle—is the ultimate perk package.

Dal La Magna, of Tweezerman, is able to dictate his own hours. "I have my own pace. I go windsurfing every day. I have only the amount of pressure that I want. I live the same life that Iacocca does. I make all the decisions. I thought about selling my company to Revlon, getting myself a job as a vice-president and working my way up, but for what? In five years I'll make a million dollars a year off Tweezerman."

There's no shortage of advantages to working for yourself. Freedom covers a lot of territory. Here are some additional fringe benefits that no corporation will ever offer you.

NO TRANSFERS. The end of surprise postings to Bahrain or Fargo.

YOU CHOOSE WHO YOU WANT TO WORK WITH. No wonder we have a hard time getting along with co-workers when we're tossed into a den of complete strangers. As boss, it's your party, and you invite whom you please.

YOU GET PROPER VACATIONS. You can't take advantage of this for a few years, but once things simmer down, and profits and delegation of authority rule, you can break the two week vacation barrier and take civilized month-long vacations like all of Western Europe. Of course, you may like your job so much, you might not want to.

NO DRESS CODE. Many of the entrepreneurs in this book have taken full advantage of this one. No ties allowed at TGI Friday's headquarters in Dallas. It's surfer duds for OP's Jim Jenks. Hercules Computer's Kevin Jenkins wears whatever he feels like, and that includes wildly colored shirts, baggy pants and skinny ties.

YOU CREATE THE WORK CONDITIONS. Entrepreneurs hate rigid, bureaucratic systems. Most opt to loosen things up to create a worker-friendly operation. As the maestro, you call the tune, and that can mean no office Muzak or paramilitary discipline.

YOUR TURN

The lesson from today's new entrepreneurs is that you can change your mind. Career decisions are not irrevocable.

You name it, and entrepreneurs are profiting from it, from the basics of air and water (Dave Bobert's $5 million Air-Vend tire inflators; Rick Scoville's Artesia Water) to exotic hi-tech equipment. The 1986 *Inc.* 500 list of the fastest growing new businesses showed the dizzying number of money-making, life-controlling options available: hero sandwiches, trailer hitches, wastewater treatment equipment, event marketing, medical services, wooden windows, Fiberglas molding, temporary help services.

Opportunities are being spawned by rapidly changing tastes, lifestyles, and technology. Independent-minded consumers are demanding more and more alternatives, which the alternative-conscious new breed entrepreneur is only too happy to oblige. Franchise entrepreneurs, formerly content to sell burgers and fries, are exploiting the new demographics of two-income, time-short families with an astounding variety of businesses, ranging from Park 'N' Bark (pet-sitting for busy masters) to Tender Sender (franchise gift-wrapping centers).

As the nation moves from a manufacturing economy to a service economy, droves of market niches are being created for new entrepreneurs who can provide a new or better service for customers. Service businesses, from fitness instruction to travel tour operations, don't cost much to get started, and practically anyone can get one going with the right idea, desire, and tenacity.

Another golden opportunity for entrepreneurs is the area of business services. As big corporations cut back and streamline their operations to stay competitive with foreign companies and smaller firms, they're keeping their overhead low by shopping out many business services. A whole range of new clerical, computer, market research, and custom services have become available for exploitation by entrepreneurial subcontractors.

The people taking advantage of all these new market niches are not necessarily the best and brightest specimens on the planet, or molded from infancy for heroic deeds. In fact, it's amazing how unexceptional, how ordinary they are. As a study by the American Business Conference discovered, "The elite of America's entrepreneurial talent is composed of self-made people, often from lower middle class backgrounds, who demonstrate extraordinary motivation, tenacity, and will to succeed."

Rick Scoville was able to extricate himself from his sticky situation in the world of glue simply because he was observant and motivated to act. "I don't think I'm any better than you or anybody else," he says. "I was in the right place at the right time and seized the opportunity."

Michael Crete admits he wasn't "driven from birth" to be an entrepreneur. He just felt the need to break out on his own and saw his opening with California Cooler. Rod Canion told his wife just a year or two before he started Compaq Computer that as a mild-mannered, not especially driven individual, he could never see himself as an entrepreneur. Yet he wound up running one of the biggest start-ups ever.

Today's most successful entrepreneurs started out from the same place many of us find ourselves in—a dissatisfying job, with little financial means or experience to do anything else. But they did something anyway. They started from scratch. They are living proof that not only is it possible to start an enjoyable, highly lucrative new business from nothing, but also, that *you* can do it.

Bibliography

Abbott, Charles Greeley. *Great Inventions*. Smithsonian Institution Series, 1932.

Adams, Russell. *King Gillette*. Boston: Little, Brown & Co., 1978.

Aspaklaria, Shelley. "Down But Not Out." *Venture*, March 1986.

Bacas, Harry. "America's Changing Face." *Nation's Business*, July 1984.

Becker, Eugene H. "Self-Employed Workers: An Update to 1983." *Monthly Labor Review*, July 1984.

Beauchamp, Marc. "The Sugar Daddy Defense." *Forbes*, February 10, 1986, p. 76.

Belden, Thomas Graham, and Marva Robins Belden. *The Lengthening Shadow/The Life of Thomas J. Watson*. Boston: Little, Brown & Co., 1962.

Bellew, Patricia. "Fallen Entrepreneurs In Silicon Valley Find Failure Is No Disgrace." *Wall Street Journal*, April 30, 1985. Pt. I, p. 1.

Black, Gordon S. "The Life Quality Index." *Public Opinion*, June/July 1985.

Boyd, David P., and David Gumpertz. "Coping With Entrepreneurial Stress." *Harvard Business Review*, March 1983.

Brockhaus, Robert. "The Effect of Job Dissatisfaction on the Decision to Start a Business." *Journal of Small Business Management*, January 1980, pp. 37–43.

Broder, John M. "Business Adapting to New Climate." *Los Angeles Times*, November 24, 1985.

Cherrington, David. *The Work Ethic*. New York: AMACOM, 1980.

Collins, Gail. "A Dearth of Business Plans." *Venture*, May 1985.

Collins, Orvis F., and David G. Moore, Darab B. Unwalla. *The Enterprising Man*. East Lansing: Michigan State University Press, 1964.

"Business Failure Record." Dun & Bradstreet 1982–1983.

Crabb, Richard. *Birth of a Giant*. Philadelphia: Chilton Book Co., 1969.

Crowther, J.G. *Discoveries and Inventions of the 20th Century*. New York: E.P. Dutton, 1966.

Cuniberti, Betty. "Yuppie Angst: Coping With Stress of Success." *Los Angeles Times*, November 21, 1986. Pt. V, p. 1.

Drucker, Peter. *Innovation and Entrepreneurship*. New York: Harper & Row, 1985.

"The End of Corporate Loyalty." *Business Week*, August 4, 1986.

The Experts' Guide to the Baby Boomers. Interviews with Peter Francese, Landon Jones, John Naisbitt, Daniel Yankelovich New York: Time, Inc., 1985.

Furst, Sidney, and Milton Sherman. *Business Decisions That Changed Our Lives*. New York: Random House, 1964.

Gardner, John W. *Excellence*. New York: W.W. Norton & Co., 1984.

Gilder, George. *The Spirit of Enterprise*. New York: Simon & Schuster, 1984.

Gendron, George. "The Spirit of Independence." *Inc.*, July 1985.

Greene, Richard. "Do You Really Want To Be Your Own Boss?" *Forbes*. Oct. 21, 1985.

Gewirtz, Don. *The New Entrepreneurs*. New York: Viking Penguin, 1984.

Gunther, Max. *The Luck Factor*. New York: Macmillan, 1977.

Hornaday, John, and John Aboud. "Characteristics of Successful Entrepreneurs." *Personnel Psychology*, No. 24, 1971, pp. 141–153.

Hornaday, John and Charles S. Bunker. "The Nature of the Entrepreneur." *Personnel Psychology*, No. 23, 1970, pp. 47–54.

"In Quest For Security, More Employees Set Up Little Ventures." *Wall Street Journal*, September 15, 1981.

Jewkes, John, and David Sawens, Richard Stillerman. *The Sources of Invention*. New York: W.W. Norton & Co., 1969.

"Job Commitment in America." *Monthly Labor Review*, July 1983.

Johnston, Oswald. "'Boomers' Redefining Job Success." *Los Angeles Times*, October 19, 1985. Pt. I, p. 1.

Kahneman, Daniel and Amos Tversky. "The Psychology of Preferences." *Scientific American*, January 1982.

Keyes, Ralph. *Chancing It*. Boston: Little, Brown & Co., 1985.

Ladd, Everett Carll. "Americans At Work." *Public Opinion*, August/September 1981.

Lazzareschi, Carla. "Business Whizzes: No Midas Touch." *Los Angeles Times*, October 17, 1986.

Lawrence, John F. "Weigh Human Factor During Retrenchment." *Los Angeles Times*, November 24, 1985. Pt. V, p. 1.

Light, Ivan. "Immigrant and Ethnic Enterprise in North America." *Ethnic and Racial Studies*, April 1984. Volume 7, No. 2.

"Loyalty Wherefore Art Thou?" *In Business*, September/October 1985.

"Matters of Fact." Interview with David Burch. *Inc.*, April 1985.

Machlowitz, Marilyn. *Workaholics*. Reading, MA: Addison-Wesley, 1979.

McClelland, David S. *The Achieving Society*. New York: The Free Press, 1961.

"Michener's Worldly Advice." *Success*, December 1983.

Miller, Don. *Personal Vitality*. Reading, MA: Addison-Wesley, 1977.

Moskowitz, Milton, and Michael Katz, Robert Levering. *Everybody's Business: An Almanac*. San Francisco: Harper and Row, 1980.

———. *Everybody's Business Scorecard*. San Francisco: Harper and Row, 1983.

Mueller, Robert. *Inventivity*. New York: John Day Co., 1963.

Nelton, Sharon. "Surviving A New Business." *Nation's Business*, December 1984.

Nelton, Sharon. "The Trouble With Entrepreneurs." *Nation's Business*, February 1986.

"People Need Risk." Interview with Ralph Keyes, *People Weekly*, May 13, 1985.

Peters, Thomas, and Robert Waterman. *In Search of Excellence*. New York: Warner Books, 1982.

Pratt, Stanley E. "Guide To Venture Capital Sources." Wellesley Hills: Capital Publishing Corp., 1982.

Pratt, Stanley E. *How To Raise Venture Capital*. New York: Charles Scribner's Sons, 1982.

Rapson, Richard L. *Individuality and Conformity in the American Character*. Lexington, MA: D.C. Heath & Co., 1967.

"The Remarkable Rise in the Ranks of the Self-Employed." *Business Week*, January 23, 1984.

Riesman, David, *The Lonely Crowd*. New Haven: Yale University Press, 1950.

Robertson, James Oliver. *America's Business*. New York: Hill and Wang, a division of Farrar, Straus and Giroux, 1985.

Robinett, Stephen. "Blood From A Rock." *Venture*, January 1985.

Russell, Sabin. "What Investors Hate Most About Business Plans." *Venture*, June 1984.

Schere, Jean L. "Tolerance of Ambiguity as a Discriminating Variable

Between Entrepreneurs and Managers." *Academy of Management Proceedings*, 1982.

Schumpeter, Joseph. *Business Cycles*. New York: McGraw Hill, 1939.

Sexton, Donald L., and Nancy B. Bowman. "The Effects of Preexisting Psychological Characteristics On New Venture Initiation." Abstract presented at 1984 Academy of Management Meeting, Boston, MA. Published by Baylor University Hankamer School of Business.

Solman, Paul, and Thomas Friedman. *Life & Death on the Corporate Battlefield*. New York: Simon & Schuster, 1982.

Slaiken, Karl, and Steve Lawhead. *The Phoenix Factor*. Boston: Houghton-Mifflin, 1985.

Slappey, Stirling. *Pioneers of American Business*. New York, Grosset & Dunlap, 1973.

Stanley, David, and Marjorie Girth. *Bankruptcy: Problem, Process, Reform*. Washington, D.C.: Brookings Institution, 1971.

The State of Small Business: A Report to the President. Washington, D.C.: U.S. Government Printing Office, 1984.

Stoner, Charles R., and Fred L. Fry. "The Entrepreneurial Decision: Dissatisfaction or Opportunity." *Journal of Small Business Management*, April 1982, No. 20, pp. 39–44.

Sullivan, George. *The Boom In Going Bust*. New York: Macmillan, 1968.

Tyler, Leona. *Individual Differences*. New York: Appleton-Century-Crofts, 1974.

"Venture Capital Industry Estimated Fundings and Disbursements." Venture Economics fact sheet. Wellesley Hills, MA: Venture Economics, Inc., 1985.

Wantuck, Mary-Margaret. "When States Become Venture Capitalists." *Nation's Business*, April 1985.

Watters, Pat. *Coca-Cola*. New York: Doubleday, 1978.

Whitefield, Debra. "Big Firms' New Motto: Think Small." *Los Angeles Times*, November 27, 1985. Pt. I, pp. 1.

"Will Career Plateauing Become a Bigger Problem?" *Personnel Journal*, January 1985, No. 62.

Wilson, John W. *The New Venturers*. Reading, MA: Addison-Wesley, 1985.

"Working In America." *Public Opinion*, August/Sept. 1981, pp. 21–34.

Zonana, Victor F. "Labor Market Sees Sweeping Changes As Firms Restructure." *Los Angeles Times*. November 25, 1985, Pt. IV, p. 1.

Index